The Ascendancy
of Finance

The Ascendancy of Finance

Joseph Vogl

Translated by
Simon Garnett

polity

First published in German as *Der Souveränitätseffekt* © diaphanes, Zürich-Berlin, 2015. All rights reserved.

This English edition © Polity Press, 2017

Polity Press
65 Bridge Street
Cambridge CB2 1UR, UK

Polity Press
350 Main Street
Malden, MA 02148, USA

ISBN-13: 978-1-5095-0929-4
ISBN-13: 978-1-5095-0930-0 (pb)

A catalogue record for this book is available from the British Library.

The ascendancy of finance
Library of Congress Cataloging in Publication Control Number: 2016052458

Typeset in 10.5 on 12 pt Sabon by Toppan Best-set Premedia Limited
Printed and bound in the UK by CPI Group (UK) Ltd, Croydon

The publisher has used its best endeavours to ensure that the URLs for external websites referred to in this book are correct and active at the time of going to press. However, the publisher has no responsibility for the websites and can make no guarantee that a site will remain live or that the content is or will remain appropriate.

Every effort has been made to trace all copyright holders, but if any have been inadvertently overlooked the publisher will be pleased to include any necessary credits in any subsequent reprint or edition.

For further information on Polity, visit our website: politybooks.com

Contents

Preface

Economic crises are opportunities for making the politically impossible politically inevitable. This was certainly true for the recent dramas on the financial markets, which have led to a style of government whose methods and centres of command are distributed across public organs, international organizations, central banks and private corporations. Government has been usurped by expert committees, ad hoc bodies and informal consortia of political and economic actors; operating in a grey zone between economics and politics, their politics of emergency is legitimated solely by exigency and exceptionality.

Yet the situation is by no means new. The dynamics of modern financial capitalism are defined less by a dichotomy between states and markets than by a co-evolution of the two, throughout which mutually reinforcing dependencies became established. From the bourgeois financiers of royal budgets, through central banks and public credit to the current regime of finance, reserves of sovereignty have emerged with an order and quality of their own. Modernity has not only produced state bureaucracies, international corporations, powerful financial industries and decentralized markets; it has also fashioned a specific type of power that plays an autonomous role in the praxis of government. This power cannot be described only in terms of political structures or economic operations; instead, the interaction between both poles needs to be considered. This approach undermines, annuls or reduces the importance of the supposed antagonism between political authority and capital.

The workings and history of this power are the subject of this historical-speculative essay. Its thesis is that modern finance represents a concentration of decision-making power that acts in parallel to national sovereignty, bypassing democratic procedures. Over the past three centuries, finance has become a 'fourth power' in which the power of capital is inseparable from the activation of power's capital. The contemporary dominance of the financial regime is therefore seen as the latest phase in an economization of government, a process manifesting itself in an aggressive symbiosis between political structures and private capital, an effective coupling of market and might. The notorious opposition between economics and politics emerges as a liberal myth unable to grasp the genesis and form of modern power.

This premise governs the sequence of the following chapters. All deal with arenas of political-economic 'zones of indeterminacy' associated with the evolution of modern political structures and economic systems. An analysis of the character of the international politics of crisis and emergency since 2008 (chapter 1) serves as the point of departure for two different genealogies of economic government. Central to the first is the significance of economics and the concept of 'political economy' in governmental knowledge from the seventeenth century (chapter 2). The second focuses on the alliances and involvements between treasuries and private finance (chapter 3). From the Renaissance onwards, the indebtedness of royal and national budgets in Europe led to the emergence and expansion of capital markets. However, the creation of 'perpetual national debt' and the guarantee of public credit were also accompanied by the formation of strong and internationally active financial consortia. The functioning of the international financial system is connected to the systematic integration of private creditors and investors into the exercise of governmental power (chapter 4). From the nineteenth century, if not before, the nexus of state and finance was embodied in institutions – above all central and national banks – that occupy an unstable, eccentric and prominent position within government (chapter 5). Finally, in the second half of the twentieth century, structures of power emerged in which power was blatantly transferred from governments and states to the financial markets themselves (chapter 6). Sovereign rights of money creation and liquidity control migrated to the financial sphere, dictating a situation in which strategies of private enrichment impact on the fate of national economies and societies via 'effects of sovereignty'.

1

Functional Dedifferentiation

America, four days in autumn 2008. On the morning of Friday 12 September, the New York investment bank Lehman Brothers found itself facing bankruptcy, triggering a rapid series of emergency meetings between the American and British governments, the heads of central banks, large international banks and private investors. In March, the investment bank Bear Stearns had been forced to merge with JPMorgan Chase & Co., the deal secured by a state loan of $29 billion. Having bailed out the mortgage banks Fannie Mae and Freddie Mac with $140 billion in the summer, the US treasury secretary Henry Paulson now ruled out freeing up yet more taxpayers' money for Lehman Brothers. On Friday evening, in the conference rooms of the Federal Reserve Bank of New York, representatives of US and European banks – including Bank of America, Goldman Sachs, Morgan Stanley, Citigroup, Barclays, Credit Suisse, Deutsche Bank and BNP Paribas – were told that a private sector solution would be necessary. Various investors would be involved, the risks shared. Bank of America, based in North Carolina, and Barclays of London both expressed interest. The insurance company American International Group (AIG) was now also reporting liquidity problems, and by the morning of Saturday 13 September it was apparent that, as one bank manager put it, the 'wellbeing of the global financial system' was at risk. The equally troubled investment bank Merrill Lynch was also seeking additional capital investment, fearing that a bailout of Lehman would defer the crisis to the next weak point in the system. After short and secret negotiations, Bank of America took over Merrill Lynch in the hope of gaining entry to the international investment sector. A bailout of Lehman Brothers was now off the cards.

Over the course of the Saturday, it emerged that the losses from Lehman were more drastic and the liquidity problems of AIG far greater than had been assumed. Barclays' efforts to take over Lehman had also run aground. The bank had tabled a plausible finance plan, but before going ahead was required under British law to obtain the consent of its shareholders. Until then, it needed a financial guarantee of up to $60 billion, which no private investor was willing to put up. Time was short before the start of trading on Monday morning. In a series of telephone calls on Sunday 14 September between the US Department of the Treasury, the New York Federal Reserve, Barclays, the British chancellor of the exchequer and the British Financial Services Authority, it emerged that London was insisting on the consent of the Barclays shareholders, and would not approve a deal without a full financial guarantee. While London was pressing for a clear go-ahead from the US side, the Americans felt that they had not yet received a solid and unequivocal offer. At around midday, the Barclays option fell through. The US government and the Federal Reserve ruled out releasing more capital and, hoping that under the circumstances the financial markets would be prepared for the event, allowed Lehman Brothers to go bankrupt in the early hours of Monday 15 September 2008.[1] Banks are always rescued at the weekend. Or not.

Although the 2008 financial crisis began earlier, with the collapse of the American mortgages and property market in 2006 and the repeated liquidity squeezes on the interbank market from 2007, it was only after the 'Lehman weekend' that it escalated into a collapse of the global system. What happened next is well known. Measures taken to solve the problems only made matters worse. The Lehman bankruptcy triggered eighty insolvency proceedings in eighteen different countries outside the US. By the end of the year, fifty-three banks had folded or been nationalized. In the US, AIG was propped up with a $182 billion loan from the Federal Reserve. Washington Mutual and Wachovia went bankrupt; Bank of America and Citigroup were bailed out, and an aid programme of $700 billion was launched. After the failure of Bear Stearns, Lehman Brothers and Merrill Lynch, the only two investment banks left on Wall Street were Goldman Sachs and Morgan Stanley. Even these had to undergo a hasty and improvised transformation into bank holding companies under the umbrella of the US government. As events unravelled, international money market funds collapsed, the trade in money market instruments came to a standstill, share prices tanked, the capital and bond markets crashed, interest rates and risk premiums rocketed, and the vicious circle of liquidity crises, credit squeezes, insolvencies, bailout packages and state guarantees spread from the USA to Asia, Europe and Latin America. The collapse of the financial markets brought with it fiscal crises and developed into the notorious global economic crisis, with declining world trade, recession, tax deficits, contracting GDPs, state bankruptcies and growing unemployment. The impact of the autumn weekend of 2008 continued in the upheavals in the Eurozone and – however indirectly – has dictated government action in the form of debt caps, austerity programmes, privatizations, and employment and social policy.[2]

An Unheard-of Incident

In 2007, experts had still been confident that the worldwide financial system was stable and in robust health. As late as 10 September, representatives of high finance such as the CEO of Deutsche Bank, Josef Ackermann, were convinced that there would be no Lehman collapse. The events of September 2008 were hence inevitably seen as the end of a finance-capitalist *belle époque*, as an 'Armageddon', an 'epochal catastrophe', a 'huge earthquake', a 'turning point', and the 'greatest melodrama' of recent economic history.[3] Remarkably, however, the fateful decision to let Lehman fail was not a real decision at all. Instead, a law of 'unintended consequences' set in, the events between 12 and 15 September 2008 taking on the dynamic of a novella by Heinrich von Kleist. Honest intentions, false hopes, misjudgements, adverse circumstances and inconsistencies, a mass of business interests, and public and political considerations merged with legal concerns and pressure to act, different worldviews, abrupt reversals, misunderstandings and obstinacies to produce a sequence of events in which the protagonists appeared responsible and yet utterly insane. Although the unprecedented events of 2008 were momentous for the global economy, subsequent reconstructions struggle to provide a reliable explanation. At best, it is possible to discern a kind of 'structural irresponsibility', action delegated and re-delegated many times over, distributed variously between private companies, central banks and government departments; taken as a whole, these produced an 'unforeseeable accumulation of effects, a lessening of inhibitions, sudden irreversibility'.[4] Finally, one is left with the observation that the decision was as unfortunate as it was unavoidable and that its logic found expression only in the subjunctive. As the US Federal Reserve director Ben Bernanke put it: 'I think if we could have avoided letting [Lehman Brothers] fail, we would have done so.'[5] At the end of Karl Kraus' *The Last Days of Mankind*, a despairing God, referring to the disaster of the First World War, comments: 'I never wanted this.' Similarly, one of the protagonists of September 2008 remarked: 'I don't know how this happened.'[6]

If that week of September 2008 can be seen as a key moment in the course of recent economic events, as a critical conjuncture at which the essential determinants of these events coalesced, then this is because the processes, practices and agencies active in them belong to the factors that impact directly upon the formation of political-economic power. Whether one interprets the events of September 2008 as the result of misfortune, as the cause of the global financial crisis or as its unexpected trigger, they should not be remembered simply as a bizarre episode with unpredictable consequences. What happened needs to be understood as an exemplary endgame, as an illustration of the creation, development and logic of policy-making processes in the financial-economic regime. The consortium of public and private actors, the improvised meetings, the secret deals, the urgency dictated by the movements of the financial markets – the events of 2008 demonstrate how all this determines the actions of government and the fate of contemporary economies and societies. From the hectic negotiations over the bailout of Lehman Brothers to the response to the European debt crisis, it is possible to observe an informalization of policy-making in the grey zone between economics and politics, a deregulation of its procedures and authorities. Expert committees, governmental bodies, commissions, working groups, 'Troikas' and 'Merkozys' legitimized solely by special circumstances, extraordinary events, exigencies or exceptions, have effectively taken over government.

In 2008, the emergency paragraph 13(3) of the US Federal
Reserve Act was used for the first time. It allows the Fed, in
'unusual and exigent circumstances', to exceed its legal remit
and support 'individuals, partnerships and corporations' with
'discounts', i.e. public loans. The British government declared
the bankruptcy of Iceland's banks to be an 'extraordinary situation' and used new counter-terrorism laws to freeze Icelandic
assets. The 'roadmap' for the stabilization of the Eurozone,
announced several years later, was justified as a response to the
dangers of the situation and the 'backdrop of urgency'.[7] In an
incessant series of 'crucial' and 'very crucial moments', references
to emergencies and existential threats became the norm in
international crisis management. This was accompanied by a
rhetoric of 'exceptionality', consisting of variations on the idea
that 'times of emergency' call for 'emergency measures', that
'unusual circumstances' require 'unusual measures' – or, more
trenchantly, that the 'financial equivalent of war' inevitably
required 'wartime powers'.[8] From the rescue services of the US
government to the controversial interventions of the European
Stability Mechanism (ESM) and the European Central Bank
(ECB), these extraordinary measures generally operated in an
unregulated sphere; they crossed 'red lines' and pushed the
boundaries of political and legal norms. Escalatory potential
unaccounted for within the scope of legal normality elicited the
proverbial *necessitas non habet legem* – necessity knows no law.[9]
Finally, that problematic realm of policy-making was entered
where the wellbeing of one or other group (whether the companies
concerned, American home-owners or Greek pensioners) was
inevitably sacrificed to the higher good and the common interest.
New and urgent imperatives for the preservation of the system
were announced like the word of a merciless Gospel. As the
German chancellor put it, rescue measures 'must be geared not
towards the weakest, but the strongest. I know that is hard.
Economically, however, it is an absolute must. Otherwise, we
would be jumping from the frying pan into the fire.'[10]

From 2008, in connection with the recent financial and
economic crisis, an emergency politics has formed whose quality
and character demonstrate a number of basic features: exceptional
situations that require extraordinary instruments and measures;
negotiations that take place behind closed doors, that are
determined by the rhythm of the financial markets, and that

clash with the lengthiness of formal procedures; an urgency that forces decisions to fall firmly in favour of the common good; and the informality of powerful executive bodies that might be described as hastily convened 'committees of public safety'.

Coup d'État This style of politics displays a bewildering lack of definition between political 'form and formlessness',[11] if not a crisis of government as such, one characterized by an indistinct and ad hoc distribution of powers between state and commercial actors and a corrosion of established institutions and procedures. Yet this is by no means a new feature of government. The first point of reference is the older discipline of 'reason of state' – in other words, a tradition of political rationality that, from early modernity, was concerned with how best to defend existing political structures. Here, interventions born of necessity are legitimized by the need to secure the welfare of the state. This procedure obtains greater formal precision through a concept that, from the seventeenth century on, described the technique of effective crisis management and the contravention of the norms of lawful action in the face of acute danger. In his *Considérations politiques sur les coups d'État*, published in 1639 in a print run of twelve, Gabriel Naudé, the French librarian and secretary to Cardinal Mazarin, categorized various types of political emergency. Under the concept of 'coup d'état' he assembled the very same components marking the dramas of the most recent crisis regime.

According to Naudé, it was necessary to distinguish between two forms of political intelligence, and to concede that in exceptional situations and in the *casus extremae necessitatis* the usual rules of politics can no longer apply. This state of emergency was defined by sudden and unpredictable turns of events, potential threats and future unknowns, forcing pre-emptive action and rapid strikes against potential troublemakers. Again, it was a question of unconventional means and measures; again, it was a question of creating undefined scope for action, about the 'Bold and extraordinary Actions, which Princes are constrained to execute when their Affairs are difficult and almost to be despair'd of, contrary to the common right, without observing any order of form of Justice, but hazarding particular Interest for the good of the Publick'.[12] With the concept of the coup d'état, analysis of disorder, of critical situations and exceptional cases assumed a systematic place in political knowledge. Violated norms, the transgressive act and various forms of sanctioned illegality became the point of departure for a theory of politics.

If, following Naudé, one understands the term 'coup d'état' less as a polemical category than as a *terminus technicus* in the political knowledge of modernity, then it denotes not merely a type of baroque power that combines the surprise coup with the éclat of a dramatic and overwhelming political act; and it is not limited solely to cloak-and-dagger operations. Rather, the 'bitter-sweet' process of the coup d'état needs to be understood as an extreme case of 'good government', as a borderline instrument of political rationality, motivated by concern for the maintenance of the dominant order, whose overall character is both defensive and conservative.[13] Unlike the modern concept, the early-modern coup d'état was by no means defined by the forcible takeover of the state, by putsch, overthrow and the removal of the existing regime. Its ambiguous status derives from the fact that, while it includes actions in the interests of the common good, it cannot be justified via universal principles and maxims of government. It requires a situational, pragmatic and at the same time casuistic appraisal of concrete circumstances characterized by extremity. It takes shape secretly, operates 'off the cuff', severs reliable connections to reliable rules; it detaches itself from procedural, legal and institutional frameworks and manifests itself in pure informality. It combines uncommon knowledge about unprecedented actions in extraordinary situations; it entails the application of suitable methods in concrete cases to obtain concrete success.

Beyond its original use, the concept's systematic meaning can be defined in two ways. On the one hand, its validity emerges within a sphere of governmental rationality geared not to legal institutions and procedural norms, but to the efficiency of heterogeneous practices and stratagems. Its criterion lies not in law and legality, but in the adept use of methods that under certain circumstances secure the ruling order. It draws less on a common fund of principles of government than on the resources and relations of power that embody the strength, dynamism and vitality of the political entity. It is no coincidence that a central place in Naudé's treatise was given to the governmental practice of Cardinal Richelieu, who as first minister under Louis

XIII combined tactical finesse in domestic and foreign affairs with early attempts at mercantilist trade and fiscal policy. On the other hand, in the concept of the coup d'état, crises and emergencies take on an exemplary character as manifestations of the latent instruments of governmental power. Despite the emphasis on unusual responses to extraordinary circumstances, the methods and potentialities of the coup d'état are always available, lying dormant, latent and unused. Their deployment in extreme situations means the violent self-expression of existing forces and instruments. Manifesting itself here is the 'direct relationship of the state with itself when the keynote is necessity and safety', a resolute, immediate and unregulated operation of the ruling order upon itself.[14] In the *ultima ratio* of political self-preservation, an 'apocalypse' or revelation of the origins of power occurs.[15] In other words, states of emergency and extraordinary measures activate and reveal the forces underlying the existing order, which in calmer times remain discreet or unnoticed.

The Financial-Economic Regime　　　Historical distances and discrepancies aside, the morphological correspondences between baroque theories of power and contemporary governmental practice indicate how executive processes and their objects, procedures and actors might be located in the present financial-economic regime. They have formed within a general mentality of emergency. Informal committees, secret resolutions, the suspension of formal procedures, the parenthesizing of legal concerns, the emphasis on the preservation of existing systems of order, the dictate of extraordinary measures governed by political urgency – all this has shaped a political style that, with its effects and transgressive dynamic, effectively operates as a permanent coup d'état. It is not only a question of how, compelled by financial-economic exigency, to bypass complicated parliamentary involvement, to avoid popular referenda, to eschew democratic convention and preserve the current market order from the 'tyranny of the random majority of a national parliament'.[16] Two further aspects are also crucial: first, governmental rationality has claimed an intergovernmental range, setting new standards for the execution of the extraordinary and for the suspension of laws. This is particularly the case in Europe. From the fight against legal and political restrictions in the approval of the first rescue package, through the suspension of national budgetary rights, to the special executive power of various EU organs, figures of exceptional political power have formed beyond national borders. As if Milton Friedman's advice had been taken to heart to take economic crises as chances for making the politically impossible politically inevitable,[17] the window of opportunity represented by the recent crisis was used to open up new possibilities for governmental action, to set political priorities, to secure the interests of the finance industry, and to re-organize executive power regardless of constitutional misgivings. To save capitalism, events could not be left solely to the financial markets; the crisis was to be understood not just as a collapse, but also as a pretext for capital accumulation. The emergency powers that had been granted were immediately made permanent: whether through the ESM, a special-purpose entity under Luxembourg law, whose organs enjoy total immunity in deciding on emergency credit, and whose directives are not subject to any kind of parliamentary and judicial control; or through the European Fiscal Compact and the reform of the Stability and Growth Pact, which empower the EU Commission and the European Council to intervene directly in national domestic policy under special circumstances. European legislative procedures were thus circumvented, for the sake of haste, in the interests of an 'unwritten emergency constitution'. An informal secondary structure has been created within existing legal orders that functions as a reserve for exceptional action in the case of permanently possible crisis. Co-dependency relationships, such as have long existed between the International Monetary Fund (IMF) and developing countries via structural adjustment programmes, have now been installed on a European scale.[18]

Second, the recent crisis has caused several latent features of contemporary power to surface. It has been possible to gain insights into the *arcana imperii*, into the mysteries of financial power, and to observe that it by no means functions according to a strict separation of political and economic remits. Its efficiency instead results from the close intertwining of state, supra-state and financial-economic agencies, whose activities supplement and permeate one another. This depth of integration is ubiquitous: at the systematic level, where governmental practice is aligned with economic governance; at the technical level, where debt ceilings and structural reforms fix fiscal policy to the financial markets; and at the level of staffing, which is marked by rotation between private banks, corporations, government departments and central banks.[19] The manoeuvres, tactics and techniques employed to manage the most recent crisis reveal a mode of political-economic power that, for all its division of labour, cannot be represented in terms of functional differentiation.

The same applies to the origins of the contemporary financial system, which the processes of deregulation in recent decades made possible. For example, the major political interventions carried out by the heavily equipped state under Thatcher and Reagan laid the foundations for the financialization of modern economies and the emergence of so-called 'ownership societies'. The test case for these policies was 11 September 1973, the date the military coup in Chile installed the dual figure of political authoritarianism and radical market liberalism. The next day, proponents of the Chicago School presented the military junta with a 500-page economic programme; this provided the blueprint for the privatization of state-owned companies, education, healthcare and pensions, cuts in social spending, the deregulation of markets and especially the financial markets, the abolition of price controls and the breaking of unions.[20] An authoritarian capitalism reared its head that caused even neoliberal economists to realize that 'good things – like democracy and market oriented economic policy – don't always go together'.[21] The fundamental question that arises here is whether the conventional dualism of economics and politics is capable of grasping this kind of corporate and concerted action and, by extension, the financial-economic regime as such.

Zones of Indeterminacy   A well-rehearsed concept of liberalism has, for over two centuries, caused political theory to labour with the dichotomy or tension between the state and the market. This concept holds that the state, as an ensemble of legal and administrative practices, is opposed to the sphere of bourgeois society, which finds its spontaneous and natural order in the economy and the laws of the market. A clearly demarcated terrain is imagined where, in an endless process of negotiation, the markets limit state power and are in turn restrained by it. In this theoretical myth, spaces of freedom are weighed against concerns of security, the idea being that the free play of economic forces is invoked to hinder an all-powerful Leviathan, while a protective sovereign tames the wilderness of the markets. On this basis, a Carl Schmitt and a Friedrich Hayek meet easily. While one holds an entirely liberalistic concept of liberalism, seeing the economic as a danger-ous neutralization of the political, the other recognizes in the political the threatening figures of tyranny and force.[22] Characterized by the opposition between state apparatus and market mechanisms, the choreography of conventional political and economic theory misconstrues concrete reality; it fails to do justice to the dynamic of financial capitalism, to the governmental practices connected to it, and to the operations carried out during the recent crisis. The antagonism between politics and economy generates a blind spot; it distorts the porous boundaries of the system and the processes of functional dedifferentiation.

The recent politics of emergency have drawn attention to the escalatory potential of power structures at the interface between state form and economic process. The finance industry in particular appears to act as an essential relay in the mediation between political and economic global organization. At stake is the modus operandi of a zone of indeterminacy, in which the state and the market are not opposed to one another as hermetic entities, but exist in a relation of power formed by continuous transitions, alliances, fluctuations and mutual reinforcement. The public/private distinction is deactivated.

Although provisional and oxymoronic formulas are sometimes used to describe this phenomenon (from Hillary Clinton's 'economic statecraft' to Angela Merkel's 'market-compatible democracy'), it is an area whose historical, conceptual and theoretical dimensions have been explored sporadically at best. The most recent politics of emergency and the hegemony of the finance sector therefore require a stereoscopic analysis of the co-evolution of state structures and economic dynamics, a search for the point at which the organization of power connects to the accumulation of capital. It would be absurd to deny the strategic difference between political and economic types of action; however, the form of modern financial regimes, their authority and their history can only be understood by transgressing such dualisms. If power can be understood as the precondition for the channelling of events, actions and forms of behaviour, and if its totalitarian moment consists – according to the definition – in the domination of all aspects of social life, then one of its most effective modern forms lies in the combination of political and financial forces and operations. This applies to the aims of concrete governmental practice, as well as to the question of how and where dominant executive processes constitute themselves within the capitalist economy.

2

Economy and Government

The distinction between economics and politics is insufficient, then, to define the structures of power in the contemporary financial-economic regime. Indeed, the processes of functional dedifferentiation connected to it refer back to a history of older constellations and procedures. Even during its emergence, the modern craft of government was marked by the interpenetration of both realms; and what might be termed the 'governmentalization' of the state since the late seventeenth century refers to the systematic integration of economic objects and principles into the practice of politics.[1] After the end of the Thirty Years War, a new field of state intervention entered the frame in connection with major social and economic change – including demographic growth, an increase in agricultural production and the monetization and internationalization of the markets. Pertaining to the complex relations between territories, populations and resources, this henceforth received the title of *Oeconomy* or 'political economy'. Absolutist theories of sovereignty had defined the state as a legal construction, as an autonomous and unitary source of power, and as 'rightly ordered government';[2] in view of the state's new role, however, a separation took place between legal principles and the maxims of government. All legal formulas, 'all supposed laws of nature that flow from borrowed theorems', now seemed to be mere 'chimeras of the learned'.[3] The concrete, historical existence of state entities henceforth manifested itself alongside legal abstractions, assuming an objectivity evoked less by governments and laws, constitutions and dynasties, than by a range of factors and data, such as the size, character and condition of the population, forms of production and commerce, quantities of mobile and immobile goods, climate, moral constitutions, illnesses and accidents, the circulation of money, and the fertility of the land.[4] The question of government was determined by the manifold relations between people and things, by social interaction as a whole; it ceased to concern merely the rule of force and *potestas* and came to refer to a potential or a capacity, to a specific form of power, whose early and perhaps most concise definition was provided by Leibniz: 'regionis potentia consistit in terra, rebus, hominibus' ('the strength of a land is constituted by territory, things and people').[5]

The category of the economic is thus connected to an extensive re-organization of governmental knowledge from the end of the seventeenth century. The concept of 'economy' became synonymous with a form of government operating at a specific level of reality in modern societies, one that cannot be understood in terms of laws and legal forms. Symptomatic of it were new varieties of knowledge, ranging from German cameralism to French physiocracy, which inherited older forms of mercantilism and focused on an expanding field of political empiricism. This 'economic' knowledge assumed a privileged position in the self-conception of state entities, distinguishing itself through its reference to a materiality in social life, in which people transacted with one another prior to appearing as legal subjects or moral persons.

One of the early systematic studies in this field, Christoph Heinrich Amthor's *Project der Oeconomic in Form einer Wissenschaft* ('The project of the economic in the form of a science') of 1716, set out the various dimensions of this new economic form of governmental knowledge. It is characterized, first, by its empirical approach. Measuring itself against the experiential sciences, it is concerned with 'nothing but real things' and strives for an encyclopaedic broadening of its topics – from state finances to trade, from farming to manufacture, from cattle rearing to mining. Second, the new economic science claims universal validity and can refer equally to private households and royal courts, to towns and countries, kingdoms and, ultimately, the 'whole wide world'. Third, it focuses not only on the constitution of objects, but also on the relationships between them; in other words, it is directed at the balance of forces and modes of exchange. The object of economic science is the interaction between things and beings. Connected to this is, fourth, a specific set of aims and interests: to guarantee, via the proliferation of wealth (both of populations and of resources), the strength and 'welfare' of the political entity, a mutual reinforcement of state power and economic potency. Finally, economic science is inseparable from types of intervention that privilege forms of indirect government; associated with the figure of economic knowledge is a shift in the aims of political government. Just as political empiricism refers to the interdependencies of human beings and things, individuals and wealth, populations and territories, so government now means a form of intervention that, in various contexts, takes on not only a negative and restrictive role, but also and primarily a positive and stimulating one. The function of the state is not solely protective and limited to the generation of internal and external peace. Rather, its economic definition requires that it be present in all contexts, and that it capitalize on these contexts; that it 'keep an eye' on people's transactions and affairs and at the same time hold them in permanent 'motion', constantly inventing new means and techniques for the convenience of all.[6] What is referred to as 'economy' is thus defined both by a particular thematic *topos*, by a mode of cognition, and by certain procedures of governmental technology.

'Leviathan' and 'Oeconomica'   The copperplate frontispiece at the beginning of Amthor's work could be understood as a response, as a supplement or as a counter-image to the famous allegory of the Leviathan, the figure of the sovereign ruler in Thomas Hobbes. At any rate, the composition and the structure of both tableaux reveal characteristic differences and alternative conceptions and operations of political power. Hence, the frontispiece for the first edition of *Leviathan* (1651) – probably made, with Hobbes' involvement, by Abraham Bosse – documents an ascending, vertical order recognizable as the transition from practical rule to the theory of state (fig. 1). While the panels in the lower half assemble various emblems of state and ecclesiastical power – castle and church, crown and mitre, cannon and lightning bolt of excommunication, symbols of battle and weapons of logic, battle and disputation – the towering figure in the upper half of the image appears as the allegory of Hobbes' concept of sovereignty:

the *makros anthropos* or *homo magnus*. The 'mortal god' of the state is portrayed as the representative of all citizens, as the personification of all legal persons, in whose name it acts and passes judgement; a constellation in which the multitudes dispersed across the land are sublated and metaphorically extinguished in the timeless fiction of the state corpus.

This prince or sovereign stands entirely beyond the rural and urban topography spread out before him, dominating these with his countenance like an immobile sun at the centre of a galaxy, while towering over the panorama symbolically. There is no interaction between the perspectival landscape image and the figure of the state behind it. This conceptual and symbolic detachment is also conveyed by the horizontal arrangement or readability of the surface of the image. The emblematic accoutrement of the figure – whose central royal crown unites the sword on the left with the bishop's mitre on the right, worldly power with the power of the church – not only repeats the title of the work set centrally below, in other words all that can be subsumed under 'the Matter, Forme and Power of A Common-wealth Ecclesiasticall and Civil'. It also marks the theoretical pivot and moment of unity in Hobbes' theory of sovereignty: 'justice' and 'true religion', 'justitia' and 'fides', merge in the prince's embodiment of 'peace'.[7] Hobbes' Leviathan thus contains a transcendent convergence of ecclesiastical and earthly power; the *corpus politicum* and the mystical body of Christ merge in the figure of the sovereign. The Leviathan manifests the basic premise of the theory of sovereignty as political theology; the political definition of God is combined with the divine sanctioning of the state, justifying the caption at the top of the illustration from Job 41, 33: 'Non est potestas Super Terram quae Comparatur ei'('Upon earth there is not his like'). The Hobbesian emblem thus stands for a concise concept; it is a conceptual allegory showing the sovereign or the prince 'in the generic universality of the concept developed by theory'.[8] For Hobbes, who repeatedly cited Platonic philosophy, 'Leasure' was the mother of philosophy', while the sovereign commonwealth was 'the mother of Peace, and Leasure'.[9] The frontispiece can thus also be understood, via the reciprocity between the concept of state on the one hand, and philosophy, theory and *vita contemplativa* on the other, as an emblematic self-description of Hobbes' conception of a political philosophy *as* philosophy.

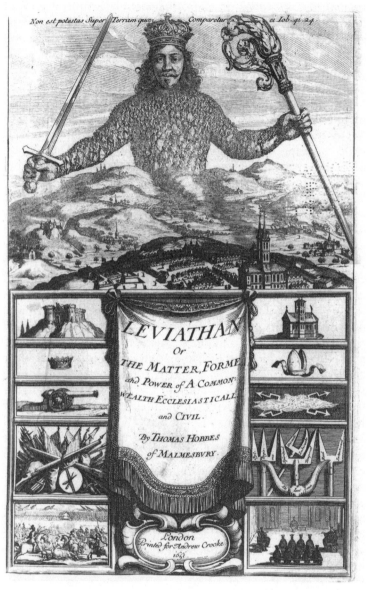

Figure 1: Thomas Hobbes, *Leviathan, Or the Matter, Forme and Power of a Common-wealth Ecclesiasticall and Civil* (1651), frontispiece.

The markedly less ambitious frontispiece of Amthor's treatise, with its representation of the economy or 'Oeconomica' (fig. 2), takes another approach. Notwithstanding similarities in the vertical and horizontal composition of the image, it formulates what are almost antitheses to the Hobbesian conceptual allegory.

Figure 2: Christoph Heinrich Amthor, *Project der Oeconomic in Form einer Wissenschaft* (1716), frontispiece.

For example, sitting at the feet of the economy are not practical figures that are subsumed and dominated by a personified theory of state. On the contrary: on the ground, devoid of function, sit diverse incarnations of leisure, which – as the inscriptions and Amthor's commentary confirm – are readily identifiable as variations of idle philosophy and speculation – from 'Divinus Plato' and 'Summus Aristoteles' to 'Philosophus Plagiosus' (the figure of a courtier) and a monk-like 'Eremita'. From the mouth of the allegory of the economy falls the verdict: 'Odi ignarum vulgus' ('I despise the ignorant people'). Not only are Platonism, Aristotelian science, courtly dalliance and monastic contemplation disqualified as examples of 'shameful indolence' with a 'predilection for leisure', as Amthor puts it in his caption; they are also identified as the enemies of economic science. For them, the constitution of the new empirical knowledge is 'all too impure and dangerous'. This is typical of the modern use of the concept of economy and the 'practical philosophy' associated with it, which seeks to liberate technology and the arts, and 'bourgeois activities' as such, from their slumber at the 'heart of contemplation'.[10]

It is not surprising, then, that economy raises itself above all this, as the representation of active life uniting (political) 'wisdom' (*Prudentia*) and (economic) 'industry' (*Labore*). Here, the ascent from practice to theory in Hobbes meets the dominance of political-economic practice over whimsical figures of theory. The economy now stands not beyond but in the world, which encompasses land and sea, and which – via the ship on the left-hand edge of the picture – is described as a space of transaction.[11] This is supplemented by the horizontal axis of reference. The right arm of 'Oeconomica' is draped with an exhaustive collection of symbols of various activities, crafts and trades: farming, cattle rearing, mining, architecture, manufacturing, trade. The left arm embraces a castle, a crown, a sceptre and a dagger, referring to 'cameral matters' and the 'economy of the land', and therefore the budgets of the state and court. Here, the personification of economy is portrayed less as a figure of unity than one of mediation. Running from the left to the right-hand edge of the picture (from the right to the left-hand arm of the figure) is a sentence explaining the symbolic syntagma, the connection between productive activity and the 'respublica': 'His fulcris nititur respublica.' This translates literally as, 'The welfare of the state rests upon these supports'; in Amthor's commentary, that means that 'the entire commonwealth / and high and low persons alike, / rich and poor, from the fields, / the cattle farms and the mines, / just as merchants and tradespersons, must feed and maintain themselves'.[12] In other words, the trades on the left support the state and the common good on the right, and the arm of 'Oeconomica' supports both at once. While the male sovereign in Hobbes personifies the multitude as a single entity and is furnished with the symbols of power, representing a union of worldly and divine rule, the significance of the female allegory of economy consists not in its unitary or conceptual form, but in its mediatory function: in the negotiation between trades and activities, between people and things, between the wealth of the individual and the welfare of the state. The less this figure of 'Oeconomica' can claim theoretical dignity and sovereign power, the more her activity pertains to the close and mutually reinforcing correlation between the public and the private, the political and the economic. The economy presents itself as a form of government that operates under the conditions of reciprocal permeation. One might say that the two illustrations together form an emblematic double portrait of modern power, in which legal-philosophical concepts of sovereign rule are contrasted with the economic-practical dimension of government.

In terms of the history of theory, the introduction of the economic into the modern science of government can be understood as the end of political Aristotelianism. The emergence of the concept of 'political economy' at the beginning of the seventeenth century interrupts the subordination of *oikonomía* – as mere domestic economy – to the political agenda. While the Aristotelian *oikonomía*, including its sub-categories such as chrematistics, trade and barter, was limited to the administration of the household (*oikos*), since Montchrétien's *Traicté de l'œconomie politique* of 1615 an extension of the concept's range of application and deployment can be traced. Efficient budgeting becomes the benchmark of the craft of politics, and the 'science of acquiring goods applies equally to states and to families'. From now on, the economy is the coordinate and criterion of political knowledge; it is only by studying industry, trade, the circulation of money, resources and population figures that the state can gain precise

Doctrine of Order

knowledge of itself, and thus a full picture of its own strengths.[13] Even if, in authors such as Montchrétien, the overall architecture of rule has a mercantilist orientation and is still held together by the sovereign, who dictates the principles of government through his authority as *oikodespotes* alone, a number of older terminological elements return with the transfer of the concept of economy to the political realm as a whole.

In the context of a long classical and Christian conceptual history, the modern use of the concept of economy reassumes the character of a universal order. *Oikonomía* or *oeconomia* had, since Xenophon's *oikonomikos*, been associated with the 'most beautiful' arrangement of things, with effective organization and careful administrative technique. All the way into the eighteenth century, the concept assembled a range of ordering operations and activities, its diverse semantic substrates evidencing a generalization and dissemination of this aspect of orderliness. This included a rhetorical economy that draws on planned and considered composition and adept use of representational means; a general 'economy of nature', entailing the wise order of natural things in the constant preservation of species and kinds; and the special economies of the earth, of human beings, of the animal body and of plants, all of which indicate a coherent harmony between parts and the whole.[14] Given this semantic breadth and the various – natural historical, medical, physiological, rhetorical – elements of meaning, the neologism 'political economy' simply means an ordering figure inherent in the political; the assumption that, here, order as such either exists or can be created, an 'order, through which a political body principally subsists'.[15] This was the case up to the beginning of the nineteenth century. Novalis still defined economy as 'the theory of the order of life'.[16] The economic presents itself as the science of order as such.

The dissemination and diversification of the concept of economy as an ordering category – up to and including the concept of political economy – are linked to a transmission of basic theological principles. Despite the vast semantic diversity generated by the Christian use of the concept of *oikonomía* since the New Testament, ranging from the correlative form of a Trinitarian deity through the incarnation of Christ to varieties of ecclesiastical and pastoral activity, the modern theological reception is marked by one semantic aspect above all.[17] This concerns the realization of a divine plan of deliverance and the proper distribution of salvational goods. In his extensive conceptual genealogy, Giorgio Agamben has shown how the classical concept of *oikonomía*, meaning household budgeting, private economic management and administrative practice, entered the theology of the Christian era, where it entailed the dimension of divine rule, the historical dispensation of redemption, the historical revelation of God through salvation, ultimately opening up the perspective of Providence. *Oikonomía* means the action and the rule of God and, since the Middle Ages if not before, appeared in the form of a world-order that claimed to represent God's will.

Agamben could thus prove that the modern dichotomy between sovereign rule and government, between the rationales of political theology and economic practice, was theologically prefigured, and that the tension between these poles was equal to that between a transcendent God and his worldly influence. Agamben thus reconstructed a process in which Christian theology 'economized' itself and increasingly understood itself as a kind of divine management. Agamben also pointed out the critical moment in the theological reception of *oikonomía*, namely the problematic transition from the essence to the action of God, from rule to government, from transcendence to immanence.[18]

It is precisely this theological semantic that at the same time enables the concept of economy to become detached from the limited concerns of the *oikos* and to broaden and universalize. The transfer of the concept to the realms of nature, the universe and politics should therefore not simply be understood as the secularization of theological motifs of order. Rather, its secular use was preceded by the theological borrowing of profane concepts. A conspicuous semantic shift occurred: just as, in its theological appropriation, the local sense of the concept of *oikonomía* as 'housekeeping' transformed into 'universal divine rule', claiming for the Christian God the role of universal administrator, so with the secularization of the economic, the course of the world itself was now structured according to the model and the laws of Providence. The theological concept of an *oeconomia divina* linked the divine order of the world with providential expectation, and could thus serve the modern desire for order in the cosmic, sublunary, natural, social and political realms. This is demonstrated in the concept of an 'economy of nature'. Eighteenth-century natural historians understood this as a 'wise arrangement of things', in which the relationship between individual objects and beings, their distribution, propagation and preservation, was based on uniform proportions and consistent laws for the 'generation of common ends and the achievement of mutual use' – as a revelation of 'God's splendour'. At any rate, the 'hands' of the creator had taken pleasure in creating a universal equilibrium between all natural things; and just as the bustle of the marketplace concealed an order, so in the apparently confused appearance of nature there existed a systematic 'divine plan'.[19]

Oikodicy   The concept of economy appeared on the horizon of modernity as a general category of order, and was simultaneously indistinguishable from theological and 'oikonomic' substrates. It indicates a twofold problem: first, the connection between lawfulness and Providence and, second, the critical relationship between ruling and governing. This unitary theological-economic figure manifests itself most clearly in the Enlightenment's attempts to construct a theodicy. The question was now not just how the existing world could be justified as 'the most perfect', as an 'admirable machine', as the best 'commonwealth or 'meilleure des républiques' – which would imply that all worldly evil was at best a side effect, collateral damage, an accidental result of what was, all in all, a wise 'structure and economy of the universe'.[20] If, as Leibniz maintained, disparate world events were indeed compatible with the divine common will or plan, and were evidence of a pre-established harmony and hence of Providence, then the universe as a whole must also offer itself as the solution to a universal problem of order.

Hence, the disorder and 'confused chaos' of the world are put down to limited perspective and an incomplete knowledge of the world:

> Look at a very beautiful picture, then cover up all but a small part. What will be evident in it, no matter how closely you look at it, but some confused chaos of colours, without selection, without art; indeed, the more you look at it the more chaotic it will seem. And yet when that covering is removed, you will see the whole picture from an appropriate position, and then you will see that what seemed to be thoughtlessly smeared on the canvas was in fact accomplished with the greatest skill of the author of the work.[21]

While, when contemplating the sky, one may recognize merely 'a wondrously confused being', to the eye that is 'placed in the sun' it will be proven that 'the supposed disorder and confusion was the fault of our reason, and not of nature'.[22] While, when observing a random series or line, one perceives merely 'twists and turns, ups and downs, points of reflexion and points of inflexion, interruptions and other variations', the 'geometrician' can provide an equation and a construction – or the graph of a function – and thus 'the reason and fittingness of all these so-called irregularities'. Any number of points drawn randomly on a piece of paper can be connected by a curve, which appears regular and predictable when observed as a whole – and 'that is how we must look upon the irregularities constituted by monstrosities and other so-called defects in the universe'. The world is a matter of representation. What *en detail* appears as erratic, subordinates itself to the order of the whole; what presents itself to the mortal eye as confused and unconnected, proves – in the eye of God, the absolute reader – to be coherent, determinate and predictable.[23]

If, however, the existing world can indeed be said to be the best of all possible worlds and if, because of its manifest virtues, God has chosen to realize the real world, thereby proving an 'admirable economy', then this is because this realization follows a maxim of efficiency, generating with minimum expense and the simplest of means and measures the best results – 'it is as if one said that a certain house was the best that could have been constructed at a certain cost'.[24] A kind of container problem has thus been solved. The best world, i.e. the real world, realizes the greatest abundance, the richest content, and as much 'as is possible in accordance with the capacity of time and space (or of the order of possible existence); in short it is just like tiles that are arranged so that as many as possible occupy a given area'.[25] Belonging to this optimization and maximization of existence is also a game of combination, in which the greatest number of compossibilities are created and, at the same time, the greatest density of relations and the greatest cohesion.[26] From the range of what is possible, combinations are selected that between them contain the most possibilities. The result is the simplest and richest world, a world that accommodates the greatest diversity in unity and, like a sphere, accommodates the greatest volume in the smallest space.[27] A world in which all parts – in time and in space – fit together seamlessly, in which the smallest change to a single body impacts on the totality of the others, marks the optimal realization of the possible. A higher degree of reality is revealed in an ordered society than in a mere crowd, and in an organized body or a machine a higher degree than in a society – precisely because in each of these respectively there appears to be 'a greater number of relationships between the components'.[28]

Leibniz offers a range of further examples for this criterion of efficient realization: for example, the work of a 'geometer', who 'knows how to find the best' – that is to say the shortest and most rational – 'constructions for a problem'; the prudence of a 'good householder who uses his property so that nothing is left uncultivated or barren'; the skill of the engineer 'who achieves his result by the least complicated way that could be chosen' ; or the activity of an experienced author 'who includes as much reality as he is able in the least space'. This economy, in which God's economic activity is proven, follows a course of progressive optimization and a criterion of minimum loss. Just as the perfection of the state consists in the 'happiness' of its inhabitants, which in turn depends on none of the latter's forces being wasted, so the moral and physical economy of God is arranged such that 'this city should lose no person just as the world loses no substance'.[29] This means that in the limitless dynamism of the world – whose striving for reality is reflected both in the driving force (*conatus*) of physical bodies and in the driving force of the passions in spiritual beings – there is no stasis or final point of rest. The world manifests itself as in inherently mobile force-field, which obtains a perpetual balance between disorder and order, harm and gain only as a whole. As a system, it is characterized by constancy of sum and the preservation of energy. The divinely arranged world budgets sparingly and avoids all superfluity. Every harm produces a gain, every disadvantage is compensated by an advantage, every evil is 'repaid with interest' in the economy of the universe.[30] Hence, the act of the theodicy concerns the realization of the best possible world in the double sense of *efficere*, namely as an effectuation that connects the force of Providence with the form of a rational order.[31] The riddle of Leibniz' metaphysics and his theodicy is solved through the principle of a universal economy, in an economy that constitutes the order of the world according to the criterion of minimum waste and maximum use. At the core of this theodicy, which seeks to justify the rationality of God in view of apparent accidents and misfortunes, the theological argument is ratified economically. It obtains the status of an 'Oikodicy', in which the divine economy dictates the consistency and the concealed regularity of the manifest world.[32]

The modern concept of economy opens up a field of intervention that directs political concern at complex and extensive relationships between resources, populations and types of transaction; it describes the economic as a field of objects, a mode of cognition and a practice of government. Moreover, the ordering categories connected to the concept of economy also import a theological grid that lends administrative operations a providential orientation. This leads to the coining of the concept of 'political economy', which begins its career as the term for a specific field of political operation and goes on to become the title of a universal science of prosperity. Rousseau's article on 'économie politique', written for the *Encyclopédie* in 1755 – the original title is 'Économie ou Œconomie (Morale et Politique)' – can be seen as a transitional text that reflects on the older uses of the concept, while also adapting and amplifying these for the purpose of political government.

[margin: Political Economy]

Rousseau resolutely and demonstratively abandons an Aristotelian horizon of meaning, thus marking a double shift and hiatus. Using a questionable etymology, he again recalls at the start of his text the origins and the range of the concept of economy: economy is composed of the words *oikos*, house, and *nomos*, law, and 'originally merely means the wise and legitimate government of the household'. The 'économie domestique' or 'particulière' is then broadened to the 'government of the large family which is the state', becoming an 'économie générale' or 'politique'.[33] However, the analogy between the economy of the home and the economy of the state is immediately dismissed. This is because the family and the state are distinct in quantitative, qualitative and representational terms. Not only are they different in size and extent; more importantly, the father's control over his domestic affairs contrasts with the position of a civil government, which can understand the destiny of the state only through 'the eyes of others', in other words through complex administrative data. The family order is characterized by its basis in nature;

it is dominated by the strength of the father and his natural emotions and property rights, and by the propagation of heirs, and is subordinate to the cycle of natural reproduction. The administration of the state, on the other hand, requires qualities and operations that are antithetical to these things. Here, the connection is not natural but arbitrary, based on consent; the actors of government are guided not by their emotions, but by their public duties and the law; they do not administer their own property, but protect that of others; they do not increase the wealth of the state, but guarantee its balanced distribution. While it is the fate of the family to be poised between extinction and self-reproduction, the state stands for permanence and constancy. As Rousseau put it: 'Although the functions of the father of a family and of the foremost magistrate should aim at the same goal, they do so in such different ways; their duty and rights are so distinct that it is impossible to equate them without forming false ideas about the fundamental laws of society, and committing errors fatal to mankind.'[34]

That is one cardinal difference, a precondition for the constitution of political economy's subject matter: the family and the house are no longer the deceptive exemplar and model of sovereign rule, as was the case with Montchrétien; at best, they are now a segment or instrument in the government of populations. John Locke had already contrasted 'political power' with the rule of the paterfamilias, and the German cameralists also formulated this similarly: 'The welfare of the whole state has a very different composition to that of an individual family.'[35] Paterfamilias and regent now part company, with the house and the family ceasing to figure as a metaphor for complex economic relationships. The more that modern government is defined economically, the more the economic becomes detached from the semantic scope of the *oikos*.

Connected to this is a second hiatus, which Rousseau – in his treatise on political economy and later in *The Social Contract* – emphasized just as firmly:

> I invite my readers also clearly to distinguish *public economy*, which is my topic, and which I call *government*, from the supreme authority, which I call *sovereignty*; a distinction which consists in this, that the one has the legislative right and in some cases obligates the very body of the nation, whereas the other has only the executive power, and can only obligate individuals.[36]

In *The Social Contract*, this distinction is again accentuated, this time through the contrast between 'will' and 'force', between general will, in other words legislative power, and government, in other words executive power.[37] Interesting here is that the concept of political economy is used synonymously with that of government, so that it encompasses the entirety of governmental practices and fields of interest. Also recognizable is a specific configuration of modern politics, in which the image of political corporality divides and doubles itself in a peculiar way: political-economic government now appears in opposition to the legal form of sovereign power. The 'king's two bodies', the phrase used by Ernst Kantorowicz to describe the specific doubling of the political body in medieval legal theology – between the mortal and imperishable, the physical and invulnerable bearer of royalty – finds an analogy in what one might call 'the state's two bodies': a symbolic or representative body, which displays itself as the configuration of a common will, which incorporates this will and makes it timeless; and a physical or empirical body, which pertains to the correlation between population, individuals, interests and goods, and in which is organized a complex of forces and resources. Rousseau recapitulates this division or doubling with his use of corporal metaphor and imagery: the head as the seat of 'sovereign power' is opposed to the movement of a machine, which is maintained through the 'wise economy', the vital principle of the heart.[38]

In short, the question of political economy and of political-economic governmental practice causes the model of the family and the rigid framework of sovereign authorities to become both redundant and incoherent. Rousseau's political economy withdrew from mercantilism's sphere of influence; government is no longer justified through sovereign rule and its organization is no longer based on the example of paternal care. It is not only political form and economic intervention that are now in tension. More importantly, the question is how the two sides interact, and how political categories and formats are reformulated on the basis of economic government.

Bipolar Machine

This does not mean that the issue of sovereignty becomes obsolete. On the contrary, it became all the more persistent under the new conditions. Using Rousseau's thought as an example, it is possible to trace – so it will be argued here – the construction of a 'bipolar machine' (as Giorgio Agamben put it), whose composition throws light on the structure of Rousseau's theory and the new remit of political economy. The emergence of the concept of political economy, together with the issue of the economic as such, is connected to analysis of the processes and mechanisms able to coordinate political or state power with the administration of the social field. The reformulation of theories of sovereignty using concepts of the social contract and general will produce a matrix supposed to give equal space both to the legal aspects of sovereignty and to the elements of political-economic praxis, as well as to the correlations between them. It is no longer a question of deriving maxims of government from sovereign positions; the issue now is which institutional forms of sovereignty can be reconciled with given – that is to say, economic – forms of government.[39] The key concern therefore becomes the transformation of structures of control and command, in which external, legal limitations combine with internal regulations.

Rousseau himself argued entirely logically that government (and thus political economy) was an 'intermediate body established between subjects and sovereign so that they might conform to one another'.[40] He also identified the 'difficulties' and 'contradictions' that are to be resolved in this process of mediation. The first of these is the question of how passions and natural inclinations such as 'greed', 'vanity' and 'personal interest' are to be reconciled with the common good and the 'public interest'. The second difficulty is the task of efficient allocation, of balanced satisfaction of need, in other words of taking care of the distribution of 'food, money, and commodities in just proportions, according to times and places'. Third, all of this is guided by the principle that the divergent 'particular wills' must 'take their bearings' from the 'general will' – an operation bound up with the 'difficulty' of 'securing both public freedom and governmental authority'.[41] Here, the government or the political economy is expected to perform a multiple coordinating role, a complex task that is notable in two respects.

The first concerns the internal logic and the implications of Rousseau's construction. Although a doubling of the body of the state emerges clearly in his theory, he insists equally strongly that the function of sovereignty and the function of government cannot be separated in reality. On the contrary, as Rousseau writes in *The Social Contract*, the crafts of government and the executive are nothing other than 'emanations' of the sovereign, and thus of the general will.[42] The government, as catalogue of concrete operations, is distinct from the sovereign authority and yet, as its emanation, coincides with it. Given this constellation, it has been shown that Rousseau's concept of emanation is related to the emanation of the persons of the Trinity in Christian theology, which up until the seventeenth century taught that the divine principle was neither diminished nor divided through its Trinitarian structure or through its intervention in the preservation of the world. On the other hand, with the concepts of the 'general will' and 'individual' or 'particular will', Rousseau received or inherited a central topic of debate in eighteenth-century theology. As Agamben has demonstrated with reference to research on Rousseau, these concepts occupy a critical position in the discussion on Providence and providential government of the world. Hence, the general will in Malebranche's *Treatise on Nature and Grace* (1712) includes all the universal laws decreed by God that, as natural laws, guarantee the order of Providence in worldly government. God's individual wills, on the other hand, which at the most account for exceptions such as miracles, are excluded from Providence and reduced to the occasional causes and collateral effects of a wisely arranged world. The individual wills, which alone would produce only chaos and a pandemonium of miracles, are absorbed by the universal law of the general will (or by the general will as law). The more this approximates the pre-established harmony of the theodicy, the more the theological origins of the modern concept of economy emerge: as a general theory of order, in which the rule of divine Providence guarantees government on earth.[43]

Entirely consistently, Rousseau understood the general will as the 'first principle' of political economy and the 'most important maxim of government'. He spoke of a government that 'in all things follows the general will', and that has eradicated and annulled the divergences among the particular wills in favour of a 'most just' and 'most general will', out of which, ultimately, speaks the 'voice of God', a 'celestial voice'.[44] However, the theological roots of Rousseau's theory of economy go beyond the derivation of the concepts of the general and the particular will. Rather, the structure of the entire 'providential governmental machine' is transferred from the theological to the political realm. The connection between sovereignty and government, between

law and executive power, is theologically determined; the question
of political economy, the question of its principles and procedures,
installs a programme of earthly Providence. Providence is absorbed
completely into the order of the world.[45] In short, by opening
up new fields of intervention, Rousseau's political economy
demands a reformulation of political categories; it assumes a
bipolar structure, in which the interplay between political rule
and economic government appeals to the establishment of
Providence in social life. The 'economic' constitutes itself as an
empirical field in the eighteenth century only insofar as its
structures and mechanisms simultaneously represent the activity
of a providential dynamic.

Liberalism The concept of political economy as it emerged in the eighteenth
century is thus marked by a significant internal tension. On the
one hand, it refers to a new realm of facticity. In terms of its
procedures and subject matter, political economy – understood
as a specific, indirect form of government – is distinct from
sovereign practices of rule. It becomes synonymous with both
a governmental practice and a political science, whose concern
is the welfare of modern societies. At the same time, as Rousseau's
treatise showed, the concept of political economy imports a
providential paradigm that implies a continuum between rule
and government, between sovereign authority and the exercise
of power. In the 'intermediary body' of government, in other
words the political economy, a reciprocal conformity of general
law and particular efforts takes place, as well as a social rationalization of the providential economy as a whole.

This sense of political economy prefigures the way in which
the economy is understood towards the end of the eighteenth
century, namely in the particular sense of economic or market
activity. This is the second notable aspect of its modern use. For
example, the 'economic science' of the physiocrats conceived of
itself as a theory that 'applied' and transposed the 'natural,
immutable, and essential order instituted by God' to the government of societies. In questions of livelihood, the distribution of
goods and of resources, it saw at work both a natural law and
the prospect of a 'natural order'.[46] Above all, however, the
emergence of political and economic liberalism showed how
the market would go on to establish itself as the realization of
the providential principle of government.

The religious bias of liberalist doctrines, the 'metaphysical dignity' of liberal economic theory, and liberalism's continuation of 'deist theology' have often been pointed out.[47] Recent studies, however, have formulated plausible doubts as to whether the (self-)understanding of liberalism as a programme of individual freedoms and market utopias resistant to politics can account sufficiently for the history and the implementation of liberal conceptions. It is not only a question of tracing, in connection with liberal governmental practice, the centralization of executive activity, the expansion of the professional state apparatus, the reciprocity between expanding market societies, and the intensification of state-administrative control. Rather, the problem of liberal government as a whole becomes the focus of attention. In this respect, liberalism is understood not in terms of its notorious opposition to the state and to politics, but as a refinement and an extension of government and as a governmental-technological permeation of the social field.

This coincides with the observation that, beginning with the eighteenth-century apologists of 'commercial society', the market and market dynamics were discussed not merely as aggregates of profitable business practices but also as the arena for the foundation of the social as such, for the self-institution of civil society.[48] In the process, the aforementioned aspects of political economy were taken up and displaced in significant ways. In David Hume and Adam Smith, a rigid distinction can be seen between sovereign statutory instances and social regulations; here, the legal order, the law and the legal-political format receive a solely restrictive, defensive and negative function. 'Mere justice', according to Smith, 'is upon most occasions, but a negative virtue, and only hinders us from hurting our neighbour.'[49] Conversely, regularities are ascribed to the 'natural' system of the market, which guarantees the mutual assimilation of the common good and particular interests more effectively than arbitrary political intervention. The more that governments are exempted from governing, the more that adhesions and spontaneous associations within bourgeois society, modes of communication and mechanisms of exchange, assume a governmental function. In the second half of the eighteenth century, the liberal project is defined not by the extraction of the political from private transactions and the expulsion of government from the social sphere. Rather, what Hume, Ferguson, Smith and Paine discuss under the heading of civil society has more to do with a regime that focuses on the rules and controls emerging in the social field itself. Their various considerations concerning the system of sympathy, the cycle of passions and interests and the mechanism of the market are associated with an appeal that society be governed by enabling it to follow its own course and develop according to its own principles and laws. Society, as Paine puts it, 'performs for itself almost every thing which is ascribed to government'.[50]

This leads to the question of the laws that determine the 'natural system of freedoms' and the system of market relations organized by the division of labour, as described by Adam Smith. It has been shown that Smith's understanding of the natural order and natural law are inspired by Newtonian physics and modelled on the uniform and stable trajectories ruled by gravity; the disparate phenomena of the heavens can thus be traced back to a set of laws concealed behind them. If this invokes natural theology and the belief in a relation between natural law and Providence, so too does the notion of order in the system of social intercourse.[51] Seeking to apply Newton's method in his moral-philosophical studies – from *The Theory of Moral Sentiments* to *The Wealth of Nations* – and to enquire into the coherence and underlying principles of discrete phenomena in social and moral life, Smith claims the exemplary nature of a universal 'oeconomy of nature'. In the individual motions and tendencies, in the complex ways in which society communicates, the economy of nature realizes the 'beneficent ends which the great Director of nature intended to produce by them'. This Director, which reveals every world event to be a 'necessary part of the plan of the universe' and whose duty is to 'promote the general order and happiness of the whole', appears in Smith as an 'all-ruling Providence' with Stoic elements. This providential thrust transforms particular efforts into universal ends and is the hallmark of a 'great system of government', 'so beautiful and grand a system', a 'political machine' whose regular, harmonious and smooth functioning produces 'the happiness of our fellow-creatures'.[52] Providence has introduced the possibility of a regular order into social life.

Market Laws What goes for social communication as a whole – as explained in *The Theory of Moral Sentiments* – defines the functioning of the market in particular. The theological implications of Smith's 'invisible hand' have been extensively reconstructed.[53] If the economic connection between interests, selfishness, the division of labour, labour value and the pricing system does indeed regulate the social order without a legislature, then three things are noteworthy. First, a heuristic principle can be observed in the notorious invisibility of Smith's laws of the market that causes existing transactions, interests and distribution of resources to seem like contingent deformations and deviations that artificially distort and obstruct natural dynamics. Restrictions on import and export, customs, premiums, price and wage regulations, monopolies and privileges have created an erratic state of affairs that not only impedes but also obscures and falsifies the 'natural course of things'. If Smith's theoretical claim consists in investigating the invisible laws of a transparent order concealed behind the visible opacity of economic relations, then his practical claim is simultaneously to abolish all obstacles and barriers – and not least the mercantilist irritations – to natural processes.

The market, whose principles Smith analyses in the first and second books of *The Wealth of Nations*, is not pre-given, is no reality; if anything, it appears as the figure of a theoretical and practical prolepsis. As a regulative idea, it calls for an analysis of the observable and extant economic constitution of the world in terms of the possibility of its coherence and systematicity:

> All systems either of preference or of restraint, therefore, being thus completely taken away, the obvious and simple system of natural liberty establishes itself of its own accord. Every man, as long as he does not violate the laws of justice, is left perfectly free to pursue his own interest in his own way, and to bring both his industry and his capital into competition with those of any other man, or order of men. The sovereign is completely discharged from a duty, in the attempting to perform which he must always be exposed to numerous delusions, and for the proper performance of which no human wisdom or knowledge could ever be sufficient; the duty of superintending the industry of private people, and of directing it towards the employments most suitable to the interest of society.[54]

The natural system of the market is hidden evidence that calls for the rectification of empirically apprehensible irregularities.

Second, a kind of theoretical shift occurs that must count as a specific deployment of emergent liberalism. The divergence

between sovereign authority and maxims of government characteristic of political economy in general is now transposed
onto the system of social and economic transactions. It takes
the form of a dynamic transformation of particular interests
into the common good, representing a law that is bound neither
externally to the individual nor to an institutional guarantor,
but that emerges from the actions and inclinations of the actors
themselves. The fragile relationship between general and particular
will, which Rousseau defines as the space of political-economic
intervention and the working of Providence, is transferred to
the governing mechanism of the market. With its progressive
transformation of blind and selfish efforts into social interests
or the general will, the market now assumes the function
of law.

   This mechanism can be understood as the Columbus' egg of
modern politics. The market creates a reserve of Providence in
which the government of subjects is perfected through the 'free
rein' of individual activities. The reclamation of concrete social
freedoms becomes the pivot of liberal governmental technology.
By yielding to economic freedoms, individuals – involuntarily
and unconsciously – carry out the universal law upon themselves.
Every individual, 'by pursuing his own interest ... frequently
promotes that of the society more effectually than when he really
intends to promote it. I have never known much good done by
those who affected to trade for the public good.'[55] The sovereign
authority becomes vacant at the moment that it delegates its
functions to the laws of the market. The tension between sovereign
and government characteristic of political economy is turned
into the liberal dissociation between state and economic system;
the diminished role of the state is now opposed to the private
market as figure of sovereignty.[56] The market thus embodies a
principle of indirect government, dissolving what Rousseau called
the 'difficulties' and 'contradictions' between political form and
governmental practice. Via the medium of political economy,
emergent theories of the market and its 'invisible hand' bequeath
a lasting theological inheritance. Articulating a providential
programme that permanently interlaces rule and government,
immanent order and transcendental principle, they link the
economic administration of the social to faith in the prudence
of a concealed deity. The market defines itself as an economic
mechanism insofar as it optimizes political functions.

Third, under these conditions, state institutions, the rule of law and legal regulations can be interpreted as acts of pure tyranny. From this perspective, the state only ostensibly represents the general interest. The political measures and regulations described by Smith in *The Wealth of Nations* include all kinds of 'waste and extravagance', whose common denominator is a lack of 'reason'.[57] Compared with the rule of universal and stabilizing market laws, the laws of the state necessarily appear arbitrary, biased and particular; while market mechanisms have a stabilizing effect, the state only entrenches and protects existing inequality. The state's claim to universality is surrendered by appealing to a natural and providential market order. The integration of a universal social law into the market particularizes the law of political sovereignty. To put it another way: if a basic reflex of emergent liberalism is already evident in Smith, one that turns against the deceptions and tyranny of political government, then this is indebted to the theoretical assumption of uniform and harmonic market dynamics, in which an 'invisible hand' realizes the plans of Providence. In this respect, the isolation of autonomous economic mechanisms proves to be an eminently political process.

From the end of the seventeenth century, good government meant economic government. This implies a rationalization of government's cognitive methods and procedures. The state establishes itself as an enterprise that continually and exhaustively secures its 'assets' and 'forces'. Political reason carries out a systematic extension of its operative sphere to a multiplicity, diversity and range of new fields of expertise. The scientization of politics leads not only to doctrines of legitimation through natural law, but also to a political epistemology that premises the state as object of cognition, with its own laws and ways of functioning. The 'political' ceases to be bound solely to the scope of sovereign rule, and casts itself as a field that provokes other descriptive and operational forms of political power.

Political Antinomy

Deriving from the notion of state reason, a concept of physical state resources and a form of government develop that operate in parallel with legal laws and that concretize themselves in the field of political economy. The economic now encompasses a specific layer of reality and a field of intervention that generates new political objects (populations, individuals, territories) and new references (complex relations between people and things). These objects escape not only the crude framework of political-legal codification. The old legal system is itself opposed to capitalist development, which demands more delicate control mechanisms. Other forms of control establish themselves alongside the law, sovereign power and modern systems of political representation. These pertain not to the representative body of the state, but to its physical body, affecting questions about the demarcation, distribution and legitimacy of political rule. The 'economic' now constitutes itself as an encyclopaedia of empirical knowledge about the state as such. Its coherent survey of disparate and heterogeneous data follows a principle of government that coordinates the welfare of the individual with the welfare of the state itself. Adam Smith's definition still holds:

> Political economy ... proposes two distinct objects: first, to provide a plentiful revenue of subsistence for the people, or more properly to enable them to provide such a revenue or subsistence for themselves; and secondly, to supply the state or commonwealth with a revenue sufficient for the public services. It proposes to enrich both the people and the sovereign.[58]

The doubling of the political body can be understood as a specific antinomy of the political, in which controls and laws compete for the definitory power of political governments, in the process excluding, overlapping, interconnecting and reinforcing one another. The network of political-economic technologies and the law of sovereignty are the two outward limits to power, forming the basis of the 'welfare state problem' in modern societies. This demands a delicate calibration of rule, which is exercised upon legal subjects, and governmental power, which is directed at living individuals. Regulations are limited by law, whose authority is itself limited by the demand for finer control mechanisms.[59] The effect of this antinomy marks the architecture of political-economic knowledge, and applies particularly to the figure of emergent liberalism.

Hence, it was not solely market activity that, in liberal conceptions, was isolated from the field of political intervention; it was not solely (political) rule and (economic) government that were opposed. Liberalism can play one pole off against the other only because the duality of transcendent rule and immanent government has entered into social intercourse, where it claims a providential inheritance, naturalizing itself in market laws. This marks a fundamental theoretical hiatus. As a political theory, liberalism aims at the dissolution of feudal, absolutist or personal ties and at the maximization of individual freedom; as an economic doctrine, it understands the market as the perfection and refinement of government. In political terms, liberalism is the vehicle for the self-institution of civil society in the form of economic transaction; as the administrator of this institution, it understands state institutions solely as agents of irregular, particular and arbitrary intervention. However, the precondition for the demand that government be limited is the extension of governmental operations; the naturalization of social laws is the precondition for an aversion to law. Although liberalism evacuates the post of the sovereign through its appeal to the market, it fails to get rid of the problem of sovereignty.[60] Just as political liberalism cannot be separated from economic liberalism, so liberalism's theoretical structure does not allow the dissolution of its antinomical structure. It is precisely because liberal thought conceives the economy as a closed system, in which individual action coincides with the efficacy of universal law, that it resists attempts at genealogical self-analysis, and therefore fails to comprehend the systematic connection between sovereign power, political government and economic process.

The blind spot of liberalism – the result of its notorious opposition between politics and economy – causes the role of liberal concepts in the economic orientation of political power since the eighteenth century to be distorted. That is what defines liberalism's ideological character. On the one hand, liberalism offered an apology for 'prudent government', a continuous review of state action according to the criteria of natural laws. On the other hand, it trivialized the connection between political structures and economic dynamics, and the process by which the economy became sovereign. The naturalism of liberal concepts of the market needs to be understood not just as the continuation of providential concepts of order, and thus as an elementary figure of political justification, but also as a distinct step in the history of the economization of government action as such. Since the eighteenth century, the development of economic government is determined by the alteration of the aims of political control. From now on, government is primarily geared not

Value and Power

towards repression and restriction, but towards the stimulation of resources and production.

This new political-economic technology can be seen as the reaction to the growth of the population and the apparatus of production. It responds to the necessity of coordinating the accumulation of capital with the accumulation of people, with a view to increasing state power. Mechanisms of power begin to operate that no longer function via the theft and expropriation of services and goods, as in feudal power. On the contrary, power is based on general value creation, which seeks via the regulation of mass phenomena to guarantee the administration, security, development and control of life: 'a power bent on generating forces, making them grow, and ordering them, rather than one dedicated to impeding them, making them submit, or destroying them'.[61] The wealth designated by the 'economy' was not yet, as was the case from the nineteenth century, an economic system in the narrow sense, one restricted to the sphere of production, distribution, circulation and consumption of goods and values. Before an economic subsystem formed in contrast to the political, together with its own economic sub-discipline in the form of national economy, the economy pertained to material, social and moral intercourse as a whole. This is crucial in connection with the question as to the origins and genealogy of economic knowledge. Seventeenth-century mercantilism had localized wealth both in the amassment of raw materials and commercial profits, and in the population, in other words in the superfluity and wealth of people, via labour and taxation.[62] By the eighteenth century, it was the premise of political economy that the sole and basic resource lay in the population: human beings are 'the greatest, the most important wealth of a state'.[63] This is where individuals are supplied 'with a little extra life', and the state 'with a little extra strength': an economic pervasion and manufacture of life itself.[64] With the emergence of political economy in the eighteenth century, a field of operations opened up in which value creation and the exercise of power were installed as elements of one and the same governmental praxis.

More recent liberalism – or neoliberalism – perpetuates this project under new conditions. Economic government has radicalized in two respects. It is no longer, as in the eighteenth century, a question of how, in the given political context, to segregate and delimit market freedom; rather, the question is how to regulate the exercise of power itself on the basis of free-market principles. On the one hand, neoliberalism favours governmental action that tests the validity of market rules in arenas beyond the economy, action that drives mechanisms of competition into the thick of social life, dispersing these across the tissue of society, guaranteeing deep control of the social through the implantation of regulative factors. On the other hand, neoliberalism imposes an 'economic imperialism' that economizes vital processes as such, seeking to 'extend the frontiers of economics and apply the tools of economic theory to the long-neglected sphere of non-market activities'.[65] Following the principle of human capital, it subordinates marriage and fertility, altruism and delinquency, social behaviour and emotions to economic method. Individuals and households are treated as 'production units or small factories'. The concomitant to a more or less toothless popular sovereignty is the universalization of the market function. This is again driven by a desire for political-economic order, which is obtained through the strategic deployment of functional dedifferentiation. In the visions of a 'generalized liberalism', governmental practice becomes a form of social engineering specializing in the capitalization of the 'human being in its entirety'.[66] Modern liberalism derives from a conglomerate of moral theory, theological notions of order, political theory, market ideology and social technology.

3

Seigniorial Power

The Merchant's Gift At the end of the seventeenth century, in the era of the emergent field of political economy, a touching story did the rounds in France about the fortunes of an all-too-familiar ruler and his financial circumstances. In the written version of 1685, the story first gets caught up in a series of digressions, then takes an unexpected twist, and ends with an account of a grand gesture and an accompanying moral. In a rambling conversation about past intrigues on the artistic scene in the court of Louis XIII, the subject turns to the painter Nicolas Poussin, who in 1641, on the urging of the king and his cardinal, Richelieu, moved from Rome to Paris. There, Poussin was appointed director of paintings and ornaments for the royal buildings, took over the hanging of the *Grande Salle* in the Louvre, and immediately attracted the suspicion and jealousy of his established Parisian colleagues. Particularly prominent in this respect was a landscape painter named Jacques Fouquières, who had himself hoped for the commission and complained about the affront. Curiously, remarks one of the speakers, Fouquières was always to be seen walking around with a long *épée*. Poussin called him 'the baron', because Fouquières believed that unless he wore an *épée*, even when working, he would forfeit his aristocracy. Had he been related to the Fouquièreses of Germany, the conversation continues, he would have done well to show more magnanimity, since these people were said to have been very powerful and generous. Far from it, comes the reply: the painter Fouquières had nothing to do with the German family. Rather, he came from a poor Flemish background. The other family was called Fouckers, lived in Augsburg, and were the richest and most respected merchants in the city.

However, the courtly conversation doesn't end there. After moving on to the sufferings and prestige of baroque painters, to absolutist politics and courtly intrigues in the seventeenth century, it follows the Gallic association of Fouquières and Fouckers and turns to the Fuggers of Augsburg in the mid-sixteenth century. A short introduction follows: during the era of Emperor Charles V, the Fouckers or Fuggers had received the privilege of importing, via Venice, all manner of spices to Germany, which they resold in France and elsewhere. This made them fabulously wealthy, earning them so much trust and such enormous credit that several of their members henceforth occupied important posts in the army and the Habsburg court. Then, finally, comes a story about a 'unique' and very 'strange' occurrence involving these same merchants. Returning from North Africa and Italy, Charles V made a short stop in Augsburg, where he lodged at the Fuggers' home. In order to assure the emperor of their gratitude and respect, the Fuggers put on a splendid display of hospitality, among other things hanging a bunch of cinnamon sticks over the fireplace, cinnamon being one of the most expensive spices at the time. Not only that: after showing the emperor a certificate of debt or IOU that he had once issued in receipt of a very considerable sum of money, they burned the certificate and lit the cinnamon sticks in the fireplace. These emitted

> a scent and a glow that the emperor perceived to be all the sweeter and more pleasant for seeing himself released from a debt, which in view of his business situation at the time he would have been able to repay only with difficulty and which, in this so gallant a manner, was presented to him as a gift. As concerns the family of the painter Fouquières, however ...,

and so on.

The casual anecdote, first told by the French architect and art theorist André Félibien and immediately published by the *Journal des Sçavans* under the rubric 'novelty' and 'entertainment', is probably pure fantasy and without any basis in a real historical encounter between the Habsburg emperor and his creditors.[1] Nevertheless, it is significant in connection with a number of other episodes that, whether authentic or fictitious, also concern early-modern merchants' generosity towards their royal debtors. It was also reported that the wealthy Genoese patrician Adamo Centurione, on receiving a certificate of debt from Emperor Charles V, immediately burned it in the latter's presence. It was said that the emperor held his hands to the flames, remarking that he wished to 'warm them in the glow of a note, in which burned the true affection of a patrician from a free fatherland, which each served with his life and his wealth'. In another version, the emperor, after receiving an advance of 200,000 gold pieces, was simply issued with a receipt of their repayment. Similar stories were told about the Antwerp merchants Jan Daem (or Daen) and Juliano Dozzi (alias Gaspar Ducci), although the volume of credit paid to the sovereign greatly varies, at times entering the millions.[2] As kind and reconciliatory as such donations to the imperial budget might seem, these stories are only ostensibly about generous gestures, redemption and a happy end to royal debt; despite appearances, their aim is not to demonstrate the heartfelt servitude motivating the political engagement of early-modern capitalists. Félibien's anecdote in particular portrays an entanglement between financier and sovereign whose resolution is tragicomic at best.

Aside from the fact that the story of the mutual amicability between politics and capital fits neatly into an era in which sovereign power was already being circumscribed by mercantilist and political-economic governmental praxis, and which was also familiar with the proverbial 'state bankruptcies' of the Habsburgs, it describes an incident in which the emperor and the financial dynasty swap places in a surprising way. On the one hand, it invokes all the obligations, advance payments and loans with which Charles V indebted himself to the Fuggers, among other people, in order to finance the bribes for his election as Holy Roman Emperor and the costs of his military campaigns. The emperor who decides to stop in Augsburg appears there as a bound sovereign. On the other hand, the story's pyrotechnic turn inverts the political order yet further. What pleases the emperor's nose (or warms his cold and impecunious fingers) is not only the incineration of the certificate of debt and thus the eradication of an unwanted bond. More importantly, the combustion of the certificate emphasizes and potentiates the relationship between bondage and liberation. While the smouldering cinnamon sparks a demonstration of luxury and unproductive waste, re-enacting the notorious stigma of royal luxury, the burned certificate constitutes an early-modern 'haircut', at the same time acknowledging the unprecedented circumstance that the sovereign is simply no longer creditworthy. In the house of the patrician, the emperor is confronted with both a representation of courtly profligacy and a reminder of his insolvency and unmet obligation.

The logic of the story thus performs the paradox of the gift, and hence a gesture whereby release from bondage reinstates commitment.[3] More precisely, an operation takes place that must necessarily infuriate the sovereign, at least momentarily. If sovereignty in general is understood as the standard for the minimization of dependency, as the manifestation of disparity, and as the figure of last resort, then the gift of the merchant becomes a quasi-usurpatory act.[4] The merchant's gift annuls all reciprocity, all prospect of recompense; breaking the cycle of gift and counter-gift, it imposes a decisive imbalance or asymmetry. And while, in seventeenth-century theories of sovereignty, the royal exchequer is defined as the creditor of all creditors,[5] the burned notice of debt marks an irrevocably final, yet private resort of credit in the relation between monarch and finance. Things are rendered to the kaiser that are not the kaiser's, and nothing to the kaiser that is the kaiser's. That is the ambiguous resolution of the situation. In the Augsburg setting of Félibien's tale, the bound sovereign experiences his freedom thanks to an unbound act of financial deliverance. He is redeemed as that which he once was, namely ruler of the Holy Roman Empire, through the mercy of capital. What is 'unique' or unprecedented about this story is that, with the grand and generous figure of the financier, confusion is created as to where and in whom sovereign power is incorporated.

The anecdote interprets and reflects on the complex political role of national budgets and their implication in contemporary finance capital. It points back from a later epoch to the beginnings of absolutism and the emergence of modern statehood in the sixteenth century; the political-economic entanglement it tells of is already identifiable as the object of serious concern in the theories of political rule of the time. This goes particularly for the development of the concept of sovereignty since Jean Bodin.

The Question of Finance

Generally speaking, it is possible to observe in the development
of theories of sovereignty – and hence of a paradigm of modern
statehood – an increasing sense of political crisis. These theories
were concerned with ordering the multitude of different 'ruler-like'
positions, authorities and entitlements into a uniform political
format, and with asserting a reliable, 'absolute and perpetual
power of a commonwealth' in opposition to the dwindling power
of royalty to secure peace, in relation to confessional civil wars
and to the permanent conflict in Europe over hegemony.[6]
Alongside these efforts to concentrate and stabilize political
power, however, the negotiation of fiscal issues assumes a special
and problematic status. On the one hand, the right of coinage,
taxation and the national budget are claimed as the inalienable
and essential features of sovereign rule. One of the 'main rights
of sovereignty' consists in the power over the financial administration and over the 'availability of public funds'; these are inseparable from the 'person of the sovereign'.[7] On the other hand,
unlike other prerogatives – such as legislation, decisions over
war and peace, the right of pardon, the highest judicial authority
– these rights lead into controversial and confusing territory
marked by indeterminate responsibilities, peculiar considerations,
complicated distinctions and awkward structures of obligation.
For example, because of the trading of office and the cession of
privileges, and because of the interventions of leaseholders, agents,
trustees and various intermediaries, coinage and taxation questions
open up a field of activity in which the incursion of particular
interests threatens to erode sovereign state power. Where the
administration of state assets becomes an issue, beneficiaries
and parasites appear.[8] The collection of permanent duties is seen
by Bodin and others to be a dangerous limitation of monarchical
power, as a relativization of its supremacy, for example when
taxation conflicts with bourgeois property rights or with demands
for autonomous public financing by royal dominions. Whoever
relies on regular tax payments makes themselves dependent on
other people's wealth.[9] Ultimately, the fiscal complex as a whole
appears as the vessel of extraordinary risks to the status of the
sovereign. Bodin is very clear about the nature of this threat.
In the context of the notorious indebtedness of royal budgets
in the sixteenth century, he sees in the credit-like financing of
the state an absolute limit to absolute authority. The cycle of
lending and debt servicing through credit – an evil that Bodin

thought had been introduced into the world by Francis I – becomes the apotheosis of political pathology. It is symptomatic of the 'utter ruin' of the state.[10] In it, the sovereign monopoly is assaulted and undermined by economic dependencies.

The issue of state finances and their administration opens up a field whose negotiation poses a particular challenge to modern theories of sovereignty; it comes up against incompatibilities with the uniformity of sovereign power and leads to manifold inconsistencies. A resistance of objects and activities causes the theoretical text to hesitate, occasioning casuistry and, more broadly, evincing difficulty in comprehension by means of the legal concept of the sovereign state. In Thomas Hobbes, fiscal and financial matters continue to fall within the remit of sovereign rule; however, they are not counted among its defining characteristics.[11] Here, it is possible to recognize early concerns about the constraint of supreme state power and the unregulated devolution or alienation of sovereign authority. Political theory labours with this subject matter, whose propensity for integration into sovereign power simultaneously produces resistance. The fiscal complex represents a central motif for the perpetuation and stabilization of early-modern state power; however, it simultaneously marks its limits or lines of fracture. The question of state income, state debt, tax, coinage and fiscal affairs as a whole occupies a crucial position that resists explanation through a homogeneous 'concept of the political'. Taking three basic elements as examples – the concept of the treasury, the status of coinage policy, and the role of public lending – it will be shown how modern finance develops in close correlation with political remits, at the same time constituting itself as a strategic field with its own quality, its operationality characterized by a zone of political-economic indeterminacy.

This reveals itself in what, according to a long legal tradition, The Fisc is referred to as the treasury or fisc. In Roman law, the concept of the *fiscus* – the 'money basket' or 'purse' – was the subject of complex distinctions that sought to define the relationship between imperial private wealth and the wealth of the state. Questions included the legal proprietors of the treasury, periods of limitation and inalienability, the relation between the treasury and the immortal entity of the empire, and the status of fiscal matters in the organization of ruling power. The treasury assumed the character of a strange object, whose categorization remained controversial, dubious, unclear or, at best, full of exceptions. As Otto von Gierke noted, in the Roman Empire, the *fiscus Caesaris*, the imperial private purse, coincided with the *aerarium* of the *res publica*, the wealth of the state or the people. The *fiscus* was, to a certain extent, state owned, and yet was also subordinate to private commercial norms, procedural rules and legal representation. Through its public ownership, the treasury developed on the basis of a private-law concept of the person, introducing a peculiar duality in the format of imperial power. On the one hand, this represented a 'great step': 'Whilst the state raised itself ever more peremptorily above all law, the state as treasury subordinated itself to the law and, divested of its majesty, became a private entity among private entities.' On the other hand, the private status of the treasury was riddled with exceptions, which introduced into the treasury itself a tension between its public and private dimensions, leaving open questions concerning its 'substrate' and 'substantial unity'. It remained unclear, or unresolved from case to case, as to who or what – whether *res publica*, emperor or private person – acted in the name of the treasury.[12]

While there is evidence of a fundamental and consistent link between the treasury and the state in the modern era, ambiguities and equivocations of this kind remained. Fiscal law was understood as an emanation of the *summum imperium* and as a component of the *superioritas*. The treasury is the marker of sovereignty and is equally attributable to all sovereign authorities – monarchs, states, imperial cities. In this respect, the bearer of public property rights converges with the bearer of public rights of sovereignty; the treasury is congruent with the person of the sovereign. Depending on the form of government, the emperor, the monarch or the collective are identified as having fiscal rights and obligations. Again, however, it is not only the distinction between public and private property titles that becomes an issue. As a moment of sovereignty, the treasury assumes the character of an independent and 'personified fund' or asset. As Gierke writes, it becomes an immortal and abstract 'conceptual entity', an individual and 'fictive legal personality' that outlasts changes in ownership, and that confronts the sovereign as a sign of sovereignty, binding him with certain obligations – for example, the prohibition of the sale of state property.[13] The treasury occupies an eccentric position and, as the defining element of sovereignty, remains inaccessible to sovereign intervention.

Just as the treasury is separate both from the ruler as private person and from the sovereign as bearer of rights of sovereignty, so within the treasury itself a distinction is introduced between areas belonging to the sovereign powers of an inalienable and indivisible state power (such as rights of coinage) and elements subordinated to ordinary property law (such as mines or customs) – a strange conglomerate or confusion of rights of sovereignty and private-law stipulations. In the treasury, the distinction between acts of public law and mere business transactions is challenged and problematized. The objects and operations of the treasury are, in some sense, included among the sovereign rights of the sovereign. At the same time, it is uncertain whether this inclusion is essential or merely accidental; fiscal operations cannot be definitively separated from private business activities.[14] In Bodin, public domains and state property are tied to the status of the sovereign, and hence are 'sacred, inviolable, and inalienable' (*saint, sacré, et inaliénable*). Yet, insofar as fiscal law pertains to royal private property as well as public goods, it cannot straightforwardly be claimed as a distinguishing feature of sovereignty.[15] If, in the seventeenth century, the maxim 'that it is only the sovereign prince who has the right to have a treasury' applied, then this prerogative is directly tied to commitments and responsibilities.[16]

Alongside the question of public finances, that is to say the question of finance *per se*, ambiguities and dislocations emerge that evince a strange, unfamiliar and evasive subject matter both in the social and political life of modernity, and in canonical conceptions of political power.[17] ('Finance', deriving from the Latin *finis* and the medieval Latin *finare*, originally meant both 'end' and 'limit', as well as fixed 'duties' and 'to put an end to', i.e. 'pay'; initially, it referred to payments stipulated by public authorities, to all kinds of monetary transactions with the court.) Attempts at a monolithic comprehension of the problem of sovereignty are suffused by resistances and interferences stemming from the fiscal and financial field. On the one hand, the treasury constitutes a realm possessing the key features and powers of sovereign authority. On the other hand, this realm disintegrates into various public and private remits and responsibilities; only with a great deal of conceptual effort can it be associated with the standard political format of sovereignty. On the one hand, the treasury is an impersonal, timeless and inalienable entity, almost holy; like the sovereign, it stands above the law, can be addressed as the 'soul of the state', and marks a sphere of supra-personal continuity. On the other hand, the institution of an independent legal person in the form of the treasury causes tension between the ruling authority and the 'sacred' realm of finance; sovereignty appears restricted, and the quasi-eternal duration of the sovereign is made dependent on the quasi-eternal duration of the treasury.

A process was thus completed in which, as Ernst Kantorowicz observed, resolutely secular entities such as the treasury, finance and state property received the signature of the numinous, and thereby the capacity to represent the permanent and inviolable aspects of monarch and state.[18] However, the connection between the financial and the magical-theological features of sovereignty marked a weakness in the uniform structure of sovereign power; the treasury or the realm of finance became the site of a peculiar fusion between political power, societal operations and bourgeois private transactions. Attempts to define the treasury in legal-political terms repeatedly led to a zone of indeterminacy, in which the categorization of fiscal affairs – from rights of coinage, taxation and duties, through confiscations and contributions, to customs, salt works or mines – remained provisional or debatable at best. The special status of the treasury in early modernity is demonstrated by that fact that, at crucial moments, it clearly coincides with the arcane realm of sovereignty, while at the same time, and equally clearly, setting itself apart and situating itself as a sphere of action and power with its own qualities.

Coinage Policy   Similar reciprocities, transgressions and zones of indeterminacy can be seen in connection with an uncontested and inviolable fiscal right of sovereignty: the right of coinage or minting privileges. Until the early-modern period, coins and the functions of money – as well as weights and measures as such – were considered the property and the responsibility of the crown, and secured a large proportion of royal income. Alongside the notorious manipulation and reminting of coins, this happened through so-called seigniorage – a form of duty that masters of the mint were entitled to levy through the manufacture of coins.

Coinage profit and production costs were reflected in the difference between the nominal value and the melt value of coins
in circulation. The right of coinage included setting the legal
price of the currency; it dictated the conditions of circulation
and fixed the parameters for private business activities such as
trade in precious metals. On the whole, the mints were privately
run and vested with privileges. In other words, the production
of money and the processing of raw materials into legal currency
were characterized by an overlapping of commercial and royal
interests.

Seigniorage did not develop simply as a lone privilege in
connection with monopoly-like coin manufacturers. Its relation
to the formation of sovereign statehood consisted in the fact
that the monarch standardized the units of measure circulating
in his territory and verified the values set by the mints. Until
the sixteenth century, the levying of charges on money meant
that the arbitrary act of authority – as *valor impositus* expressed
in the coin's denomination – became the symbol of the recognition
of this very authority. The coin is the sovereign's locus of representation. The sovereign's minted name or portrait announces
that the coin 'is subordinated entirely to the authority of the
sovereign monarch, who stipulates its material, form, market
value, weight and price according to his wish'.[19] The financing
of the treasury underpins the mechanisms of the early-modern
circulation of money and the institutionalization of territorially
circumscribed currencies.

The formation of sovereign power was associated with a
network of actors and heterogeneous operations marked by a
close interconnection of the private and public spheres. This
was not only the case for minting privileges, which were awarded
to urban landowners and rural aristocrats; generally inheritable,
minting privileges combined royal functions with private commercial activity. More importantly, monetary-political factors
such as seigniorage and the specification of denomination
impacted on the mutual integration of political rule and private
wealth creation, whose dynamics led to the emergence of the
first financial markets. The precondition for this was the separation of different sorts of money. While coins and cash of all
kinds and provenance circulated across borders more or less
freely, the currencies stipulated by rights of coinage were valid
only within respective zones of sovereignty, and were not directly

convertible. Broadly speaking, this meant that within a particular territory the market value of foreign coins was determined not by their nominal value in the country of origin (material value plus seigniorage) but by their fineness. In other words, the exchange rate was calculated by treating foreign coins as commodities and placing them in relation to the legal means of payment. This situation – which introduced the professions of the money-changer and the banker – was an accidental result of emergent statehood, caused by acts of sovereignty, by territorial standardization and by the homogenization of coinage.

However, a systemic or systematic relationship was also established through private operations, namely through one of the most prominent commercial practices of the time. Since the thirteenth century, bills of exchange and the transactions associated with them had become the most important financing instrument of the European economy, playing a central role in the rise of a new caste of traders, the merchant bankers. Insofar as cashless payments with bills of exchange consisted in transferring money from one territory to another, or borrowing in one place in order to pay back money in another, exchange transactions were always tied up with money-changing operations. Payment using bills of exchange linked the trade in commodities to exchange-rate relations; the currencies of different territories or countries were placed in relation. The wealth of merchant bankers, and of early-modern banking as such, was commonly attributed to their disregard for territorialities, to concealed interest charges and to speculative exploitation of variations in exchange rates.[20] Most importantly, however, merchant banking enabled a mechanism whereby sovereign right of coinage became directly intertwined with private commercial contracts.

For example, when a merchant banker purchased a bill of exchange above a certain sum, with which the issuer wished to finance a business deal elsewhere, the price was determined according to a rate, calculated in the place of issue, based on the ratio between local currency at face value and foreign coins at melt value (in other words, their value minus the seigniorage). The sum was calculated according to the legal value of the coins in their place of origin. However, it was payable at the place of destination or transaction, where it was calculated according to the local exchange rate; in other words, it was changed into the local currency (including the seigniorage). Through the transfer, the merchant banker earned the difference corresponding to the seigniorage of the foreign coins. However, this profit could only be cashed in when the transaction went a step further and the sum was, via any number of stages, returned by means of bills of exchange to its place of origin, where the local seigniorage was now added to the original currency.

This process should not be seen as mere arbitrage or the clever exploitation of profit-making opportunities. Rather, it was a necessary function of the structure of the early-modern monetary order, in which political measures and commercial practices were interwoven. It is possible to speak of a 'seigniorage effect': the relation between the rate of exchange in transactions using bills of exchange, and legal value in transactions using cash or coins, allowed the merchant banker to make a profit on the difference whenever a deal was made with a foreign country where seigniorage was charged.[21] In other words, the capitalist form of enrichment that took place was due less to a conscious profit-making strategy than to a systemic interlacing of political structures and commercial practices.

If these dynamics are seen as exemplary moments in the fiscal and financial order of early modernity, then two aspects are noteworthy. First, there is the mutual reinforcement of private and political forces. On the one hand, royal seigniorage enables private enrichment on the part of the merchant banker; on the other hand, the exchange business indirectly secures and confirms the autonomy of royal prerogatives in monetary matters. A complementation and combination of responsibilities takes place. While the right of coinage pertains directly to money in circulation within a particular territory, guaranteeing fiscal income, the trade in bills of exchange involves foreign money, constituting an international currency system and at the same time promoting the accumulation of private capital. There is no opposition here between a centralized state and a decentralized market; on the contrary, a financial-economic dynamic results directly from the complementarity and coordination of sovereign acts and commercial conventions.[22]

Second, the circulation of money and the monetization of Europe are characterized by the contrary movements of nationalization and privatization. While the mints – sanctioned by rights of coinage and royal privileges – transformed commodities (precious metals) into legal and territorially bound currencies,

Monetization

thereby connecting the circulation of coins to the requirements of the treasury, in prevailing business practices a reverse process took place. As the circulation of bills of exchange shows, this gave rise, via the trade in two or more legal currencies, to a kind of private mintage. Public money, including seigniorage, was thereby privatized. In parallel with royal mintage, the trade in bills of exchange converts private book money into legal currency. The royal monopoly on mintage is matched by a private monopoly on money on the part of the merchant banker, who owes his wealth to the interaction of both forces. Sovereign power to specify the value of money emerges as the accidental condition for the systemic duality of public and private money.

Local differences and peculiarities aside, the monetary system in sixteenth-century Europe thus has two essential components. Parallel to the multitude of public coinages legally valid on sovereign territories was a private 'mintage', practised across borders by the merchant banking monopoly, which validated foreign money.[23] This is the context in which the concrete functions of money emerged in early modernity. Whether money is understood as an emergent medium of exchange or as a standard for relations of debt, the monetization of Europe in the Renaissance produces a nuanced picture, revealing a form of money defined by a relation between the public and the private.[24] Social and economic intercourse is structured by an elementary relationship between sovereign regulation and commercial practice. The distinctions between legal monetary value, the price of precious metals and 'fictitious' book money determine the dynamic of monetary relations, making plausible a 'nominalist' interpretation of the monetary function.[25] If money means what money does, then it denotes a space in which the requirements of territorial statehood and the privileged status of merchant bankers are expressed in one and the same act (of payment).

The monetary system in early modernity and the monetization of European commercial transactions cannot, therefore, be described in terms of an opposition between state structures and economic dynamics. At the political end of the spectrum, the right of coinage is not identical with the state entity, but is characterized by an indeterminacy between public and private actors and operations. Conversely, the private business activities of merchant bankers and others results not in an atomized market, but in a hierarchical and quasi-monopolistic network of exchanges directly dependent on royal prerogatives (such as seigniorage). A mutual integration and co-adaptation took place between sovereign acts and commercial activities. The right of coinage and its evolution into a state prerogative created space for specific forms of enterprise and profit. This is the background for the emergence of various related processes of capitalization affecting public finances and royal power in equal measure. All these aspects can be situated within the parameters of a general development, whereby – somewhat paradoxically – the extension of sovereign rule over several centuries takes place in parallel with the alienation of official responsibilities and functions.

If these processes marked the start of the gradual decline of the feudal understanding of money as a matter for the ruler, then from around the end of the sixteenth century – in connection with monetary crises and emergent absolutism – it is possible to observe a theoretical and practical restructuring of the monetary system, a transformation that affected the relationship between the sovereign and the right of coinage in particular. Fourteenth- and fifteenth-century analyses of monetary and coin policy had already criticized the fact that the coin belonged to the domain of the regent and claimed that the right of coinage as such belonged to the community. Here, the sovereign appeared not as the author or owner of the money in circulation but as the 'most public person' and 'highest authority' (*persona magis publica* or *maioris auctoritas*), whose function was solely to represent the public order.[26] The turbulences connected to the manipulation and debasement of coins led repeatedly to demands that monetary value be protected from arbitrary royal interven- tion, and that the resultant fiscal losses be compensated via indirect charges and excise duties.

These considerations are linked directly to modern concepts of sovereignty. Jean Bodin observed the ruinous effects of debase- ment, condemning such interventions – which were mostly used to finance extraordinary expenditure on war and suchlike – as confiscations and as a 'barbaric injustice' that was responsible for a general loss of confidence in public and private affairs as a whole.[27] It was to prevent this happening that the sovereign, as representative of the people, was entrusted with maintaining the quality of coins. This meant, on the one hand, that in theories of sovereignty from the end of the sixteenth century, rights of coinage continued to fall exclusively within the remit of the

Money and Law

crown as 'one of the most exceptional features of sovereignty'. The prerogative was therefore guarded jealously; any violation of it constituted high treason and was a capital offence (counterfeiters received the cruellest of punishments, such as being boiled alive in oil).[28] On the other hand, the royal right of coinage was not unconditional. It was argued that the value of coins and money was analogous to the law: 'The right of coinage is of the same nature as the law.' Here, the theoreticians of sovereignty fell back on an Aristotelian precept, as Nicolas Oresme had done in the fourteenth century, understanding *nummus* (coin) as a derivation of *nomos* (law), and money itself as an institution with its own inherent laws. Fineness, value and standard were thought to have legal status; just as sovereignty represented the indivisible and unassailable measure of all relations, so the purity of minted metal provided the unalterable value of things. The relation between melt value and nominal value was placed beyond the reach of arbitrary intervention. This meant that the coin was 'inseparably' bound to the crown and could no longer be alienated via privileges or lease, as the financial situation required. More importantly, however, the sovereign himself was bound by the law. Any alteration of monetary value, any change in the relation between fineness and denomination, was now equivalent to royal counterfeit; it injured rights of sovereignty and was permissible only in extreme emergencies.[29] Connecting monetary value to metal value represented an important step in the evolution of state sovereignty over money; however, while prohibiting the alteration of coin value limited the scope for speculation, it was simultaneously an act of sovereign self-constraint.

Here, too, a kind of sovereignty paradox emerges. Defining coinage as an inalienable power of the sovereign disqualified sovereign manipulation and seignorage; the authority of the sovereign over the institution of money was precisely what bound the sovereign to its law. Absolute sovereignty – *legibus solutus* – was limited not only by divine and natural law, or the law of dynastic sequence, but by the integrity of fiscal and monetary prerogatives.[30] The unconstrained sovereign was confronted by the barrier of an inviolable monetary system.

Public Credit   Even if the forms of sovereign statehood in Europe proposed by Bodin and others existed only embryonically, and were more prospective than real, they can be understood as articulations of an interest in the stabilization of state structures and finances.[31] It was only in 1577 that the French king carried out a monetary reform obliging him to prevent coin manipulation and to guarantee the fineness of the various coins. The problems connected to this kind of regulation raise more fundamental questions about state financing that go back to the fifteenth century. These questions concern the transformation of occasional, extraordinary and arbitrary charges into permanent fiscal revenues, and are closely linked to the institutionalization of national debt and taxation, in other words to the genesis of the modern state itself.

After the Hundred Years War, fiscal debt and royal budgets in Europe increased drastically. The dawn of 'public credit' – in other words, private lending to the sovereign or the state – was attended by the dual concern as to how European royal houses could prove to their creditors that they were reliable debtors and, conversely, how state financing was to be permanently secured. It was by no means guaranteed that monarchs would take over the debts of their dynastic predecessors; this meant that obtaining money in emergencies was consistently problematic. Financing via tax and duties therefore had the character of temporary confiscations born of emergency, enforceable only in the face of resistance; and they were supplemented by a range of other instruments, such as the mortgaging of crown goods, the leasing of property, and the issue of compulsory bonds and short-term securities. An exception to this was the city societies, whose citizens vouched for public debts with their private assets; the creditworthiness of city societies led to their being characterized as abstract, 'eternal' legal personalities, regardless of changes of government.[32]

At play in the system of public credit and national debt was the interpenetration of the state administration and the financial economy, together with the emergence of modern political-economic systems and the agenda of the 'finance state'.[33] National debt in the strict sense was unknown in antiquity; during the Middle Ages, because of weak central government and uncertain dynastic succession, it was only possible to a limited extent. However, by the fifteenth century it had become systematic. Contemporaries and older economists – from Bodin to Boisguilbert – saw the financial policy of Francis I of France as a prime example and, while drawing various conclusions, noted the emergence of national borrowing and the budgetary interconnection between fiscal debt and state financing. Whether in admiration or with alarm, they noted how, in connection with the wars with the Habsburg Empire, the state accepted advance payments and loans with interest in order to cover not only exceptional financial requirements but also regular and permanent expenses.

In around the mid-sixteenth century, this financial policy led to the formation of financial consortia and financial markets, in particular at the Lyon stock exchange. Simultaneously, the city of Paris issued annuities (*Rentes sur l'Hôtel de Ville*), interest on which the city covered by raising indirect taxes on commodities like meat, fish and wine. The Parisian municipal administration was charged with administering these taxes, setting in motion a cycle of debt servicing and taxation beyond the direct intervention of the regent. After numerous failed attempts, the financial administration was also centralized; earnings from the crown lands were combined with tax revenues in a single state treasury (*Trésor de l'Épargne*), intended as a reserve for unforeseen and exceptional events. This led to an organizational form in which sovereign state power was divided into complex branches (fig. 3). As a result, ordinary revenues such as income from the crown lands gained an extraordinary status, and what had until then been extraordinary, such as taxation, became normal. More generally, a taxation state emerged whose origins go back to the thirteenth century. Tax law and its usurpation by the regents were an essential characteristic of sovereignty, catalysing the administrative permeation of the social field and the development of sovereign state structures. These structures established a fiscal connection between national debt and tax duty; the exceptional became normal, temporary distress became an ongoing necessity, and acute external emergencies (such as war) became 'internal administrative needs'.[34] The connection between national debt and the continuous raising of tax could now be seen as a fiscal and administrative perpetuation of emergency and exceptional situations in the name of state sovereignty. From this angle, the demands of the treasury and the financing of the state instituted the dictate of permanent *necessitas* or emergency at the heart of the architecture of government.

On the one hand, this normalization of extraordinary capital requirements – the trinity of defence, public borrowing and taxation – could be seen as the motor for the emergence of

Figure 3: Tree diagram of the French estates and authorities. Source: Charles de Figon, *Discours des estats et offices, tant du gouvernement que de la justice & des finances de France*, Paris 1579 (the branches of the mint and the financial executive, including the knot of the state treasury, are on the right).

modern state structures and their executive apparatuses. The tax farmer became an official functionary, and the prototype of the 'public servant' emerged from the royal financial executive.[35] A further indicator of the birth of the modern state from the spirit of national debt is that, given the complex bundle of obligations, leaseholds, securities, mortgages, bonds and pensions from which modern public financing emerged, the concept of 'eternal debt' was used in the financial sector before a sovereign and 'eternal' state authority was recognized in principle.[36] Private creditors yearned for a national debtor that took responsibility for and survived its debts. The connection between royal financial needs, national indebtedness and private creditors created a situation that required the establishment of a permanent cycle of debt. Interest payment demands and repayment deadlines on the part of the financial consortia meant that the royal budget needed to be secured through the continuous raising of tax. Fiscal debt guarantees state sovereignty; sovereign debt precedes political sovereignty. If sovereign is he who decides on the exception, then equally sovereign is he who enables this decision – for example the financers of national debt. The financial problems of early-modern states are the context of theoretical and practical efforts to comprehend sovereign rule. The rise of European trading houses, financial consortia and monopolies, and their ties to the European monarchies, prompted the centralization and entrenchment of the absolutist state machinery.

On the other hand, the fiscal introduction of national debt – and of a sovereign state burdened by repayment obligations – led to a mobilization of commercial forces and private financial power. National debt as an entity became the strongest source of private wealth.[37] Here, it was not only a matter of temporary alliances between regents and merchant capital, like the one that bound together the Fuggers of Augsburg and the Habsburg emperor Charles V from their ascent to their decline. Rather, a process occurred in which the antagonisms between political structures and money capital themselves collapsed, if they even existed in the first place. This gave rise to the aggressive figures of early-modern capitalist power, the first prominent example of which were the northern Italian city-states.

Genoa   As early as 1148, the Republic of Genoa was forced to issue bonds, its creditors forming societies which, for the purpose of interest payments and debt servicing, were delegated the administration of tax revenues. During the permanent wars in northern Italy, this system expanded. These societies or *compere* (literally 'purchases') multiplied along with the loans; in 1407, the majority merged to form the Casa di San Giorgio. This supplied the Genoese government with regular credit into the eighteenth century. It has been described as one of the first ever public limited companies and the model for what were to become clearing banks, lending banks, banks of issue and deposit banks. However, as an embodiment of early financial power, it was only able to operate by virtue of its origins in a systematic fusion between public or sovereign components and private interests. The Casa di San Giorgio incorporated a consortium of private creditors into the Genoese government and the administration of the republic. Traders occupied positions in the political executive and rentiers or *comperisti* gained a permanent place in the legislature, controlling government revenues, state borrowing and public finances. The Casa received monopoly rights on taxation, it mortgaged state property, operated armies and fleets, waged war and signed treaties; it was ceded judicial authority, colonies and rights of sovereignty. Genoa has therefore been referred to as the plutocratic or 'capitalist city par excellence', and the Casa as a 'state within a state'.[38]

Crucial, at any rate, is that national debt became the locus and motif of the mutual integration of political institutions and commerce; only once these had become indistinguishable did the power of Genoese finance emerge. By the mid-fifteenth century, the Casa was the most powerful financial institution in the Occident. Increasingly, Genoese merchant bankers transferred trading profits into public bonds and securities. In the sixteenth century, they allied with Spain; their bills of exchange mobilized capital for German trading houses such as Fugger or Welser, at the same time forcing these out of the credit business with Spain. Genoese bankers developed new strategies in the securities trade and organized the conveyance of a large portion of Spanish silver assets from Seville to northern Italy; they financed Spanish troops in the Netherlands and dominated the money markets at stock exchanges and trading centres in Lyon, Besançon, Antwerp and elsewhere. In Venice, trade and finance were controlled by the municipal authorities; this state-centred system enabled the city to assert territorial dominance in northern Italy. In Genoa, on the other hand, the fusion of socialized debt and privatized state revenues created the conditions for supra-territorial networks, enabling the city-state to dominate European finance and to be seen as the prototype for cosmopolitan capital accumulation.[39]

The emergence of money and financial markets was, in turn, the result of the direct or indirect interconnection between state financing and private commercial practice. From the 1530s onwards, under Genoese dominance, the money markets developed into mobile trade fairs, based first in Besançon or 'Bisenzone' and later in Piacenza, asserting their supremacy up until the seventeenth century. The main protagonists were the Spanish monarchy and its financial needs, the armies stationed in Italy and in particular in the Netherlands, the Spanish silver imports from the American mines, and the Genoese businesspeople and merchant bankers who organized the fairs. Contemporaries noted the peculiarity of these events, the isolation of the money trade and its connection with the dictates of Spanish politics. The Genoese 'exchange fairs', wrote one contemporary, 'are the heart that gives nutrition, motion and life to the mysterious body politic'.[40] It was not only about providing the Spanish royal house with regular and continuous credit, in view of the irregularity of Spanish fiscal revenue and silver imports, but also about organizing transactions that ranged from Madrid to the distant outposts of the Spanish military. The basis of the trade was contracts or *asientos*, with which the Spanish crown transferred large sums of money to troops stationed in the Netherlands or Italy, making use of Genoese commercial connections to do so, and offering American silver imports in return. Contracts covering an entire annual demand were sometimes signed, deals done via a complex system of financing.

For example, when the Spanish financial authorities signed a contract with Genoese bankers for ten million *scudi* to cover costs in the Netherlands, the bankers undertook to pay out the amount in advance in Antwerp. Simultaneously, the Genoese had to ensure that they received reimbursement from Spain. At the quarterly fairs, they bought bills of exchange issued for Antwerp, as well as securities from Spain, in order to schedule Spanish repayments. The deals were carried out via various routes and intermediary purchases, exploiting discrepancies in value and demand at the various trading centres. The securities themselves were, in turn, mostly paid for using bills of exchange of various origins, depending on the favourability of the purchase price. These operations could, in principle, be carried out without cash and even without one's own capital; personal risk was also minimized by involving foreign assets and investments. This series of deals – the so-called *ricorsa* – culminated in the fulfilment of payment obligations in the Netherlands (in gold) and reimbursement by the Spanish crown (e.g. through the shipping of silver from Seville for resale in Genoa). The strategic and logistic requirements of the Spanish crown thus led to an extensive system of financial transactions linking up trade across the whole of Europe. The Genoese trade fairs served as clearing houses for the settling of obligations and demands. A new currency – the *scudo di marchi* – was created as the unit of payment at these fairs. This was tied to gold and had no equivalent in any minted currency. As a pure measure of value, it had several advantages: it was not territorially bound, it was independent of royal monetary policy, and it made the money markets independent.

Simultaneously, however, a private credit business emerged, triggered by the Spanish monarchy's financial requirements and global power politics. Dominated by the Genoese *banchieri di conto*, this business exploited the existing system of exchange and in doing so generated a European-wide financial market. The trade fairs came to resemble informal banks, the cascades of *ricorsa* transforming conventional bills of exchange into credit instruments – while bypassing traditional prohibitions on usury. Money transfers became credit operations. The trade in investments, and in investments in investments, established an expanded market system based on private advances and public loans. This implies that Genoese wealth and Spanish military power were enabled not so much by gold and silver resources as by the use of credit techniques. The *asientos* combined the trade in bills of exchange, currency swaps, the circulation of payment, loans, advances, national debt, public credit and precious metal imports in an international network of financial transactions. Bernardo Davanzati, the Renaissance theorist of money, described this system in 1581 as a liberation of capital flows and a perturbing deterritorialization of commercial dynamics:

> The Genoese have invented a new kind of exchange trade, which they call the 'fairs of Besançon', because they originated there;

today, they take place in Savoy, in Piedmont, in Lombardy, in Trento, outside Genoa, and elsewhere, and are better described as 'utopia', i.e. fairs without a place. ... No trade in goods happens at them; rather fifty or sixty bankers assemble, each with a small book of papers, in order to control the exchange trade through almost the whole of Europe, and by re-exchange renewing it at a rate of interest agreed among themselves, whereby they are guided by one and only consideration, which is to guarantee the duration of the game for as long as possible.[41]

The interaction between Spanish global politics and Genoese bankers thus gave rise to the decentralized networks and centrifugal forces of the early financial markets. If Genoa was the prime example of the genesis of the capitalist 'world-system' (to use Wallerstein's term) in the fifteenth and sixteenth century, then this is due to a policy of public borrowing and the systematic 'alienation of the state', which 'marked the capitalist era with its stamp'.[42] The rise of Genoese financial power in the form of the Casa di San Giorgio and the emergence of the first international capital markets at the Genoese fairs were a result of the dynamics of national debt and the connection between sovereign policy and private commercial activity.

Seigniorial Power Modernity gave rise not only to sovereign state apparatuses, international trading companies, influential financiers and decentralized markets. A specific type of power also formed, one that is properly described neither in terms of political structures nor in terms of economic operations and strategies alone. Rather, it constituted itself through the interaction of both poles. The emergence of this type of power follows no inexorable logic of historical development; instead, it is contingent upon the problematic status of fiscal affairs, the expansion of territorial states and monetary systems, and the circumstances surrounding the financing of royal and national budgets. Given the increasing monetization of the European economy since the Renaissance, and the connections between fiscal policy and the generation of wealth, one might refer here to 'seigniorial power' (deriving from seigniorage). Seigniorial power differs from other kinds of state power insofar as it coincides neither with the political-legal institutions of sovereign power, nor with technologies of administration and government. Instead, it is based on the integration of private actors, trade and commerce. Nor is it synonymous or identical with financial power, despite its close proximity to it. The vaguely defined concept of financial power pertains primarily to the complex of high finance, the concentration of private financial capital, the banking sector and 'big business', including its political and social influence. In contrast, the specific genealogies, figures and modes of operation characterizing seigniorial power are connected with the zones of political-economic indeterminacy emerging alongside modern political orders and economic systems. They have an ambiguous relation to both sides, they are encouraged and restricted by state authorities, they can either boost or inhibit the exercise of political power, and they can stimulate or obstruct (for example through monopolization) market mechanisms.

The theoretical framing of seigniorial power is also difficult because political and economic theories of modernity are, for reasons of consistency, organized according to concepts of system, form and structure. While political theory, in its variations up to the present, is characterized by a constructive or deconstructive discussion of the form of political sovereignty, economic theory is above all oriented towards the formation of autonomous systems of economic functioning. The figures of seigniorial power, however, cannot be characterized by the fixity of forms, the coherence of systems or the stability of structures. Rather, their composition is informal, diffuse, unstable, resisting translation into a concise system. One might speak of an open and constellatory amalgamation, a fusion and interaction of forces of various provenance, whose power consists precisely in their lack of institutional or systematic character. There exist, at best, 'diagrammatic' arrangements, defined by fluid correlations between heterogeneous elements, by the development of informal fields of force and specific tactical and strategic modes of operation.[43]

Seigniorial power emerges alongside and in correspondence with particular features of modern state sovereignty, such as national debt and authority over taxation and currency, and at the same time includes the economic dynamics unleashed by these, such as the financial and capital markets. Its conceptualization therefore requires no prior entity such as the state or the market. The issue in connection with the concept of seigniorial power is not whether the modern state is the creature of the capitalist economy or its impulse and motor. There has been no conclusive answer to these questions; it has been conceded that the 'state' both prompted and delayed capitalist development, and was in turn both reinforced and impaired by it.[44] Nor is it a question of placing developed state apparatuses in complementary and crucial relation to capitalist modes of production, of interpreting them as the epiphenomena of property distribution, as the instruments of class war, as the guarantors of the regime of accumulation, as the superstructure of relations of production, or as ideal 'collective capitalists' and suppliers of material infrastructures.[45] Undoubtedly, seigniorial power and its components, such as company structure and modes of financing and accumulation, are linked to the process of capitalism. However, its defining feature is its autonomous strategic movement, one whose coordination with and subordination to market dynamics and state structures cannot be conclusively determined. The concept of seigniorial power expresses, at best, that the separation or dichotomy of politics and economics distorts the relation between value creation and the organization of power in the name of a theoretically ratified, abstract ideal. Seigniorial power was and is the blind spot of canonical political and economic theory.

Four Characteristics As a quality peculiar to the organization of relations of power in modern societies, seigniorial power has four characteristics. The first of these is its heterogeneous arrangement. Laws, social processes, political interventions, infrastructures (such as trade and finance) and private and public actors form an alliance, in which the formation of capital power is inseparable from the activation of power capital. The antagonism between 'state' and 'capital' is weak or absent altogether. The dominance of Genoese bankers in the Renaissance, for example, was based not just on the association of private financial resources, but also on the ability to transform potential for political action into commercial wealth – and vice versa. The *conversion of state power into capital*, and thus the capitalization of power as such, is – second – linked to fiscal operations; it occurs through the alienation of the state at the moment of its emergence. It denotes a dynamic in which the beginning of the 'epoch of statehood' coincides with a determination of its limits and end. This process is exemplified in the marketization of national debt, in the system of government bonds underwritten by taxation; originating in the northern Italian city-states, this linked executive activation of means of coercion with the creation of new fields of commerce. Just as permanent taxation establishes an immediate relation between individuals and the state, bypassing other, traditional or feudal forms of association, so public credit, loans and bonds embody a form of obligation that is an essential resource of seigniorial power.[46] Guaranteeing future fiscal revenue, seigniorial power coordinates itself via the *permeation of the social field*.

Third, cycles of credit and debt are thereby triggered that have rightly been referred to as the primal scenes of capital and finance. If 'capital' is broadly understood as an exploitable and processable sum of values that bears the hope of future profit, then the private management of national debt institutionalizes a speculative, 'capitalist' form of financing. 'The modern fiscal system, whose pivot is formed by taxes on the most necessary means of subsistence', plays a crucial role in the 'capitalization of wealth'; together with national debt, it is one of the 'secret foundations' and 'most powerful levers of primitive accumulation'.[47] Well into the eighteenth century, a 'capitalist' was someone who, alongside movable goods and liquid assets, owned government bonds.[48] As mysterious and primitive as this combination of treasury and *regime of accumulation* is, it cannot claim to be unique or particular; like all things 'primitive', it has a lengthy history. It caused the extraordinary to become the rule, the exceptional to become the norm. Accumulation is not antecedent (for example via forceful expropriation or 'enclosure'), but coincides with the formation of seigniorial power. Insofar as the financial economy since the Renaissance represents a precondition for industrial capitalism, one might, with respect to the operation of seigniorial power, speak of permanent primitive accumulation.

Fourth, this led to a movement as powerful as it was ambiguous. Just as the modern state secured its continuity through the perpetuation of national debt and taxation, so it obtained a quasi-sovereign power in fiscal affairs. At the same time, through the permanent state of exceptionality, this power evaded sovereign intervention (and later obtained institutional form in central banks). This indicates the precarious status of seigniorial power. In it, the alienation or privatization of state resources comes up against the political occupation of private finance. It is this two-way public–private charge that gives seigniorial power a special status. On the fiscal side, seignorial power claims arcane components and sovereign dignity; as the embodiment of private capital, on the other hand, it resists acts of arbitrary political power. The formation of the sovereign state unleashed, together with private trade, a dynamic which manifested itself in an eccentric becoming-sovereign of seigniorial power. With finance, a *reservation of sovereignty* forming a category of its own established itself alongside and apart from state authority.

4

Apotheosis of Finance

The relevance of political economy as a branch of knowledge Model and enquiry is connected to the emergence of specific figures of Capitalist power that accompany the formation of modern states, yet evade Nation immediate association with political structures and economic dynamics. This process involves, on the one hand, an economization of government, whose access to forms of social intercourse extends and intensifies the operative field of governmental regulation. On the other hand, a field of fiscality and finance is installed in the zone of indeterminacy between sovereign statehood and commercial practice. The development of economic government and seigniorial power was not synchronic, but was dictated by various sets of interests and issues. In the context of modern state reason, political economics – from mercantilism to liberalism – focused on the indirect control of the social field; it thus developed as a branch of governmental knowledge. In connection with fiscality and finance, on the other hand, the limits, aporias and 'perversions' of sovereign power became acutely problematic. For political economics, the concept of which was coined in the seventeenth century, the central issue was the social-technical suffusion of complex processes of exchange in emergent market societies. Seigniorial power, on the other hand, was formed by the exceptional private–public agencies that, since the sixteenth century, had gained important decision-making prerogatives in the organization, extent and exercise of state authority. Political-economic know-how and finance were thus the coordinates

according to which the operationality of economic power, a
dominant element in the development of modern societies, was
constituted.

An initial intersection of the two areas can be observed in
the 'model capitalist nation' of the seventeenth century: the
Dutch Republic, and in particular the province of Holland.[1]
Since 1566, the Netherlands had been involved in a war of
independence (lasting until 1648) with the Spanish monarchy;
as early as 1611, the Dutch Republic was referred to as the
prototype for a 'good regime and government' (*bon regime &
gouvernement*). It exemplified how the prerequisites for a strong
and stable society were best found in a 'free, competent, industri-
ous, mercantile nation' liberated from absolutist rule. It was in
this connection that the concept of 'political economy' was coined
to refer to a harmonious order in the movement of people and
things.[2] A few decades later, this tendency became marked in
canonical commentaries on Holland's political form. Against
the background of long-running debates about the role of the
(Spanish) governor, about resistance to monarchical authority,
and about the federal and republican order, Dutch governmental
practice was measured on the basis of its promotion of 'welfare',
'wealth', population growth, commercial activity and 'private
interests', and hence on its systematic economization of political
maxims and principles.[3] This accounts for the fact that, at the
turn of the seventeenth century, Simon Stevin, the Dutch math-
ematician and advisor to Moritz von Oranien, complained about
the introduction of commercial, 'Italian' or double bookkeeping
in the management of public budgets.[4] However, if the Netherlands' combination of a strong and hegemonic state power with
a weak central administration was seen as atypical,[5] then this
was not least due to an extensive fusion of political institutions
and capital, to a proliferation of public–private junctures, and
hence to a dispersal of seigniorial power. In the Netherlands,
the economization of government and the integration of private
finance into the exercise of politics gave rise to a new 'diagrammatic' structure in the organization of power.

The In the Netherlands, too, the roots of this development were
Politics the politics of national debt. Charles V urged the Dutch provinces
of Debt to buy Spanish government bonds, which were guaranteed by
granting the provinces tax sovereignty and by levying permanent
poll taxes and duties in the Netherlands itself. These new

instruments (*nieuwe middelen*), employed from the mid-sixteenth century, installed a system of credit and tax capable of financing not only Spanish rule but also, from the end of the sixteenth century, the struggle for Dutch independence. The system was characterized by heavy taxation, permanent national debt and low interest rates on government bonds. The cycle of public borrowing and tax revenue was supplemented by the decentralized dissemination of state bonds, which could be issued by individual provinces, tax districts or the admiralty. This established a molecular permeation of public institutions by private financial investors, who because of guaranteed returns were unconcerned about the repayment of public debts (records show that in the 1660s there were around 65,000 rentiers in the province of Holland). Conversely, as was observed at the time, heavy taxation – including the taxation of the poorest of the poor – enabled the capillary *étatisation* of the social field. The acceptance of tax or tax bondage, primarily justified through the permanent state of war (*staat von oorlog*), ratified the political agenda and can be seen as an indicator of the state's penetration of society.[6]

Just as continuous taxation was an economic expression of the disciplinary cohesion between the state and individuals, so the financing of national debt through taxation expressed the dependency of political structures on private finance (see fig. 4). Holland's exceptional status in the seventeenth century was, among other things, due to the perfection of the cycle of credit and taxation, which manifested itself in the antithetical and unlimited movements of economization and *étatisation*. These can be understood as two halves of a political-economic 'apparatus of capture'.[7] The realization that high taxation could be productive, that it could be beneficial not only in terms of the volume of national debt, but also in terms of rents and profits, was an important moment in the history of capitalism. The fusion of the public and private was achieved through the systematic insertion of creditors, rentiers and pensioners into political administrations, causing the interests of the municipalities to converge with those of wealthy investors. Political institutions gave merchants, bankers and investors in government securities a significant degree of control over public affairs. The interaction between taxation, national debt and the rentier class was the reason for the continuous availability of credit and the success of the Dutch provinces as a whole.[8]

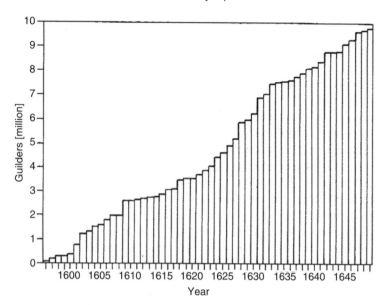

Figure 4: Public debt of the States-General in long-term bonds. Source: Marjolein t'Hart, *The Making of a Bourgeois State: War, Politics and Finance During the Dutch Revolt* (Manchester 1993, 167).

Corporations, Institutions   Another crucial factor in the convergence of political and economic interests was the United East India Company (*Vereenigde Oostindische Compagnie*, VOC), founded in 1602 on the orders of the States-General to eliminate competition and monopolize foreign trade. This business consortium, whose Juvenalian motto was *orbis non sufficit*, organized the exploitation of the East Indian colonies – including forced labour, massacre and occasional genocide – by means of new financial instruments such as shares and regular dividends for investors. Its foundation also represented an important step in the emergence of effective corporate structures, connecting institutionally and legally private commercial activity with sovereign authority. In its operations in the Far East, the VOC – and later the Dutch West India Company – was ceded a range of sovereign rights, for example the right to wage war, to sign treaties under international law, to diplomatic representation, to judicial authority, to keep a fleet and an army, and to seize territories. The internalization of protection costs and the privatization of the military budget were concomitant with the private financing of state functions. Although the business policy of the VOC, with its reliance on a purely extractive colonial economy, was rendered obsolete by its English competitors in the eighteenth century, there was no doubt that its merging of capital interests, methods of financing and rights of sovereignty was an organizational innovation in corporate management.[9]

The Netherlands became the nucleus of the capitalist world-system by systematically arranging these political-economic agencies into a network of capital and financial markets. Amsterdam's growth from the early seventeenth century into a centre of international finance – replacing Genoa and Antwerp – was the result of an interplay of institutions ensuring the mobilization of financial transactions, the money market, and the trade in public and private securities. The Wisselbank in Amsterdam, founded in 1609 on the orders of the city authorities and based in the town hall, was originally intended to be a deposit and clearing bank. However, it subsequently began purchasing, selling and exchanging currencies, regulating transfers and cashless transactions, granting overdrafts and transferring promissory letters, IOUs and bills of exchange, thereby becoming the most important point of exchange in the European financial system. Even though the bank did not issue money or banknotes, it gradually transformed, contrary to its statutes, into a credit institute. It provided liquidity to the government and the VOC during war and times of crisis, and towards the end of the seventeenth century also began lending to private companies. It was regarded as the guarantor of confidence in Dutch public finances. Because of its domestic and international dominance in the movement of capital, the Wisselbank – which had been established under republican conditions – was soon seen as a quasi-monarchical and sovereign entity, if not the *arcana imperii* of the United Netherlands.[10]

With the foundation of the Amsterdam stock exchange in 1611, a venue was created that supplemented commodities and futures trading with a market for securities, funds and bonds. The first extensive commentaries record trading in financial instruments such as options and securities; the 'spume of specula-tion' above all included the shares of the VOC and later public bonds. On the resultant secondary market, the reduction of transaction and information costs accompanied greater mobility in capital transactions.[11] A study of 1766 noted that the credit operations of a dozen traders in Amsterdam could, in an instant, move bank money of up to 'two hundred million guilders' across Europe: 'There is no sovereign who is able to do such a thing. … This credit is a power that ten or twelve traders exercise in all the nations of Europe with absolute independence of all authority.'[12] Amsterdam's emergence as a centre of capital and finance, and the Dutch regime of accumulation as such, were enabled by the connection between public borrowing, semi-oligarchic associations of investors, private limited companies, banking institutes and securities markets. One might therefore speak of a modern 'financial revolution'.

Political Anomaly   The political anomaly of the Netherlands in the seventeenth century – namely its hegemonic status despite a weak state and lack of administrative centralization – is defined by multiple overlaps between economic and political structures. On the one hand, cooperation between public institutions and private finance intensified and proliferated at various organizational, local and personal levels. On the other hand, the nexus of state and finance obtained institutional stability and permanence. This nexus was expressed in the coalition between fiscal debt, public credit and taxation, in the company structures of the United East India Company, and in the operations of the Wisselbank; it became a coherent financial system through the securities trading of the stock market. That the Netherlands was able to assume 'arche-typal' capitalist form despite its atypical and extraordinary status in Europe was due to the systematic enforcement and entrench-ment of seigniorial power.[13]

The Dutch regime of accumulation and bourgeois state-formation overcame various obstacles: Spanish rule, domestic revolts against heavy taxation, the Portuguese and English naval powers, and the local economies in East India. At the same time, it appeared as a combination of 'solutions' that minimized and even resolved the tension between political power and private wealth. Dutch predominance in the seventeenth century – arising from contingent circumstances, including the *Grand Privilège* of 1477, Spanish occupation policy, confessional conflicts, minimal territorial coherence, the absence of strong feudal structures, and a loose federal arrangement – entailed the historical potentiation of seigniorial power, together with its social and economic innovations. These were characterized by a diagrammatic form and fluent transitions between moments of sovereignty, practices of government and market dynamics.

It is no surprise, then, that the predominant descriptions of these political-economic formations emphasize – above and beyond geographic factors – a society with diminished territoriality, weak striation, high mobility and a prioritization of spaces of traffic and transmission. The Dutch were perceived as 'the *Carryers of the World*, the middle Persons in Trade, the Factors and Brokers of *Europe*',[14] and the Dutch ports, particularly Amsterdam, as disorderly demographic conglomerations, as the 'mouth of Europe's drain, through which surges the waste and detritus of all the corners of our continent'.[15] The political anomaly was figuratively described as a 'semiaquatic existence', a border-zone between land and sea, an 'amphibian habitat' – iconographic elements that belied the economic dynamism of the political body.[16] They can be understood as emblematic references to the fact that – as had been calculated in the eighteenth century[17] – the liquid capital of the Netherlands far exceeded the value of the territory of the state, including its fixed assets. In these images, the Netherlands and its political *raison d'être* appear as the plague of an old-European 'Nomos of the Earth', for which the state and the law existed only on terra firma, far removed from coasts, ports, economic activity and promiscuous social transactions.[18]

At the same time, the intensification and dissemination of seigniorial power and its enclosure in the nexus of finance and the state can be understood as a central agent of what would later be referred to as capitalism. This is because the concept of capitalism, which, as historians have demonstrated, made a comeback having previously been rejected,[19] cannot be reduced to a mere signifier of free-market principles, or a term for economic systems as such. Rather, from the end of the nineteenth century, the concept is linked to a line of historiographical enquiry that, alongside economic forms, corporate structures and property relations, includes the historical parameters of politics, culture and mentality.[20] The various 'spirits' of capitalism can be defined in countless ways: as the rational tempering of irrational drives, as the dissociation of labour from the means of production, as the privately run free-market economy, as the dominance of a

'Capitalism'

dynamic class of business owner, as unrestricted capital accumulation by ostensibly peaceful means. However, across the spectrum of attempts to define capitalism, one problem asserts itself more or less constantly. This is that the 'capitalist' question, the question as to capitalist form, has two implications: first, that modern and early-modern economic forms cannot be reduced to the dynamic of a closed subsystem, which functions in concert with other social subsystems; second, that what is at stake is the arenas where social reproduction in general is linked to the self-reproduction of capital and market mechanisms in particular.

In this context, seigniorial power can be understood as an essential factor and prerequisite for the capitalist dynamic. Seigniorial power generates, guarantees and propagates the connection between political structures and private commercial activity; it links processes of financing with the organization of the social field; it creates a class of dominant rentier; it founds and stabilizes cycles of fiscal debt and public credit, and thus a dependable system of credit as such; it provides the infrastructure for the expanding movement of money and capital. A continuous capitalization of state power thus occurs in the form of private wealth. Simultaneously, a form of speculative financing is institutionalized, whose operations and investments provide the locus for the self-reproduction of functional private–public dependencies. It is by no means coincidental that the concept of investment, which became common in the seventeenth century as a term for the realization of capital advances with the prospect of future profits (in connection with trading in East India), derived from the older word 'investiture', signifying the ceding or 'beclothing' of feudal rights of property in order to create subaltern dependency.[21] As an elementary mode of capitalist operation, investment transfers financial resources in order to reproduce relations of social dependency and structures of obligation.

Marxist intuition would suggest that capital and capital accumulation should be understood not just as economic and commercial units or determinate quantities of value, intervening at various moments in processes of production and exchange. Embodied and circulating in these measurable quantities is a combination of political and economic forces; and it is these forces that precipitated and enabled the financial regime. The key question is not whether and how processes of accumulation are to be understood as 'primitive', as the logical and historical condition for capitalism. Rather, modern capital accumulation was only possible through the existence of seigniorial power, in other words through the systematic combination of state authority and private enrichment, for example the systematic combination of the 'colonies, the national debt, the modern tax system and the system of protection'.[22] What took place in the Netherlands from the end of the sixteenth century cannot be understood simply as a broad transition from feudal orders to capitalism; rather, it was a process in which disparate forms of seigniorial power coalesced and concentrated into a coherent order, enabling private property to circulate as capitalized state power. From a genetic or genealogical perspective, finance capital is a quantifiable, exploitable and mobile quantity of private–public dependencies.

Seigniorial power, the aggressive linking of state structures and private finance, inaugurated 'one of the most brutal and most bigoted [periods] in the history of modern Europe'.[23] And yet, because of its informal and diagrammatic character, its conceptualization is largely absent from political and economic theory. With its elementary significance for the establishment of capitalist processes of financing, seigniorial power becomes the focus of crucial questions concerning the production of institutional persistency. Particularly important in this respect are all those experiments and projects that from the seventeenth century served to embed creditors in the structure of national debt, and that gradually and with varying degrees of success led to the foundation of central banks, national banks and banks of issue. The debates that accompanied this process revolved around issues such as the guarantee of long-term or unlimited lending to the state, the avoidance of state bankruptcy as a result of war, and the normalization of fiscal states of emergency. Together with the associated 'masterpieces' of financial technique, they led to a Brave New World of private lending, and to the surprising observation that states could flourish precisely on the basis of their ruin.[24]

Fiscal Desperation

Probably the most influential establishment of all was the Bank of England, founded in 1694. Inspired by the new enthusiasm for 'projects', the Bank of England emerged from various proposals for ways to create money, including lotteries, alchemical experiments, trading companies, tontines, bonds, tax increases, and banking institutes along the lines of Genoa or Amsterdam. It was the response to a variety of emergencies: the dramatic national debts contracted by English royalty during the wars on the European continent, the high interest rates on loans from the goldsmiths, the occasional confiscation of mercantile property, the proliferation of taxes, the defaults of the English government, the associated bankruptcies of London merchants, and the ruinous state of the royal house's own fiscal reputation. In 1640, for example, Charles I had requisitioned around £200,000 in coins and precious metals belonging to London merchants; in 1672, Charles II had cancelled payments on debt certificates issued by the crown (the Stop of the Exchequer); and from 1689, in dire financial straits, William III had raised an endless series of taxes on stamps, windows, peddlers, carriages, births, deaths, marriages and bachelors.

Following the proposal by the Scottish merchant William Patterson that an alliance of 1,268 creditors simply lend the English king £1.2 million sterling at an interest rate of 8 per cent, the permanent threat of royal larceny was transformed into a contract between debtor and creditor. A new institution was thus installed in an act of fiscal desperation. Crucial elements and components of modern finance were ratified in the process: the monopolization of state financing by a body of wealthy tradespeople; the perpetuation of royal debt, which continues to circulate up to the present, and which might be called the original national debt; the institutional insertion of private financiers into the exercise of governmental power; the cession of permanent privileges such as taxation and the issue of notes (to the amount of the loan advanced) to private enterprises. Finally, the foundation of the Bank of England normalized the state of emergency and war in which the English nation found itself. This was explicitly formulated in the preamble to the Bank of England Act of 27 July 1694. The compensation of private loans through future customs and taxes on shipping cargo and alcohol was justified through reference to the war with France: 'An Act for granting to theire Majesties severall Rates and Duties upon Tunnage of Shipps and Vessells and upon Beere Ale and other Liquors for secureing certaine Recompenses and Advantages in the said Act mentioned to such Persons as shall voluntarily advance the summe of Fifteene hundred thousand pounds towards the carrying on the Warr against France.'[25] The fact that the Bank of England emerged and began operating at a time when the United Kingdom was either preparing for war, waging war, or in the position of having to repay the costs of war is a key feature of its institutional form.[26] Intended to last until 1705, and then until 1710, what began as a financial experiment eventually became permanent. As the 'great cashier of English finances', the bank installed a perpetually 'floating debt'.[27]

Debate surrounding the first systematic establishment of fiscal debt and private lending to the state was characterized by reflection on an unusual and exceptional figure of power, by tentative attempts at conceptualization, and by a wide range of hypotheses and expectations as to how the bank functioned. Questions were asked not only about the risky perpetuation of politically dictated states of emergency, but also about the creation of a private–public hybrid enjoying a set of privileges in which highly disparate interests – including those of the treasury, state creditors, taxpayers and rural landowners – clashed. As a public limited company and commercial bank, it accepted private deposits; and as a banker's bank, it mutated into a creditor of last resort, becoming a cornerstone of the financial system. As a public institution, on the other hand, it was tied directly to political requirements, stood at the service of the army and navy, operated as the long arm of government and, by the eighteenth century, was referred to as the 'great machine of state'.[28] While the private company competed with commercial banks, as an instrument of government it vouched for the repayment of national debt; and while the public limited company was answerable only to its shareholders, as a national bank it produced the resources to finance government. Fiscal policy and commercial finance had become systematically intertwined and indistinguishable.

Given its difficult mandate, which had no real precedent, the Bank of England necessarily attracted controversy. It was referred to, on the one hand, as 'one of the best Establishments that ever was made for the Good of the Kingdom' and as a 'glory to our nation'[29] and, on the other, as a root of the corruption and ruin of the nation, as proof of moral decline and fiscal 'disorders'.[30] It was perceived as an ill-defined figure of power with an unknown potential for escalation, an open-ended game of power. Concerns circulated that the bank, in league with the nation's rich, would turn the king into an 'absolute' ruler; and conversely, that it would corrupt government and deliver the state into the hands of the populists. While Tories and rural landowners feared that such institutions were incompatible with the monarchy and were the first step towards a republic and a commonwealth, Whigs worried that the bank would allow the monarchy to escape parliamentary control and undo the achievements of the Glorious Revolution.[31] The Bank of England thus took up an ambiguous position in the system of government and the political body; it appeared to compete with existing executive and legislative powers and was considered politically unpredictable and uncontrollable. It posed the general question as to how bound or unbound – how sovereign, singular, how 'Great and Powerful, and Dangerous indeed to be disoblig'd' – the forces behind it were.[32] It was asked whether 'our laws' would henceforth have to be passed by the bank, and whether the banking sector itself would be able to dictate laws to government.[33] Overall, the Bank of England was regarded as a dubious means of converting private wealth into political power and as a possible reincarnation of the archaic unity of the 'powerful' and the 'rich' (originating from the Old English *rīce*, meaning 'powerful' or 'noble').

Finally, the constitution of the Bank of England brought into play an art of political differentiation that attempted to locate, in the tension between sovereign rule, governmental praxis and bourgeois commerce, a specific and unidentified type of power structure. The virtue and the peculiarity of the situation in England were said to lie in the fact that a constitutional monarchy had made space for a new position of power. As Daniel Defoe remarked, while French absolutism was characterized by the king's direct recourse to private property, and thus by the impossibility of private lending to the state, the 'purse strings' of the English exchequer were held by parliament, thus preventing any intervention by the 'limited power' of the British crown. It was precisely the king-in-parliament, the contentedly contained sovereign, that provided the conditions under which 'boundless Credit' could become sovereign; as the crown itself had once been, credit was something that 'nothing can injure or destroy'. Banking and credit appear as an issue of sovereignty; just as the king is controlled by parliament, whose very concept resists any claim to 'absolute power', so the space left vacant by the sovereign is occupied by public credit. In the mutual restriction of political forces, credit alone remains unlimited, itself dictating how the powers of government are best contained; the 'power of credit' represents the 'masterpiece', the *coup d'éclat* through which private management makes the transition into political government. As Defoe put it, only 'fools' would relieve monarchs and states of the debts that ensure the wealth and influence of private persons.[34] As a private–public organ, the role of the new bank was to tame politics, in order to embody a quasi-sovereign power itself.

From around 1700, following the lead of the Bank of England, a power transfer took place: an independent reserve of sovereignty now emerged in parallel with existing governmental powers, stabilizing the interdependencies between private interests, finance and fiscal policy. The process can be understood as an insulation of autonomous enclaves within the praxis of government, guaranteeing the persistence of seigniorial forms of power. Its apotheosis was the founding of national banks. Following the English example, this led to permanently low rates of interest on public bonds and to favourable conditions for investors. National banks also attracted international capital (in 1738, around a fifth of British national debt was held by the Netherlands; by 1758 it was a third) and enabled the financing of imperial expansion.[35] Contemporaries saw the founding of national banks as a political experiment that implied the figure of 'unlimited power', the corruption of existing forms of government and the irrevocable delegation of political responsibilities. The Bank of England was repeatedly seen as marking the transformation of emergencies and states of exception into regular functions of government, and thus as a position of power that evaded parliamentary accountability – a position not even granted to the organs of the executive.[36]

This was equivalent to the isolation of an arcane realm, in which the private managers of a private corporation with a public mandate were left to dictate executive processes, beyond public accountability, according to their own secret statutes and protocols.[37] A similar process had already occurred in a earlier experiment: that of the Swedish National Bank (Sveriges Riksbank), which in 1668 also emerged from a private bank. Here, an arcane realm of financial-executive power had been forged through the exclusion of royal powers, with representatives of the crown being denied access to the secret meetings and ballots of the bank's committee.[38] Ever since its foundation in 1913, the US Federal Reserve, an alliance of private banks of issue and private–public management, has been accompanied by conspiracy theories about its secret executive processes. Up until the present day – and notwithstanding institutional variations – central banking has been shrouded in a numinous glow, a 'peculiar and protective political mystique' that 'thrives on a pervasive impression that central banking is an esoteric art'.[39] When the Bank of England was nationalized in 1946 in order to regulate the traditionally informal relationship between the government and the private sector, key features remained: the informality of the bank's policy-making, its arcane management, the ad hoc process of consultation between the treasury, the bank and private interests. In 1970, referring to the bank's reluctance to answer questions about secrecy and private influence in banking policy, one Labour MP commented resignedly that 'every question put in this direction is met with the answer – well we have been here since 1694, so we can't be all that bad, we must know our way round the joint'.[40]

Social Diffusion	The proliferation and systematic fusion of seigniorial forms of power from the seventeenth century led not only to the institutionalization and expansion of financial markets, but also to a capital-driven process of state-building characterized by the interlocking of governmental structures and market dynamics, and by the executive management of an alliance of heavy taxation, national debt and commercial activity. In the Netherlands, the mutual reinforcement of political organization and private enrichment, in other words the regime of accumulation, represented a thoroughgoing economization of governmental praxis and became the prototype for the architecture of modern governmentality. If the question of the successful exercise of power is connected to the question of the imitation of the successful exercise of power, then the experiments in social engineering in England from around 1700 measured themselves against England's main competitor and financier, the Netherlands.

This was particularly the case for the public and private virtues of reliable and flexible credit instruments, together with low interest rates, considered by contemporaries to be the 'envy of the present' and 'wonder of all future generations'.[41] Yet claims that the Bank of England, the model for which was the Amsterdam Wisselbank, was a political-economic novelty were not solely based on the fact that it provided seigniorial power with institutional stability; that it guaranteed the inclusion of private sector creditors in the political apparatus, the gradual normalization of the state of fiscal emergency, and the permanence of cycles of credit and debt. More pertinently, a range of legal, economic and political regulations affecting the Bank of England both directly and indirectly set the parameters for the ongoing implantation of the financial regime in the social. The centralization of national debt and public credit was flanked by measures that simultaneously led to a decentralization and extensive diffusion of its impacts.

Alongside the systemization of economic government along political-economic lines, these measures included the strengthening of property rights for private creditors. This was facilitated by the institutional changes after the Glorious Revolution of 1688/9, including the constitutionalization of the monarchy, the granting of parliamentary rights of policy-making and veto in fiscal policy, and the separation of the judiciary from the crown. Moreover, the transferability of financial titles, certificates, bonds and shares increased liquidity, lent credit instruments a monetary quality, and led to the development of impersonal capital markets and the fusion of secondary markets for public and private debt.[42] This was accompanied by the insertion of a growing class of investors in the management of national debt; initially consisting of members of the commercial and financial milieu, this group later extended to wealthy widows, members of the middle class and small investors. Its number increased from approximately 5,000 signatories of state bonds or tontines in 1694 to 60,000 in 1752; and from 1,268 shareholders in the Bank of England in 1694 to 4,419 in 1712. The other classes – from rural landowners to wage-earners – were locked in through a system of taxation that transformed emergency confiscations and charges into permanent executive acts. An efficient tax administration led to an increase in tax revenues from £2.3 million in 1672 to £5.7 million in 1712. This led to the astonishing fact that, contrary to liberal myth, tax revenues were highest under the liberal and parliamentary constitutions of the Netherlands and England after the Glorious Revolution. On the eve of the French Revolution, taxes in Britain were far higher than in absolutist France

– in both absolute and relative terms: tax *pro capita* was almost twice as high in Britain as under Louis XVI.[43] During the wars with France, English national debt rose from £6.1 million in 1694 to £78 million in 1750, despite generally favourable interest rates. The 'scrupulous exactitude' of English debt servicing, together with the volume of national debt and the military machine it enabled, provided an object lesson in political economy that 'surprised and astonished Europe'.[44]

Thanatocracy   The dramatic upheavals in the constitution of public and private finance from around 1700, as well as the emergence of a functioning financial apparatus of credit and debt, were possible only with the help of confidence-building measures provided by English criminal law. According to the statutes of the Bank of England, circulating credit was guaranteed by its convertibility into silver, while the currency system was secured by the authenticity of notes, coins and cash issued. It is no surprise, then, that John Locke, one of the first investors in the Bank of England, considered attacks on the financial system and the work of counterfeiters and coin clippers to pose a greater threat to national security than the French army.[45] Forgery had been treated as high treason and as a capital offence since 1562; after the foundation of the Bank of England, in connection with debates on the reform of the currency system, politicians, pamphleteers, preachers and political economists discussed the tightening of criminal law, the relationship between public deterrence and public confidence in money and credit, financial crime as a crime against society, and possible kinds of punishment, including the death penalty (hanging and burning), facial mutilation, forced labour and imprisonment. In a series of laws, including the 'Act to prevent counterfeiting and clipping of the Coine of this Kingdom' (1695/6) and the 'Act for the better preventing the counterfeiting the current Coine of this Kingdom' (1696/7), the unauthorized possession of tools for the production of money and the forgery of coins and banknotes was classified as high treason. The term 'capital crime' received a double meaning, both economic and legal. The multiplication of criminal offences together with heavier sanctions on debtors and property offences *per se* installed a 'thanatocratic' regime whose spectacle of public executions was an effective and inevitable adjunct of the English financial revolution.[46]

Another confidence-building measure was the appointment of Isaac Newton as chairman of the Royal Mint in 1696. Newton had been recommended to the post by John Locke and the chancellor of the exchequer, Charles Montagu. The swap from the Cambridge chair in physics, mathematics, natural philosophy and alchemy to a sinecure in London was motivated not solely by the prospect of applying the maxims of empirical science to the requirements of financial-political praxis. More importantly, Newton's responsibilities included preventing coin manipulation and counterfeiting. He went about this using a network of agents and informants, undercover investigations in prisons and public houses, methodical analysis and robust inter-rogation of witnesses and suspects. On Newton's initiative, numerous counterfeiters were convicted, appeals for pardon and reduced sentences were rejected, executions fast-tracked, and death sentences waived only for informants. In his first year at the Mint, he chalked up a number of successes: seventy-one charges of crimes against the currency and twenty-three convic-tions. In the following years, the number of charges and convic-tions dropped. The death penalty was now seen as a reliable means of deterrence, and it was not for nothing that Newton was seen as having been responsible for a 'reduction in the volume of counterfeiting'.[47] Draconian punishment was ratified as the complement of a secure currency, of public confidence and of the availability of credit.

Finally, the circulation of long-term national debt, bonds and borrowed money was secured not only by legal guarantees, commercial relief, criminal law and coercion, but also by profit expectations forming around the new capital markets. The transferability of securities, the diversification of financial transac-tions and the participation of minor investors caused a prolifera-tion in places of trading (including the coffee houses on Exchange Alley in the City of London). It also brought a rise in journalism, pamphleteering and straightforward gossip commenting on and analysing the state of national debt and the attendant opportuni-ties for profit. Emerging alongside the establishment of permanent credit and the expansion of the financial markets was an 'investing public'.[48] This meant, on the one hand, that the nexus between the state and private capital liberated itself from the local and personal ties between the crown and a handful of financiers.

The Investing Public

The relationship between debtors and creditors was now mobile, negotiable, impersonal, anonymous and disembodied, becoming subject to valuation by ephemeral market movements. On the other hand, the fate of credit, capital and finance became dependent on the 'opinions', the 'passions of hope and fear' that – as the Dutch stock markets had shown – were directly connected to prospects of yields, in other words the prediction of uncertain futures.[49] Commercial transactions assumed a passionate character, while a growing number of treatises debated not only the complex interdependency of market and opinion, the role of 'fears' and 'sentiments', 'trust' and 'faith', but also the ontology of the mutable and mysterious phenomenon of credit *per se*.

The dictates of opinion led to a realm of unstable materiality, eliciting prolix descriptions from contemporaries. According to Daniel Defoe, in an essay on 'public credit', what took place in the circulation of credit could barely be put into words:

> Like the soul in the body, it actuates all substance, yet it is itself immaterial; it gives motion, yet itself cannot be said to exist; it creates forms, yet, itself has no form; it is neither quantity or quality, it has not whereness or whenness, scite or habit. … Credit is a consequence, not a cause – the effect of a substance, not a substance; 'tis the sunshine, not the sun; the quickening something, call it what you will.[50]

In alliance with public opinion, public credit became an agile, volatile creature, its state altering with the changing news from around the world. A feminized figure of Lady Credit emerged that alluded not only to the notorious, gendered stereotype of emotional instability – of the nervous or 'hysterical' constitution veering between vitality and sclerosis, impotence and wakefulness, blush and pale; the 'despotic' lability of credit also fused with the domineering, older figure of *fortuna*, which itself called for strategies of mastery.[51]

This was clearly illustrated in one of the first crises to strike England's new financial system. In 1710, during the Spanish Wars of Succession, the exhaustion of public resources caused credit to dry up. Short-term debts to finance the military budget had run out of control, state bonds were being traded at a massive discount, the treasury was obliged to borrow under increasingly unfavourable conditions, and English treasury bills had fallen below the nominal value. All this pointed to an erosion of trust in the servicing of national debt and to a danger to the financing of the fiscal-military apparatus and the financial system as a whole. The investing public now dictated the value of government bonds, which had in turn became an index for the stability or instability of governments.

In 1711 a project was launched that proved beyond doubt that in the realm of credit and capital circulation, the real fact was the anticipation of facts, and that opinion dictated the course of events.[52] Thus, a double stake was in play in the foundation of the notorious British South Sea Company – officially known as 'The Governor and the Company of the Merchants of Great Britain, trading to the South Seas and other parts of America...'. On the one hand, a further variation of seigniorial power had been conceived: a corporation born of the spirit of private–public partnerships. The founding of the South Sea Company involved transferring unsecured national debt and critical loans (used, for example, by the army or navy to finance the war against France) to the capital stock of a new trading company. Government bonds could be exchanged for shares, with the treasury promising to pay 6 per cent interest on debts capitalized by the company. Around £9.5 million of national debt was converted into private shares, in anticipation of a trading profit corresponding to guaranteed annual dividends of approximately £570,000.

On the other hand, this conversion was intended not only to eliminate the critical amount of national debt. Its purpose was also and primarily to restore trust in public credit generally. This was achieved by ensuring monopolies in the South Sea Trade, which were above all based on slave-trading between Africa and the Spanish colonies in the West Indies and South America. The slave trade, which initially did not exist at all, began slowly, with a contract for the delivery of 4,800 slaves annually for the next thirty years signed only after the Peace of Utrecht in 1713. However, shares in the company were taken up quickly, their price rising from £65 to £81 between September and November 1711, reaching £97 in summer 1713. The announcement of a lucrative slave-trading deal guaranteed the creditworthiness of the securities.

What matters in this context is less the widely documented significance of the slave trade for the development of free markets and the Atlantic economy as a whole than how the practices of

The Power of Opinion

public credit and the financial markets were connected to justified confidence in some of the most aggressive forms of European state-building and colonial expansion.[53] The South Sea Company project was supported by a journalistic campaign by a consortium of authors, including Daniel Defoe and Jonathan Swift, who together with the chancellor of the exchequer, Robert Harley, associated British fiscal and financial skill with the 'Power of the Imagination'.[54] Spiced up by travelogues and the usual exoticisms, the cheery prospect of the 'Opportunity of Vending great numbers of Negroes to the Spaniards' inspired the spirit of investment, restored trust in the government, and stabilized the system of credit with the promise of inexhaustible resources.[55] Although it was never certain how far the South Sea Company actually made a profit, and despite the fact that it collapsed in 1720 following the South Sea Bubble, going down in history as a prime example of corruption and fraudulent bankruptcy (prompting investors like Isaac Newton to sue for five-figure sums), the original concept behind the public–private financial experiment was based on compelling financial-economic principles. It reveals how the power of opinion worked in early capitalism. In its founding years, the experiment carried out a multiple and, if the promises were to be believed, rewarding conversion, through which West African slave forts and West Indian plantations were linked to London as a trading capital. This was the conversion of public finances into private finances, of anticipated wealth into present-day value, of the realm of fantasy into tangible profit, of market opinion into the stabilization of governmental power.

The permanent installation of the financial regime was due not just to the fusion of public authorities and private commerce, but also to an investing public sphere, one aroused by opportunities for profit, inclined to brutal business ideas, which did not necessarily draw a distinction between the real and the imaginary. This was the birth of public opinion from the spirit of investment. It might be described as a blatant structural transformation of the public sphere, not in the sense of the emergence of a rational, bourgeois public, but in terms of the transformation of financial markets into institutions of political-economic opinion.[56] The depersonalization of the creditor–debtor relationship and the expansion in trade in financial securities generated expectations and emotionalized contingent futures, in which financial-economic dynamics combined with fluctuations in public opinion, laying the basis for a universal 'credit mentality'.

Against this backdrop, and in view of the perpetuation of national debt, two concomitant and conflicting zones of political empowerment emerged in England after the Glorious Revolution. On the one hand, the sovereign monarch was restrained, via the House of Commons and its parties (the Whigs and the Tories), by the franchised representatives of the gentry and the City. This gave rise to the outlines of a procedural logic that, with the figure of parliamentary representation, offered a blueprint for the division of powers in bourgeois society. On the other hand, investing publics emerged that acted as the agencies of direct feedback between financial exigency, political decision-making and investor behaviour. The processes that manifested themselves within these publics were disorderly and informal; connecting price fluctuations with governmental action, they represented the basis for a new zone of political-economic influence. An elementary division is thus visible in the originary scenes of civil political participation: the mediatory processes in the parliamentary system contrast with the occupation of executive functions by a nascent 'financial-market public'.[57] Parliamentary control over government is supplemented by financial-economic restraint of governmental practice, whereby important financial investors were also members of the British parliament. The establishment of a permanent system of credit and debt not only forced the formation of financial markets and constitutionally structured government; it also gave rise to an influencing machine, through which rentiers, investors and bondholders privatized significant portions of the executive.

A social implementation of the English financial system thereby took place in the interplay of institutions, policies, laws, economic practices and an investing public sphere. The management of public credit since the beginning of the eighteenth century emerged as the aggregate of governmental functions, as the result of a coalition between royalty, government, parliament and the public sphere, between efficient administration and sound business. It was only from around 1700, in connection with modern state-building, that public credit can be said to have been permanently instituted in England.[58] In this context, the foundation of the Bank of England in 1694, together with its political and economic

The Social
Bond

status, triggered long-running debates over the meaning, purpose and function of such institutions, over their problematic localization, ambiguous profile and indeterminate potential to exercise power.

In terms of seigniorial power, the Bank of England, and modern financial regimes as such, reveal several partly contradictory tendencies. Public credit was promoted in tandem with the rise of constitutional government, so that the stability of the financial system corresponded directly with the guarantee of property rights, the protection of creditors and large capital assets, and the elimination of arbitrary acts of government, particularly confiscations. Conversely, the entrenchment of national debt and the circulation of credit continued to have the exceptional character of a 'dangerous money power' – a consequence of war, the constant preparation for war, and the ensuing financial emergencies.[59] This represented a political double bind: the constitutional arrangements for securing credit could simultaneously be seen as a risk to that very order. The integration of private investors into government created an enclave that, overall, occupies an 'obscure constitutional position'. The Bank of England embodies a splitting of reservations of sovereignty; it represents a kind of 'marriage' between state and finance, thus replicating the older 'alchemical wedding' between sovereign and treasury. It places itself in structural independence of other – legislative, executive – powers of government, employing a style of policy-making that is as informal as it is secretive.[60] The Bank of England takes the form of an executive power with an individual quality, deserving to be called a fourth power of the state. Moreover, its guarantee of the perpetuity of credit – the basis of modern financial systems – created an institutional tenacity. More clearly than other public institutions, the Bank of England vouched for the permanence of the national community, representing its immortality, as the sovereign royalty once did. One of the canonical texts of English banking of the nineteenth century put it thus: 'You might as well, or better, try to alter the English monarchy and substitute a republic, as to alter the present constitution of the English money market, founded on the Bank of England.'[61]

Given its ambiguity, it is no surprise that the institution of public credit has plagued political and economic thought since the eighteenth century. It raises questions about how and where political authority is to be limited; about the relation between the constitutional order and the fiscal state of exception; about the cycle of tax burdens, interest payments and private profit; about the tension between legally guaranteed equality and economically perpetuated inequalities. On the one hand, the interpenetration of state power and economic dynamics ruled by finance was probably a reason why people saw credit and its institutionalization as a particular kind of social contract. If – in the canonical formulation of Thomas Hobbes – an agreement regarding a promise to future fulfilment can be called a 'contract', involving an obligation whose binding power is secured by 'coercion', then the deals circulating in the English financial regime, the agreements of 'trust', must be seen as the social-contractual basis for a generalized system of obligation and coercion.[62] As early as 1695, some saw paper money, in other words credit, as a guarantee for the stability of the political order after the Glorious Revolution, a bond of obligation that applied to relations among citizens as well as to those between the monarch and his subjects, a conflation of the social contract with the contract of rule. Conversely, the abuse of credit appeared as the collapse of the social order. The culture of credit became the 'great bond of society', the inviolable law in social transactions. National debt was seen as a precarious 'part of the constitution', credit as a 'national good', with the first systematic theories attributing to it the capacity to create a homogeneous body politic.[63]

By the nineteenth century, it was largely unanimous that the national bank represented the 'centre of the state', national debt the 'chain of society', and public credit the 'great bond of obligation and faith', the 'cement of the state'.[64] When the Bank of England was granted the monopoly on issuing notes by the Bank Charter Act of 1844, the prime minister, Robert Peel, commented on this contractual dimension, together with the social diffusion of the banking institute, thus:

> There is no contract, public or private, no engagement, national or individual, which is unaffected by it. The enterprises of commerce, the profits of trade, the arrangements made in all the domestic relations of society, the wages of labour, pecuniary transactions of the highest amount and the lowest, the payment of National Debt, the provision for the national expenditure, the command which the coin of the smallest denomination has over

the necessaries of life, are all affected by the decision [i.e. over the Bank Charter Act] to which we may come.[65]

Banknotes cause national debt and private lending to circulate as a new alliance, as a new social and political bond.

Enclave of   On the other hand, a despotic potential could be identified
Authority in credit and its impact, and hence a critical political situation in which 'either the nation must destroy public credit, or public credit will destroy the nation'.[66] Whether the situation was seen to consist in the private confiscation of government power or in the political productivity of private wealth, it represented a political abnormality, a 'most formidable monster' of national debt and public credit, capable of 'striking terror into those who had cherished it in its infancy'.[67] In the debates over the constitution of the French Revolution, if not before, the inevitability of national debt and public credit led to reflection on a political system confronted with the irreconcilable demands of, on the one hand, society and the nation and, on the other, finance and private creditors. National debt and the emergency policies associated with it conflicted with an architecture of government that defined itself through constitutionality and the division of powers. In particular, Emmanuel Joseph Sieyès' reflections on the constitutional concept of the republic were marked by the attempt, through complex institutional regulations, to guarantee credit repayment and at the same time to banish its dangers. Sieyès spoke of the 'sorry situation of a society' in which 'private investors fear for their wealth and their existence, while the mass of taxpayers fears a crushing burden'.[68] He argued that the question of national debt lacked any constitutional solution. However much credit and creditor rights may have been constitutionally guaranteed, they were still capable of eroding the stability of the republic. The vertically structured division of powers was insufficient to contain the 'totalizing' power of public debt, credit and finance; what was required was a broader administrative balance between constitutional order and financial power.[69] Duties to society were irreconcilable with duties to creditors.

What has occasionally been referred to as the modern 'financial revolution' not only involved the decentralization and the social diffusion of financial-economic operations. Equally significantly, the sporadic procedures of seigniorial power that developed at the juncture of political strategy and private finance capital obtained varying degrees of institutional persistence and, in the form of the emergent central banks, prominent representation. As official bodies for the conversion of fiscal and financial-economic interests, central banks like the Bank of England became crucial functional elements in the entrenchment of state apparatuses and the consolidation of the financial regime. Thus, the Bank of England – in combination with other institutions such as the fiscal bureaucracy, national debt and parliament – was the prerequisite for British military and colonial expansion. Simultaneously, it stabilized the markets, as the 'ego' of the credit system dictating the conditions under which credit, debt and financial instruments circulated.[70] The Bank of England operates on a fluid terrain where political decisions (e.g. war and public financing) translate directly into events on the financial markets and where, conversely, financial-economic cycles (e.g. quotation and interest rates) call for political intervention. With its private–public structure, it can be seen as both the motor and the control centre for the reciprocity of political and financial-economic policy-making.

This is guaranteed by a form of organization that annexes and integrates the antiquated and unstable institutions of the treasury, national debt, coinage and money. Central banks and their functions were part of the process of 'governmentalization' taking place with modernity; they belonged to an ensemble of political technologies that, via an economization of governmental praxis, aimed at increasing state power. By the nineteenth century, the remit of central banks included older rights of sovereignty such as the monopoly on money, executive functions such as the control of national debt, and direct participation in markets. One logical consequence of this was the Bank Charter Act of 1844, which established in the Bank of England, alongside a department for the issue of notes, a department for commercial operations 'to be managed in the same way as any other private bank'.[71] It was this diffuse and heterogeneous remit that led to the segregation and insulation of central banks, so that while their interventional power belonged to the modern praxis of government, it was also independent of other executive and legislative powers. The curious situation emerges whereby it is precisely the democratization of government – as in England following the Glorious Revolution – that drives the formation of new enclaves of authority. The increasing participation of the public sphere in political institutions was offset by the establishment of new economies of power alongside the constitutional order – by the segregation of an arcane realm in the form of the central bank, and by the informal power of an investing financial public.

5

Fourth Power

The economization of government from the seventeenth century
not only involved the differentiation of state apparatuses and
economic dynamics. It also stabilized a form of seigniorial power
characterized by the systematic interconnection of treasury and
finance, of political interests and the interests of private business.
The expansion of financial markets correlated with the normalization of (financial-)political states of emergency, the perpetuation
of national debt and public credit, and the permanent involvement
of private finance in the exercise of politics. As a part of the
executive, these forms of power – the Bank of England being
the first example – obtained a privileged and eccentric institutional
status within the spectrum of governmental practice. Constraints
on the sovereign entailed an apotheosis of finance; the emancipa-
tion of financial power was guaranteed by the self-restriction
of political sovereignty. This means, on the one hand, that the
emergence of modern governmentality cannot be described in
terms of concepts of homogeneous statehood. Even at its incep-
tion, the state reveals itself as an ensemble of heterogeneous,
'disaggregated' elements lacking clear demarcation. On the other
hand, sporadic and occasional arrangements, such as that between
royal debtors and private creditors, took on the character of
discrete enclaves for the accumulation of a new form of political-
economic policy-making power. The Bank of England acted as
a channel for the integration of finance capital and investors
into government.

That is one reason why the Bank of England soon inspired the foundation of similar institutions – with varying degrees of success and longevity – in Europe and the US throughout the eighteenth and nineteenth centuries. Originally, the Bank of England was not a central bank or bank of issue in the modern sense. It had no autonomous monetary policy and was entrusted solely with administering state deficits and guaranteeing the reliable servicing of debt and the satisfaction of the creditor cartel. Only gradually did these institutions gain an independent remit. Mostly as a result of the concrete historical situation, what had begun as privately run government banks now became responsible for issuing notes and creating money, for safeguarding the banking system, for acting as lenders of last resort, for overseeing the value of the currency, for regulating the money supply, and for matters concerning price stability, interest policy and inflation.

Regardless of the diversity, incompatibility and heterogeneity of their historical forms and functions, and whether they were founded and run as private companies or as public facilities, these institutions are integral elements of modern governmental practice. As monopolists in the system of credit, central banks are agencies for the consolidation and expansion of financial markets. Moreover, with their fusion of sovereign, fiscal and private economic roles, they demonstrate how power is organized under the conditions of finance capitalism. Central banks are evidence of the emergence of a powerful finance capital from a complex synergy of political institutions and private agents. Together with the routines of government, the modern financial system developed beyond executive and legislative controls.

At the same time, there was constant debate over these institutions' legal and technical status, on the definition of their remits, methods and powers, and on their internal organizational structure. Probably the most famous project of the previous century, the US Federal Reserve System (established 1913), emerged from a series of controversies and temporary enterprises, finally assuming a somewhat peculiar institutional form. The involvement of rich investors and the short-lived central bank projects of 1791 and 1816 had initially been prompted by perennial questions of state financing and fiscal emergency, along with the exigencies of wartime and military spending. Familiar debates arose on how and whether private interests should be reconciled with sovereign powers, whether the necessary financial and fiscal measures interfered with democratic procedures, and whether a central bank with state authorization was even constitutional.[1] If the many banking failures and legislative discrepancies between the different states indicated a 'state of confusion' in the nineteenth-century American banking sector,[2] then in the ensuing debates there emerged new criteria and coordinates, new stakes and entities in the organization of the financial system.

From the end of the nineteenth century, in the context not only of a growing economy but also of financial crisis and economic recession, the problems of state financing, public credit and debt servicing were increasingly joined by urgent questions concerning the stabilization of the money markets and the banking system, and hence the protection of the structures of finance capitalism as such. Particularly intense and controversial was the discussion about the instruments and measures necessary to provide a security apparatus for the financial economy. On the one hand, there were claims about the dominant positions of money trusts, the 'despotism' of economic and financial oligarchs such as the Rockefeller Group or J.P. Morgan & Co., and the political divisiveness of 'big business'.[3] On the other hand, there was a confusing situation marked by conflicts between finance capital and agriculture, by immobile reserves, credit crunches, inflexible money supply and high interest rates on borrowing, by an increasing decentralization of the banking system, by the growing significance of regional state banks, and by a proliferation of banks (from approximately 10,000 in 1900 to 25,000 in 1912).

During the banking panic of 1907, the government in Washington was forced to bail out the financial system with emergency aid and low-interest national bonds, following defaults and runs on the big New York banks such as J.P. Morgan – which not long ago had itself helped out generously in financial and economic predicaments and played a prominent role in state financing – and the collapse of numerous companies and smaller banks. After the crisis, it was primarily the banks themselves that called for legislation and reform of the banking sector. The cacophony of proposals included privately financed guarantee funds, the creation of emergency money underwritten by the government, municipalities and railroad companies, and even calls for a currency that would be secured by various commercial

The Federal Reserve

investments. Finally, a plan emerged for regional private reserve banks to form a central National Reserve Association that would function as a government-controlled central bank, and would acquire a monopoly on issuing and printing money and holding credit reserves.[4]

Although the controversy did not end with the Federal Reserve Act of 1913, which was seen either as a triumph over the money trusts and a 'communist idea', or as the victory of financial capital, the 'creditor caste' and the 'banking fraternity', the final compromise met with the approval of the majority of bankers.[5] Yet the Federal Reserve System, designed by, among others, the parliamentarian Carter Glass and the economist H. Parker Willis, was not simply a new institution. Its uniqueness and subsequent success consisted in the fact that it operated as a security mechanism for existing financial structures, translating these into an organogram that resembled not so much a closed, institutional unit as a loose aggregate of established business practices, private corporations, supplementary administrative units and executive bodies. The responsibilities of the Federal Reserve were to include the establishment of regional reserve banks for decentralized lending, the standard issue of banknotes and the creation of credit money, the rediscounting of private bills of exchange, the guarantee of minimum reserves, and the stabilization of the banking sector and financial system as such. This mandate was to be carried out through a complex fusion of centralized and decentralized powers, of public duties and private interests, and of formal and informal executive processes.[6]

The territory of the USA was henceforth divided into twelve districts crossing state boundaries, each represented by a reserve bank or central bank. Their capital stems from the private member banks resident in these districts, whose investments yield a statutory dividend of 6 per cent. After the payment of overheads and dividends, surplus profits are paid partly into the reserve fund and partly to the Department of the Treasury in the form of a licence fee, which is used among other things to underwrite notes and government securities in circulation. The reserve banks and their capital stock remain tax exempt (apart from real estate). These public limited companies operate as privileged fiscal agencies of the US government; alongside issuing banknotes, they engage largely independently in all kinds of open market operations, including the purchase and sale of government securities, financial transactions, trade in precious metals, remittances and giro transfers. Six of the nine governors of each reserve bank are taken from representatives of the member banks and representatives of trade, agriculture and other sectors of the economy; all are elected by delegates of the member banks and their shareholders. The three remaining governors are nominated by the Federal Reserve Board in Washington. One of them – a professional banker – functions as the chair of the Board of Governors and as a Federal Reserve Agent, in other words as an official representative of the Federal Reserve Board, with reporting duties.

The central Federal Reserve Board directs the operations of the system as a whole. It supervises and controls the management of the reserve banks, determines base and discount rates, monitors reserves, regulates the issue of notes, and acts as a clearing house for the individual banks. Its governors – originally five, then six or seven – are nominated by the US president; the initial ten-year term was later, with the agreement of the Senate, extended to fourteen years. Governors are meant to represent the various sectors of the economy throughout the country, with no more than one candidate per Federal Reserve district able to stand for election. Two governors must be proven financial and banking experts, one of whom is nominated – again by the president – as chair. Until 1935, the other members of the Board of Governors were the secretary of the treasury and the comptroller of the currency. Finally, the Federal Reserve Board (or Board of Governors) is supplied with a Federal Advisory Council, whose members are delegated by the twelve Federal Reserve Banks and which carries out an advisory function vis-à-vis the policy of the board.[7]

Its unique status notwithstanding, the Federal Reserve System is, in terms of the developments leading to the Banking Act of 1935, exemplary of the organization of policy-making power in the financial-economic regime. This is true for its hybrid *duality* – the result of an uneasy mix of executive processes and informal policy-making, of decentralized responsibilities and central bodies, of a political mandate and financial-economic functions, of fiscal policy and monetary policy. Both the Fed's complex structure and its unstable status within the system of government are marked by this duality. The Federal Reserve is not merely a public organization in private ownership, an

Double-Sidedness

arrangement that perpetuates the privatization of sovereign tasks, such as money creation. More importantly, with its organizational guarantee of fusion between fiscal-political and private-economic interventions, it became a converter for governmental power and market dynamics, operating on the basis of indefinite powers, an unclear status and different sources of authority. It is both a network of private banks and a central institution of government; and although the monetary system is now placed beyond the exclusive control of the private economy, public affairs are nevertheless delegated to commercial banks. The Federal Reserve enjoys special privileges unlike any other institution in Washington. It generates its wealth on the money markets and administers its budget independently of Congress. The legislation of 1913 was based on the principles of central banking; however – as one banker put it at the time – it transformed the banks belonging to the system into 'joint owners of a central dominating power'.[8] While the nominated governors of the Federal Reserve Board occupy the summit, they share their powers with the directors of the twelve Reserve Banks, which in turn represent the interests of the private banks in their district.

An alliance formed between public and private interests that was deliberately situated alongside and apart from elected governments. Contemporaries describing the system used a cumbersome rhetoric of 'not only ... but also' and 'on the one hand ... on the other'. Entitled 'The Place of Reserve Banks', the first report of the Reserve Board to Congress stated that while the Fed was not an emergency agency, it was also not a conventional participant in the banking business; it participated in the market yet stood outside it; it was both a player on the stock market and the 'guardian of banking reserves'; it was not profit oriented, yet it was interested in generating revenues.[9] In a letter from the Reserve Board to the president of the Senate in 1921, it was again emphasized that the law of 1913 had established a central body but not a central bank; that the reserve banks were private companies that nevertheless acted on congressional authority; that they were to be understood not as government banks in the 'strict sense' but as 'quasi-governmental institutions'; and that while the directors of the reserve banks did indeed represent the government in some sense, they primarily acted on behalf of the commercial banks.[10]

Even regarding the functioning of the Federal Reserve Board in Washington and its financing, the question is whether it acts as an 'independent government body' or is dependent upon the Reserve Banks.[11] Such ambiguities have sometimes led to bizarre conflicts. When the District of Columbia charged property tax on the Washington building, the Federal Reserve refused to pay on the basis that it had been established in 1913 per congressional resolution as an institution of government. This prompted the objection that the land upon which the building stood had been purchased from the federal government, and that the government hardly sold property to itself. Threats to tax or auction off the land were only dropped after years of legal dispute and confirmation that the building was indeed the property of the nation.[12] Today, the Federal Reserve has mastered the art of fine distinction and understands itself less as 'independent of government' than as an 'independent entity within the government'.[13] However, long-serving members of the Department of the Treasury and managers of the Federal Reserve System have emphasized the deep ambiguity of this self-conception: 'Constitutionally, the Federal Reserve is a pretty queer duck.' And: 'To some extent, the Federal Reserve considers itself government. Other times, when it serves, it considers itself not government.'[14] In other words: the Federal Reserve System means that the government is not the sole source of government.

These complexities, ambiguities and tensions indicate that agencies such as the Federal Reserve emerge as specific, technical interventions within the praxis of government and that, indeterminacies notwithstanding, they pursue a clear course. The notorious public–private duality of the Federal Reserve is suffused with *fundamental asymmetries* that were already inherent in its design, and that became entrenched throughout subsequent reforms. These asymmetries underlie the political and economic status of the Federal Reserve and the quality of its executive power. It is worth recalling that the Fed emerged in the context of political conflicts from the end of the eighteenth century, above all the farmers' revolts against extortionate interest rates, the formation of the Farmers' Alliance, and the struggle of the agrarian-populist People's Party, the labour movement and the Socialist Party against the dominance of banks and finance capital. The establishment of the new system was also connected to the

Asymmetries

search for political solutions to these acute social conflicts. It could be placed too in the context of discussions on the limits of self-government, representative democracy and public opinion. For the reformers around Woodrow Wilson, 'good government' entailed the systematic restriction of mass-democratic control over the institutions of government. As Walter Lippmann wrote in 1922, 'It is not possible to assume that a world, carried on by division of labor and distribution of authority, can be governed by universal opinions in the whole population.'[15]

The extent to which this expressed a fundamental constitutional hiatus in the USA was documented in Charles Beard's study on the 'economic interpretation of the constitution of the United States' of 1913. Beard, who published his analysis quickly and in instalments, in the hope of contributing to an understanding of the 'real economic forces which condition great movements in politics', described the American constitution as an enterprise through which wealthy property owners sought to minimize the risk of the federal government being controlled by debtors and small farmers.[16] Although Beard's cursory account was at first barely noticed and then heavily criticized, his underlying thesis contained a degree of factual truth. Alexander Hamilton, a founding father of the American constitution and initiator of the First National Bank of the United States in 1791, explicitly supported privileging large-scale wealth within government. In a declaration during the Confederation Congress in 1787, he commented on the nature of a 'good government' thus:

> All communities divide themselves into the few and the many. The first are the rich and the well born, the other the mass of the people. The voice of the people has been said to be the voice of God: and however generally this maxim has been quoted and believed, it is not true in fact. The people are turbulent and changing; they seldom judge or determine right. Give therefore to the first class a distinct, permanent share in government. They will check the unsteadiness of the second, and as they cannot receive any advantage by a change, they therefore will ever maintain good government.[17]

In this context, it appeared only logical that the functioning of the Federal Reserve should be shielded from the 'tyranny of the random majority' (in Knut Wicksell's phrase) and that the financial public receive minority rights. Legally, the Federal

Reserve is independent of the president, and in the years following its foundation its insulation against governmental intervention was reinforced. Since 1935, the secretary of the treasury (as the representative of the elected government) and the comptroller of the currency (as the representative of the financial executive) have not sat on the Board of Governors. Moreover, while the US president is responsible for the nomination of the governors, he or she can dismiss these only 'for cause', and is excluded from the board's negotiations. The status of the Federal Reserve is therefore characterized by fundamental liberty with respect to the legislature that created it and to the executive that nominated its governors.[18] This gives rise to a further peculiarity. While the executive function of the Fed developed in strict isolation from the democratically elected and procedurally legitimate organs of government, its communications with political representatives – for example between the chair of the Board of Governors and the president or treasury secretary – were increasingly informal, unregulated and personal. Although the boards of the Fed are heavily inoculated against the disapproval of government authorities, the mechanisms of coordination between the Fed's own policy and that of government remained indeterminate and undefined, inspiring an extensive and polemical body of literature on the impact of these indeterminate zones of influence.[19]

The insulation of the Federal Reserve is supplemented by a systematic opening up to an interested financial public. This primarily concerns new forms and fields of intervention. If the central banks originally emerged from the dynamic of state debt, from the convergence of political and commercial exigency, and from the entanglement of fiscal policy and finance, then by the nineteenth century a new set of tasks had emerged. The Bank of England, for example, only gradually assumed the function of guarantor of credit in circulation, of bank of issue, and of lender of last resort. It remained unclear and debatable whether these bailout functions applied to market operations alone, in order to secure liquidity, or also extended to the insolvency and illiquidity of individual institutions, in connection with concerns about bank runs.[20] At any rate, the stabilization of the banking and financial sector as such became a new and crucial responsibility for central banking projects such as the Federal Reserve System. The frequent banking panics and failures had led to the

The Financial Public

concept of the Reserve System in the first place; unlike its predecessor projects, the Fed responded directly to the demands of the banking sector for security mechanisms in financial transactions and credit circulation. From that point on, the history of central banks – and the debates around them – is marked by an immanent tension between the requirements of public financing and fiscal policy, and the status of a 'bankers' bank' and its relation to the system of finance and currency.[21]

Although the Federal Reserve is a conglomerate of commercial banks, public limited companies and boards with various degrees of authority, it cannot be seen solely as an 'anomaly' or 'hybrid institution', as merely a mixture of public and private roles.[22] Rather, the informal freedoms built into the system enabled the development of privileged relationships to the world of finance, which in turn guaranteed the predominance of the banking sector in the economy as a whole. While the 1913 law stipulated that the staff of the Federal Reserve Board reflect the spectrum and geographic diversity of the economy ('the President shall have due regard to a fair representation of the different commercial, industrial and geographical divisions of the country'[23]), a management strategy was pursued that supports the claim that US banks were in fact taking over the task of self-regulation. This goes for the selection and nomination of the governors, who generally had and have a background in banking, particularly in the major banks.[24] Despite a few exceptions, agriculture, artisanship, small business and above all labour and the trade unions were excluded from the staff of the boards. Conformity and continuity in the relation between the Board of Governors and the banking and financial system were thereby guaranteed.[25]

The Federal Reserve System consolidated the financial power of New York in an equally informal manner, contributing to the dominance of Wall Street on the international markets. In 1916, the Reserve Bank of New York, with the approval of the Federal Reserve Board, began trading internationally on behalf of the entire system; this was in turn financed by the New York money market. Wartime spending brought further centralization. Alongside the operations of the reserve banks, which carried out lending at the local level and, in the case of credit crunches, lent money to the commercial banks, the open market operations of the New York Central Bank gained significance from the 1920s. Rapidly increasing short-term investments on the New

York Stock Exchange involved the Fed in securities trading, with the New York discount rates becoming the benchmark for the entire Reserve System. Hopes were soon raised of 'wresting the sceptre from London' and 'making New York the financial centre of the world'.[26]

This development was entrenched by the centralization of commercial activities. The Board of Governors was granted greater authority, in administrative and commercial terms transforming the individual Reserve Banks into subordinate organs of the central body. Insofar as varying rates of interest were connected to the open market operations of the reserve banks, attempts were made from the 1920s, on the initiative of the Central Bank of New York, to coordinate these operations in an Open Market Investment Committee. From 1933 onwards, this led to the gradual creation of the Federal Open Market Committee (FOMC), henceforth the most important executive body within the system. Its twelve members were made up of the seven governors of the Reserve Board and five governors of the Reserve Bank; the governor of the New York bank was reserved a permanent place on the committee and the vice-presidency. The chair of the Board of Governors occupies the presidency of the FOMC up to the present day, despite there being no statutory regulation to this effect. This is where the crucial monetary-political decisions are made. The FOMC regulates money supply and discount rates, operates on foreign exchange markets, and above all trades in securities and national bonds, thereby involving itself closely in the dynamics of the New York financial and money markets.

The intimacy of the institutional relationships within the Federal Reserve at the institutional, staffing and strategic levels between policy-making and the financial markets (in particular Wall Street) requires that it be understood as the agent of a *fundamental divide*. In the eighteenth century, in connection with the Bank of England, the key issue had already been the involvement and influence of an investing public. With the Fed and its ambiguous status within government, however, a strict separation took place between the voice of the democratic electorate and the moods of the investing public forming on the markets. The immunization of the Fed with regard to the representatives of the (national) citizenry combined with increasing sensitivity towards the opinions of the (international) financial

Gatekeeper Function

public. Even if the commercial activities of the Federal Reserve System were repeatedly subordinated to fiscal political emergencies, for example during the two world wars, its organizational structure and legal and technical status ensured its gatekeeper function in the political process. While its business operations took place independently of direct government intervention, its governmental power accumulated in direct correlation to the dynamics of the financial markets. The resistance of the Fed to procedures and institutions of representative democracy is the precondition for its predominance in the financial regime.

This divide, or functional asymmetry, marked the final migration of reserves of sovereignty. For the Founding Fathers, the system of coinage, the monopoly over the issue of notes, public borrowing and money creation counted among the absolute rights of sovereignty of the confederation. However, these functions were now irrevocably implanted in the commercial relations between the central bank and finance.[27] Despite its informal relations with the government and its duty to report to Congress, the institutional autonomy of the Federal Reserve is linked to policy-making processes whose status and mode of execution are thus equally autonomous, in other words arcane and sovereign. Concern for the reactions of the market means that the negotiations of the FOMC are conducted in strict confidence, and its resolutions made irreversible. Short reports about the sessions are published only six to eight weeks later. Internal memoranda and analyses remain secret for five years. When, in 1966, a bill was drafted in Congress on the right of the public to view the files of the executive, the FOMC stopped taking complete minutes of the sessions of the committee altogether: a privilege granted to no other institution of government, including the intelligence services. 'The Fed', it was stated casually, 'could not be forced to release minutes that did not exist.'[28] A few years later, the Fed won a case concerning the secrecy of FOMC resolutions. After all, neither the president nor the Supreme Court could revoke the decisions. As Alan Blinder, the vice-chairman of the Fed in the 1990s, remarked, 'this makes FOMC decisions, for all practical purposes, immune from reversal. Without this immunity, the Fed would not really be independent, for its decisions would hold only so long as they did not displease someone more powerful.'[29] Behind the complicated organization of the Fed, a process of becoming-sovereign demonstrates activities and resolutions that cannot be revised by 'someone more power-ful'. As a financial-economic reserve system, it functions only by absorbing reserves of sovereignty via a combination of esoteric knowledge and irrevocable policy-making power.

Deriving from historical circumstances and conceived as safety nets for capital markets and as welfare providers for the banking and financial sectors, institutions such as the Federal Reserve need to be understood as central capitalist institutions. Despite the diversity of the projects and institutions determining the development of the financial system in the twentieth century, in particular after World War II, and despite differences in terms of distance from or proximity to government, a number of convergences and common types of problem can be identified. As the Federal Reserve System demonstrates, central banks develop a decision-making power that is connected to the migration of older rights of sovereignty, leads to the formation of enclaves or islands within government, and obtains its critical moment in the management of different logics of address.

Double Foundation

These institutions were thus founded and insulated twice. Initially, they represented the private creditor cartel. As government banks, they were granted privileges and extraordinary rights and were facilitated through a restriction of arbitrary sovereign acts. This was the case for the Bank of England from the end of the seventeenth century. From the nineteenth century, central banks became 'bankers' banks' and 'lenders of last resort', assuming responsibility for the stability of the financial system as a whole. This prompted the creation of legal barriers against elected governments. Fiscal policy and creditor protection on the one hand, monetary policy and the stability of the banking sector on the other: this dual mandate forms the profile of central banks up to the present day. At the same time, unequal emphasis is placed on the two roles. This has occasioned extensive debate and controversy in economic science. From a *systematic* angle, clear disparities have been noted. Government banks, it is argued, owe their privileged status to fiscal emergencies, public deficits and guarantees of public credit, all of which were central to the emergence and expansion of financial markets. Conversely, the security apparatus of modern central banks was itself engendered by expanding market forces. In matters of liquidity control and reserve formation, central banks are intrinsically linked to corporations, operations and movements in the finance sector, and hence cannot be harmonized directly with the interests of government and the organs of the state.[30] Central banks' primary task of financing the state becomes distinct from their task of stabilizing the monetary and financial system. A historical closed circle can be observed in which – broadly speaking – these institutions take on the regulation of the very dynamics that they themselves prompted.

Precisely for that reason, however, from a *genealogical* angle coherent lines of development emerge concerning the economization of government on the basis of finance. Close connections between public and private interests can be observed throughout the development of central banking, from the emergence of seigniorial power, through the involvement of investors in the practice of politics, to the formation of executive enclaves operating as preserves of autonomy within the practice of government. More broadly, the consolidation of a 'fourth power' in the form of central banks was facilitated by three connected processes: first, the bureaucratic delegation of authority among governmental bodies; second, the legal insulation of central banks against the organs of representative government; third, strategic and technological adaptation to the investing public. While administrative and legislative measures were used to gain autonomy within government, the banks' independence from the financial markets was 'unattainable and undesirable'. After all, monetary policy can only be carried out in concert with market agents; 'there is no escaping this'.[31] Central banks integrated the mechanisms and dynamics of the financial markets into the practice of government.

It has never been a secret that the banking sector has nothing whatsoever to do with 'democratic activity'; that independent central banks exceed democratic control; that they display a 'democratic deficit' and an 'undemocratic nature' and restrict 'democratic possibilities'; that they cause a 'deformation of the democratic principle in general, and democratic accountability in particular'.[32] However, the question is not how central banking can be more or less successfully brought into line with democratic procedures using legal and administrative instruments, despite its continuing relevance. Rather, the question needs to be reversed. Just as central banks were unable to gain economic and political autonomy under authoritarian regimes, so they are themselves the creatures of modern democratization processes. It was the division of powers and systems of representation that provided the conditions under which they could establish themselves as para-democratic, isolated enclaves of government, operating as essential organs for the stabilization and preservation of capitalist structures of financing. They are the central elements of what is now referred to as 'democratic capitalism'. Their significance lies neither in a consolidation of the state monopoly, nor in the straightforward conveyance of economic interests into the political sphere. Instead, their institutional entrenchment intensifies economic government through the inhibition of government's public functions.

If central banks are today more powerful than ever, then this is because of a further, effective division of powers.[33] Indeed, demands for greater independence accompanied the realization of central banking projects throughout the twentieth century. At the Brussels Conference in 1921 on the economic and political order in post-war Europe, calls were already being made for the liberation of all banks from 'political pressure' of any kind; and at the Geneva Conference in 1922, the independence of central banks was declared a condition for the restoration of the worldwide economic and financial order. The governor of the Bank of England, Montagu Norman, tirelessly called for independent central banks in all countries.[34] The credo of independence was immediately put into practice in Austria (1922), Hungary (1923), Germany (1924) and elsewhere. However, the model for central bank autonomy was widely considered to be the West German Bundesbank, which its own officials referred to as 'a state within a state' and a 'counterweight to the government'.[35] After lengthy deliberations, above all over the degree of centralization and whether this banking entity was to be independent of government, the West German parliament ceded control over the currency and monetary policy to an organization that systematically evaded parliamentary accountability.

With the passage of the Bundesbank Law in June 1957, an institution was created that was authorized to act 'independently of the orders of the Federal Government' and obliged to support the 'general economic policy of the Federal Government' only insofar as its legally defined responsibilities required it to do so (§12BBankG).[36] Nomination policy guaranteed the independence of the bank at the staff level, while its committees – the Executive

Independence

Board and the Central Bank Council[37] – were granted the status
of 'supreme federal authorities', meaning that they were ranked
equally with ministries, and thus not subordinate to government.
No member of government has voting rights on the boards of
the Bundesbank, and while the government can, under certain
conditions, postpone the implementation of the bank's resolutions,
it cannot revoke them entirely.[38] Insofar as the Bundesbank carries
out its executive functions independently of the government, it
is not accountable to parliament, unlike ministers; in turn,
ministers cannot be held responsible by parliament for decisions
they are not authorized to make. Not only was the German
government thus prevented from intervening in money supply,
but the Bundesbank could control and set conditions on the
credit it granted, and therefore exert an influence on public
spending and fiscal policy.[39] Regulations of this sort earned the
Bundesbank a reputation as 'one of the most independent central
banks in the world'.[40] However, they also raised concerns as to
whether a 'parallel government' did indeed exist, whether a
'parliament-free' zone had been created, and whether 'unrestrained
political autonomy' towards the executive and legislature was
compatible with the Basic Law. In any case, it was possible
to see the Bundesbank as an institutional form that enabled
unaccountability to be construed as a principle of inviolable
independence.[41]

The legal status of the Bundesbank was therefore also controversial. Despite belonging to the executive branch of the
government, the Bundesbank's status as 'direct Federal legal
person of public law' (§2 BBankG) cannot easily be placed
among the types of legal person – foundations, institutes, bodies
– within the administrative system. It is occasionally classified
as an 'atypical institute' or a singular institution *sui generis*.[42]
An added factor was that the Basic Law of 1949 departed from
all precedent, its article 88 stipulating the establishment of a
'note-issuing and currency bank as the Federal Bank'.[43] This
article triggered controversy over the constitutionality of banking
autonomy. It was debated whether the automony of the Bundesbank could be derived from the Basic Law's stipulation of
minimal powers; whether the bank was an 'organ of the constitution'; whether the separation of powers and the claim that the
Bundesbank acted as a 'counterweight' within government
warranted its total control over the currency; and whether, within

the parameters of the Basic Law, the bank's insulation from parliament and government could be justified in terms of the risks that potentially emanated from democratically legitimated organs themselves.[44]

Although the debate about the legal status and constitutional character of an 'independent' Bundesbank went unresolved, all the various positions were essentially pre-empted and obviated by the fact that an independent bank had been set up prior to the existence of the political constitution, the Basic Law, the state, the Federal Republic and the government. Founded in 1957, the Bundesbank took over a large part of the obligations, staff and property of the German Reichsbank, which was formally liquidated only in 1961. More importantly, the Bundesbank was also the direct successor of the Bank of the German States, which had been founded in the Allied Western Zone in 1948 (cf. §1 BBankG). The Bank of the German States was the result of a compromise between the US and the British military governments; later extended to the French zones, it combined the regional central banks into a central, two-tier institute in a single economic zone. *The Bank of the German States*

The Bank of the German States is interesting for two reasons. First, it was conceived in response to the experiences of hyperinflation, depression and Nazi economic policy, and was intended to strike a balance between a centralized and a decentralized form of organization – thereby borrowing functional elements from the Bank of England and the Federal Reserve System. Second, as the Allies made clear shortly after the end of the war, the project was not to be a 'government-owned institution', or at least not 'an institution created at the national level and spreading downwards'.[45] Sure enough, the law or decree on the 'Foundation of the Bank of the German States' of March 1948 stated that 'the Bank is not subordinate to any political body or public authority other than the courts'.[46] After the annulment of Allied rights of supervision by an amendment to the law in 1951 (the 'Law on Transition'), the independence of the Bank of the German States from the German government remained in place.[47] In 1956, it was possible to state that 'the central bank is fully sovereign in its relationship with the government; it is responsible only to itself. We have a body which is responsible to no one, neither to a parliament, nor to a government.'[48]

The Bank of the German States was the first state institution ever to be founded in a state that did not yet exist. It was declared independent of political institutions that had not yet been created. The idol of independence could thus claim the ontological virtue of pre-existence: independence from government preceded the government's guarantee of the same. Just as the Bundesbank of 1957 was not, technically speaking, a new institution (with some modifications, it assumed the functions of the Bank of the German States), so the Federal Republic of 1949 inherited a pre-existing, independent central bank. Article 88 of the Basic Law legalized what had already been conceded. Just as the federal structure after 1945 preceded the Federal Republic, so in this case an economic order was established prior to all political organs. The Bank of the German States oversaw the commercial activities of the regional central banks, stabilized the monetary and credit system, stipulated minimum reserves and base rates, performed open market operations, carried out foreign exchange transactions, and controlled lending to the executive. Moreover, it was an essential prerequisite for the currency reform and the introduction of the Deutschmark in June 1948, and thereby pre-empted the economic and monetary policy of the future state.

Market   The Bank of the German States can be seen as the cornerstone
Society for various measures that established the economic boundaries of the West German state and made market mechanisms themselves the precondition for the establishment of political structures. At any rate, this is how one can interpret several of the recommendations of the Scientific Advisory Board of the Economic Administration of the Bizonal Economic Council, along with the decisions of the council itself, which abruptly dropped the Keynesian planning policies of the immediate post-war economy. In April 1948, it was advised that regulation of the 'national economic process' be left as far as possible to 'competitive price formation' on the markets.[49] Shortly thereafter, Ludwig Erhard – the Bavarian finance minister from 1945, then head of the 'Special Department for Money and Credit' in charge of preparations for the currency reform, and from March 1948 director of economic administration in the Bizonal Economic Council – presented a programme drawing on these ideas. These took legal form in June 1948 with the 'Law on the Principles of Economic Government and Pricing Policy after the Monetary Reform'. The law, which came about via a bureaucratic process without the involvement of parliament, and which the minutes

of the CDU/CSU parliamentary group referred to as the 'Enabling Act',[50] sought to abolish 'the ineffective system of coercion belonging to the past' and to rely on the market to 'boost the economy both in production and distribution'.[51] As Erhard himself proclaimed, it was about 'liberation from the state command economy' and from 'a suffocating bureaucracy'; about freeing the economic process from state restrictions.[52]

On the one hand, this entailed a series of measures combining monetary and economic policy. These ranged from the establishment of the Bank of the German States and the introduction of the Deutschmark to the abolition of existing price specifications and the gradual deregulation of pricing for industrial products, food and other goods – a process of liberalization that began in 1948 and that was largely complete by 1952–3. Of course, this relied entirely on the assumption that the pricing mechanism automatically guaranteed the optimal distribution of goods and the dynamic coordination of supply and demand, thus enabling the 'competition of performance' as such. In other words, currency reform and market liberalization were ways to create a 'healthy competitive economy' expressed by and realized in the self-regulating system of pricing.[53]

On the other hand, and equally systematically, a project was launched that, on the back of monetary and economic policy, was to reach into what Erhard called the field of 'social policy'. In the preamble to the 'Law on the Principles of Economic Government', the liberalization of the pricing system was justified through reference to the common good.[54] Insofar as the 'eternal tension between individual and society' constituted a basic social problem, the question arose as to the 'principles and forms' capable of organizing people 'into the higher forms of sociality but not, it should be emphasized, of subordinating them'. If – as Erhard remarked, firmly in the spirit of neoliberalism – it was the market alone that offered a solution, that steered a course between 'anarchy' and the state as 'termite heap', that underpinned a regime of 'liberty and cohesion', then the circulation of money and the pricing system were to be considered the guarantees of a new social contract. Consumer freedom, the freedom of commercial enterprise and the 'freedom of economic activity' were deemed to be not only 'economic basic rights', but also a 'democratic basic right', an 'inviolable basic right' whose injury was 'punishable as an assault on our social order'.[55]

This agenda, whose kairological virtue was that it could be rapidly implemented, was not just a way for post-war West German liberalism to realize capitalism. It was also about creating the conditions for the construction of the Federal Republic around established market mechanisms. After the collapse of National Socialism, the German state was politically discredited. Moreover, confronted with national division and foreign occupation, the difficulty lay in retrieving the moral foundations and legal legitimacy for an entity that could be justified neither through existing political structures nor through consensus and collective will.[56] Against this background, the opportunity arose to create, via the economic system, a framework in which post-war West German society could constitute itself. This would occur not through the delegation and exercise of state sovereignty, but through the freedoms and duties required by the new economic order. Ludwig Erhard formulated this explicitly in April 1948: only in the free-market system did the 'state gain the moral right to speak and act in the name of the people'.[57]

Erhard's economic policy on the one hand signalled that international corporations and lobbies were free to form contacts with West German business and industry and that the country's embryonic political institutions did not conceal the slightest totalitarian threat. On the other hand, the free market and 'wealth for all' were emphasized in such a way as to imply that their significance went beyond the economy as mere sub-system of the social. Rather, as Michel Foucault argued, a primal scene or founding moment was being played out. If history had negated and delegitimized the state, then the economy now paved the way for its reassertion. It was not a question of limiting state authority vis-à-vis the markets, but one of reinstating the state by invoking the economy. Simply put: 'The economy produces legitimacy for the state that is its guarantor. In other words, the economy creates public law.' The establishment and guarantee of economic freedoms function 'as a siphon, as it were, as a point of attraction for the formation of a political sovereignty'.[58]

The Liberal State   A founding process thus took place in 1948 and 1949 whose course ran from the economy to politics, from economic policy to law, from the free market to sovereign statehood. This antecedent foundation was guaranteed by the dual entity of pricing mechanisms and competition, on the one hand, and by the central bank and currency stability, on the other. Together, these bore the hope for a kind of pre-stabilized harmony between economic and social transactions. Price stability and inflation control were not simply partial factors of a social subsystem. On the contrary, they overrode all other social-political goals, forming the bond that allowed post-war society to renew itself and to create the conditions for the possibility of a political order. This is what characterized the unstable yet prominent status of the Bank of the German States, which would later become the Bundesbank. The Ministry of the Economy's draft of the 'Law on the German Bundesbank' of 1956 (the so-called 'Erhard Draft') predictably prioritized the protection of the currency 'inwardly and out-wardly'.[59] In its explanatory section, the draft stated that the 'stability of the domestic value of the currency' was 'particularly important'; the 'preservation of the stability of the currency', it argued, represented a 'moral and legal necessity'. This was precisely what warranted and necessitated the central bank's independence from government: 'More important than any other reason, as good as it may be, is the security of the currency; this is the foremost condition for the maintenance of a market economy and therefore, ultimately, for the democratic constitution of society and the state.' The derogation of the constitutional principle of parliamentary accountability could be justified on the grounds of a 'pre-legal concept of the whole', which at that moment included the provisional existence of an independent central bank, the Bank of the German States.[60]

The state is founded in the constitution; however, the 'liberal constitution' is founded in the freedom of the market. The question of the independence of the central bank is thus accompanied by a peculiar style of constitutional reasoning that chimes with the 'economic style' of neoliberalism,[61] ensures the central bank an informal constitutional status, and recommends 'including *currency stability among the catalogue of human basic rights*'.[62] The foundation of the Bank of the German States in 1948 can therefore be understood as a precise demarcation, by means of which a free-market society is instated on the condition that it defers and inhibits state intervention. As a pre-state, proto-democratic executive institution, the bank limits or obstructs organs of government in order to make room for economic government. If one can speak – literally – of the foundation of a 'radically economic state', in the sense that 'its root is precisely economic',[63] then the debates on the status of the bank's independence in relation to article 88 of the Basic Law point to the informal reserves of sovereignty that, in the form of a central bank, preceded the inauguration of the sovereign state. In the Erhard Draft's account of the powers of the Bundesbank, this reserve of sovereignty is briefly defined in connection with the bank's freedom to set monetary policy: 'In the monetary realm, restrictions on freedom must be accepted so that the currency remains healthy and the economy free.'[64] As in Hayek, money is declared to be the elementary instrument of freedom; economic freedom is guaranteed by the monetary-political restriction of freedoms. With the 'restoration of orderly financial relationships' that 'impact upon all areas of national life', a boundary is drawn around the system of political representation, though not around governance.[65] This political bifurcation counts among the founding charters of the Federal Republic.

The ECB Characterizing the German Bundesbank was an accumulation of powers that inoculated themselves against other governmental and constitutional organs. These powers included all the typical features of central bank autonomy. This goes for the Bundesbank's monopoly on monetary policy, its strict rules concerning direct and indirect financing of the state, the independence of its committees from electoral cycles, and its privileging of pricing stability and inflation control. This profile chimed with the political consensus over the establishment of a free-market economy, which after the Godesberg Programme of the Social Democratic Party (SPD) of 1959 preceded all other social-political conflicts. The lengthy debates about the foundation of the bank were followed by more or less complete silence over its operation, no doubt because of the stability of growth up until the 1970s, and the fact that the political dimension of the bank retreated behind technical issues such as the regulation of interest rates and money supply. A technocratic self-conception in the bank's management of the monetary and financial system kept the political implications in a latent state. Until the 1990s, economic common sense held that central bank autonomy guaranteed the desirable restriction of fiscal and political latitude and, together with the assurance of price stability, represented the basis for growth and employment in general and the success of the Bundesbank in particular; 'exceptions prove the rule'.[66]

This changed, on the one hand, with the end of the post-war economic system, a process beginning with the collapse of the Bretton Woods system in 1973 and completed by the liberalization and deregulation of the international financial markets in the 1990s. With the financialization of the economy, the welfare compromise in 'democratic capitalism' was weakened or annulled. On the other hand, the introduction of the European Monetary Union, and particularly the establishment of a European Central Bank, revived and intensified questions about the political status of these 'independent' institutions. There was little doubt that the ECB amounted to a Europeanization of the German model. The establishment of a European manufacturing and trading community was also linked to the constraint, diffusion, deferral or 'liquidation' of figures of sovereignty.[67] The completion of the common market and the introduction of the euro demonstrated the effectiveness of a jurisdiction once again motivated by the 'ideal of a market economy freed from politics by politics itself'.[68] Moreover, the foundational impulse had been radicalized. Post-war Europe demanded a doctrine of government able to assert and realize itself alongside, apart from and with complete indifference to the variety of national sovereignties. Today, there is a tendency to assess the European Union in terms of the integration of political diversity; however, its aim was once to stabilize economic government by disintegrating it politically, thus guaranteeing the functioning of market society. The criteria and procedures of this governmental mandate primarily became manifest, of course, in the emergence of the ECB.

The idea of a European Central Bank and its institutional form originated in informal meetings and discussions between the governors of international central banks at the Bank for International Settlements in Basel from the early 1960s. This circle formed the core of the Committee of Governors of the European member-states, constituted by a resolution of the council of the European Economic Community (EEC) in July 1964. The committee was not an organ of the EEC, its members did not represent elected governments, and its responsibilities were not contractually regulated. Although its sessions were supposed to be about financial and monetary policy and to facilitate communication on joint measures between the central banks, it was 'difficult to say what this special collaboration was supposed to consist of'.[69] Nevertheless, the committee very soon became part of a trans-governmental network that emerged alongside the EEC, the European Community (EC) and the EU, whose effect was to confer public functions on informal groups on the basis of technocratic expertise.[70] The institutional indeterminacy of the committee provided the framework for the conception of what would become the European currency system, while the club of central banks became the nucleus of the ECB. Vested with increasing powers, the committee went through a series of incarnations – as the European Monetary System, established by the central banks in 1978, and its successor, the European Monetary Institute, founded in 1994 – before reaching its final form in 1998 in the Governing Council of the ECB. As the highest executive organ of the new Central Bank, it stood at the apex of the European System of Central Banks (ESCB).[71] In other words, the European Monetary Union demanded that sovereignty in monetary matters be conferred on a body that began as nothing more than an informal gathering of central bankers.

In the course of its tortuous development, the ECB established a decidedly eccentric position in relation to the other organs of national and European government; it was only with the Lisbon Treaty of 2009 that it was registered as an institution of the European Union. The refrain of independence accompanied this process throughout. Radicalizing the statute of the Bundesbank at another level, what would become Europe's central bank was systematically designed as a non-public body. The guiding principle of the monetary project became the severing of executive functions – including financial and monetary policy – from the nation-states and the EC. In 1988 and 1989, the so-called Delors Committee, a body dominated by the directors of Europe's central banks, drew up a plan for the creation of the Economic and Monetary Union (EMU) of the EU. The EMU was realized in several phases, from the liberalization of capital transactions in 1990 and the consolidation of national budgets in 1994 to the foundation of the ECB in 1998 and the introduction of the euro in 1999/2002. Simultaneously, the informal discussion round of the Committee of Governors mutated into a proto-central bank and, following German recommendations, specified the necessary institutional arrangements. These included, on the one hand, an international treaty impervious to national legislation and, on the other, mechanisms that precluded the European Parliament from influencing decisions on monetary policy.[72]

Sure enough, these independencies were anchored in the Treaty Maastricht
of Maastricht of 1992. Article 107 of the treaty famously stated
that

> When exercising the powers and carrying out the tasks and duties
> conferred upon them by this treaty and the statute of the ESCB,
> neither the ECB, nor a national central bank, nor any of their
> decision-making bodies shall seek or take instructions from
> Community institutions or bodies, from any government of a
> Member State or from any other body. The Community institutions
> and bodies and the governments of the Member States undertake
> to respect this principle and do not seek to influence the members
> of the decision-making bodies of the ECB or of the national
> central banks in the performance of their tasks.[73]

Additionally, article 108 stipulated that 'Each Member State shall
ensure ... that its national legislation including the statutes of its
national central bank is compatible with this Treaty and the
Statute of the ESCB.'[74] After some debate and following the
recommendation of the Central Bank Council of the Bundesbank,[75]
article 88 of the German Basic Law was duly amended. It now
read: 'The Federation shall establish a note-issuing and currency
bank as the Federal Bank. Within the framework of the European
Union, its responsibilities and powers may be transferred to the
European Central Bank that is independent and committed to
the overriding goal of ensuring price stability.'

The foundations were now in place for a financial and monetary
policy without a state, which more or less followed the criteria
of a neoliberal 'denationalization of money' (as Hayek put it).
However, doubts emerged about the transfer of power to this
strange and indeterminate non-state sovereign entity, doubts
that expressed themselves in connection with wide-ranging and
lengthy controversies on whether sovereignty in Europe had
been 'restricted', 'divided', 'pooled', 'fragmented', 'eroded' or
even 'abolished'.[76] Exemplary of these debates on the EU, and
in particular on the exceptional status of the ECB, was the
complaint filed to the Federal Constitutional Court in Germany
in 1992. The complainants argued, albeit for very different
political reasons, that the Treaty of Maastricht, the national law
ratifying it, and the subsequent constitutional amendments
violated article 38 of the Basic Law. This guarantees citizens the
right to democratic representation in the German parliament

and the right to participate in the exercise of public power. According to the complaint, the law ratifying the Maastricht Treaty handed fundamental powers to the organs of the EC and prevented the popular sovereign from participating in the political process. This especially concerned the Monetary Union and the measures for the standardization of monetary policy, which the complainants argued were entirely detached from any form of parliamentary control or democratic legitimacy.[77]

Although the Constitutional Court predictably rejected the complaint, the reasons it gave for doing so were significant. The court began by conceding that there was indeed strong potential for conflict between the transfer of currency responsibilities to the ECB and the principle of democracy expressed in the Basic Law. It restated the opinion that

> the ability of the Bundestag, and thus of the electorate, to exercise rights of sovereignty via European organs has been almost entirely diminished, insofar as the European Central Bank is granted independence from the European Community and the member-states (art. 107 Treaty on the European Union). An important realm of politics, which with monetary value supports individual freedom and with money supply determines public financing and the policies dependent on it, is placed beyond the authority of sovereign organs and simultaneously – unless the treaty is altered – beyond legislative control over political responsibilities and means. The transfer of the majority of monetary political functions to an independent central bank removes national sovereignty from direct national or supranational parliamentary accountability, in order to place monetary affairs out of bounds to interest groups and politicians concerned with re-election.[78]

The responsibilities of the ECB begin where democratic participation ends. Yet the transfer of sovereignty, the restriction of democracy and the constraint of democratic legitimation are still deemed compatible with the Basic Law. In its dismissal of the complaint, the court referred to the amendment to article 88 of the Basic Law, which allowed powers and responsibilities to be ceded to an autonomous central bank on the condition that it was committed to ensuring price stability. According to the court,

> The amendment to article 88 of the Basic Law, made with regard to the European Union, permits a transfer of the powers of the

Bundesbank to a European Central Bank if this meets the 'strict criteria of the Treaty of Maastricht and the statute of the European System of Central Banks as regards the independence of the Central Bank and the priority of the stability of monetary value' [quoted from the 'Recommendations and report and the special committee "European Union (Treaty of Maastricht)"', 21]. The intention of the legislator in amending the constitution was clearly to create a constitutional basis for the Monetary Union stipulated in the European Treaty, but to limit the granting of the concomitant powers and institutions, given independence in the way described, to this case. This modification of the principle of democracy in order to guarantee confidence in a currency can be endorsed, because it takes into account the fact – tested by German law and proven scientifically – that an independent central bank is better placed to secure the value of money, and thus the general economic foundation both of national fiscal policy and of the private exercise of rights of economic freedom, than organs of sovereignty, whose actions essentially depend on the value and the supply of money and on the temporary consent of political forces. Hence, the placement of monetary policy under the sovereign competence of an independent central bank, a competence that cannot be extended to other policy areas, complies with the constitutional conditions upon which the principle of democracy may be altered.[79]

This prolix reasoning has far-reaching implications. A strange mix of legal reservations and economic presumptions, beyond its jurisprudential dimension the judgement provides a degree of insight into the political and economic status of the problem of central banks. First, the court remarks on the definitive withdrawal of national sovereignty from all forms of legislative and executive control. It then notes that the independence of this sovereign enclave is, as formulated in the second sentence of article 88 of the Basic Law, conditional upon the 'primary goal of securing price stability'. The concrete policy tasks and institutional form of the ECB were thus anchored in the Basic Law. Not only that, but a situation was created in which any changes to the statute of the ESCB and to the Treaty of Maastricht – insofar as they affected the ECB – breached the original conditions set by the Basic Law for the transfer of sovereign powers to European organs. The monetary-political criteria stipulated by the Treaty of Maastricht required an amendment of the German constitution, which itself required that the Maastricht criteria

The New Constitution

be observed; any modification to the institutional and functional profile of the ECB in turn necessitated an amendment of the Basic Law.[80] The transfer of power was made irrevocable.

Second, the argument of the court was based on the 'scientifically proven' assumption that an independent central bank guarantees the value of money and hence represents a stable 'foundation' for fiscal policy, for the private sector, and for reliable free-market operations. At a key moment, the modification – or nullification – of the principle of democracy was justified on the basis of the familiar liberal doctrine that central banks must be independent in order to guarantee price stability and control inflation. The claim drew on a common theory, first mooted in the early 1970s, about the 'dynamic consistency' and 'time consistency' of monetary and economic policy. To put it simply, a discrepancy or inconsistency was said to exist between, on the one hand, a government's long-term promotion of price stability and low inflation and, on the other hand, incentives created by electoral cycles to stimulate the economy and labour market in the short term by raising inflation. Independent central banks liberated governments from this dilemma, harmonized economic policy and placed monetary policy beyond the reach of ephemeral political interventions.[81]

This also appeared to be the assumption of the Federal Constitutional Court, which justified the independence of monetary policy via an institutional form that, according to the Maastricht Treaty ruling, was shielded from the dictate of 'organs of sovereignty', from 'politicians concerned with re-election', and from the dynamics of the 'temporary consent of political forces'. Disregarding the theoretical and empirical questionability as to whether an independent central bank can alone guarantee price stability, this argument turned an item of liberal orthodoxy into the basis for a constitutional amendment.[82] The convergence of legal ruling and liberal doctrine produced a constitutional anomaly. The question is why the opinion of the Constitutional Court in economic matters should bear more weight than, say, that of parliament or the minister of finance.[83]

Government of Last Resort   Third, the interlocking of free-market liberal and legal argumentation describes a position marked by a tension between singular monetary policies and their more general, fundamental significance. On the one hand, the special status of the Monetary Union requires that it have its own constitutional basis. This status is incompatible with that of other institutions and organs and cannot be 'extended to other policy areas'. Hence, the granting of independent 'powers and institutions' is limited 'to this case' only, in other words exclusively to the monetary system and the ECB. Monetary responsibilities receive an incommensurable and unique position within the system of government; financial matters are dignified as an autonomous political and legal realm. On the other hand, this exceptional status is justified by the fact that executive control over the value and supply of money determines 'public financing and the policies dependent on it', also 'supporting' individual freedom. The guarantee of an 'infrastructure of public and private planning' and its stability becomes the 'pre-condition for the exercise of individual freedom and public power'.[84] Even if some discretion prevails regarding the precise political and legal status due to this 'precondition', it is unequivocally stated that an independent central bank guarantees the stability of monetary value, and that governmental functions and basic rights (for example individual freedom, protected by article 2 of the Basic Law) can be exercised only on the basis of a stable currency. The exceptional status of financial policy is warranted by its foundational power in the social system. A kind of constitutional mission is thus formulated. The ECB represents the 'hard core' of the Treaty of Maastricht, the point at which exceptional regulations and the transfer of power are emphasized particularly strongly.[85] An autonomous monetary institution not only restrains organs of government in order to secure (economic) freedoms; it also represents a position of sovereignty from whence economic government is practised over governments. In other words, it is a government of last resort.

The European monetary system and the central banking sector, which originated in informal circles and para-governmental institutions, was thus vested with sovereign powers and responsibilities characterized by their singular, autonomous and exceptional status among national and European governmental organs. However, the transfer of power was fully completed only through a principle that combined the regulation of national debt with a prohibition on the ECB's direct participation in national fiscal policy. This, too, was a more stringent version of the German system. The Treaty of Maastricht had already stipulated that 'overdraft facilities or any other type of credit facility' (Art. 104[1]) with the ECB or the national banks of the member-states were prohibited for all public bodies at the European, national or regional levels; so too was the direct purchase of public 'debt instruments' by the ECB from such bodies. These prohibitions were carried over directly into the statute of the ESCB and the ECB.[86]

This means, first, that the central banks of the Eurozone countries can purchase the treasury bonds of non-EU states in open market operations, but can only purchase bonds issued within the EU indirectly, in other words on the secondary markets. Here, the ECB introduced a special regulation requiring a minimum credit rating for the purchase of member-state bonds. Second, this exposes the member-states and their fiscal policies to the evaluations of the financial markets (and particularly the ratings agencies) and encourages competition over levels of public debt. This became critical during the financial crisis and euro-crisis of 2008 onwards. Moreover, indirect participation in fiscal policy installs a chain of financing running from public budgets to private banks and investors to central banks. Third, it is the independent central banking sector that paradoxically ends up financing the dependency of national budgets and governments upon the private finance sector. The ECB supplies private banks with cheap money that these then lend to national governments at a higher rate, while simultaneously buying national debt that has previously been purchased by private banks. In other words, price and monetary stability not only legitimates the independence of central banks. Central bank independence has also created a situation where control over fiscal policy shifts to private banks, and where financial markets become an instrument with which to discipline governments. Sovereign power is being systematically transferred from the ballot box to the trading index.[87] The prohibition on the direct financing of member-states together with the central banks' monopoly on monetary policy has led to the involvement of private finance in the practice of governmental power.

Minority Protection Despite differences in structure and policy, the ECB performs the same function as the Federal Reserve System. This is to validate the distinction between democratic electorates and systems of representation, on the one hand, and the investing financial public and capital markets, on the other. Emerging from the agreements of informal circles, vested with extraordinary executive powers and rights of sovereignty, and prohibited from intervening directly in fiscal policy, the ECB effectively protects wealthy minorities with its isolation of monetary responsibilities. What was formerly referred to as the Bundesbank's 'right of way'[88] and consolidated in the controversial status of the ECB was also, in combination with the creation of a market society, a means of supplementing the political independence of the central bank with the increasing dependence of government on the private finance sector.

It is no coincidence that the liberalization of the international banking sector was accompanied by a wave of central bank reforms from the 1990s onwards, as well as a body of literature arguing that central bank autonomy guaranteed the credibility of monetary political arrangements vis-à-vis the financial markets. Elected governments' self-limitation through autonomous central banks was interpreted as a credible demonstration of their commitment to price stability, as a reliable signal of creditworthiness and creditor rights, and as an attraction for national and international investors. The associated 'credibility bonus' would supposedly impact positively on the social and economic costs of monetary and macroeconomic stability.[89] These theories emphasized the reputation of national governments as a factor in market competitiveness; the political logic behind the connection between central bank autonomy and price stability was treated cautiously at best. Questions aside as to whether and how inflation control correlates with other economic factors such as growth, employment and national deficit,[90] it needs to be asked how, by insulating monetary control from electoral cycles and democratic processes, independent central banks privilege particular interests. If price stability and low inflation were considered desirable by society as a whole, then central banks would not need to be autonomous. Independent monetary policy intervenes in the social field; opposition to inflation brings a political agenda.

Central bank autonomy and the prioritization of anti-inflationary monetary policy are techniques for harmonizing economic processes, but also ways of concentrating government power. This is illustrated in a case in which it was precisely the democratization of authoritarian structures of government that dictated the pace of an extensive central banking reform. The prehistory is familiar: after the 1973 military coup in Chile, an economic and political restructuring took place that entailed not only the suspension of democratic institutions and the monopolization of executive, legislative and constitutional functions by the military junta, but also privatizations, the dissolution of the trade unions, the liberalization of markets and, above all, the emergence of large-scale, internationally active financial corporations. It seemed logical to combine the rigorous implementation of neoliberal measures and particularly the growth of the finance sector with a central bank reform. Indeed, the fundamental importance of a financial system that 'impedes the President of the Republic from imposing policies contrary to monetary stability on the central bank' was soon recognized.[91] Although the mandate for an independent central bank was included in the constitution of 1980, a view nevertheless developed in the circle around Pinochet that central bank autonomy and authoritarian government were fundamentally incompatible. A 'conflict between the president of the republic...and a totally autonomous power that controls the monetary system would simply produce a catastrophe', according to the opponents of an independent central bank; 'such an organ would be absolutely incompatible with a presidential regime', would be 'politically inconvenient' and bind the presidential power with an 'iron belt', and would contradict the logic of a presidency that had no intention of 'yielding' or sharing power.[92] An independent central bank would inevitably collide with the military dictatorship's claims to sovereignty.

Authoritarian Precautions Even after the economic and financial crisis of 1982, during which 70 per cent of Chilean banks were taken over by the government and later largely reprivatized, no central bank reform took place. However, a new situation began to emerge towards the end of the decade. From 1984 onwards, links between the military regime and the private sector became even stronger. The employers' association (Confederación de Producción y Comercio, CPC) assumed a major role in the development of economic policy, top business representatives received ministerial posts, and major corporations were brought into government via advisory bodies and legislative and economic commissions. In a 1986 survey, business leaders confirmed that the policy of the military regime was almost perfectly aligned with the preferences of the private sector. Within this circle, calls again emerged for a central bank with maximum independence from government and political power. Without exceeding the parameters of the authoritarian regime, this was seen an 'indispensable pillar for the development of any society that aspires to be truly free'.[93]

While there had been numerous opportunities and occasions since the 1970s for a central bank reform, the project was realized under a completely different set of circumstances. The 1980 constitution, ratified by Pinochet's military dictatorship, had scheduled a referendum for 1988. This would decide whether the regime was to continue for a further eight years and whether a transition would take place to a democracy 'guaranteed' by military rule. Completely unexpectedly, a majority voted against the continuation of the Pinochet regime and for a presidential election in 1989. The result of the referendum signalled both a rejection of the regime's monopolization of government and a rejection of its market liberalism. The government was accused of 'redistributive illegitimacy'. Although the Chilean economic model received broad academic applause, 72 per cent of Chilean 'No' voters were economically motivated, with 38 per cent stating that poverty and unequal distribution were the reason why a regime change was necessary.[94] In further surveys, 70 per cent were in favour of the restoration of the public health and education systems, 57 per cent were for the nationalization of the big corporations, and 80 per cent were for strict controls on foreign investment. Since more then 30 per cent of the Chilean population lived below the poverty line, it was logical to link democratization with the redistribution of wealth and income.

This was also apparent to members of the Pinochet regime. Faced with the unpleasant prospect of losing the election to a well-organized opposition coalition (the Concertación de Partidos por la Democracia), and of handing power to elected politicians with economic tendencies different from its own, the regime used the time remaining to prevent, through a series of rapid decisions and measures, what it considered to be the intolerable consequences of democratization. Members of the military received permanent positions in government, presidential powers over appointments to high-ranking military posts were curtailed, an autonomous military budget (10 per cent of the revenues of the state-owned copper mines) was guaranteed, an independent radio and television board was established, electoral constituencies were gerrymandered and the system of allocation of parliamentary seats was altered to favour the regime and its supporters. These political reforms were accompanied by economic legislation that placed narrow limits on the commercial activity of the state, privatized more state institutions (including the public TV station and the national airline), and, in order to minimize the influence of the state in the future, changed government loans to troubled banks into debts to the central bank.

Most significant of all, however, was a law reforming the central bank, passed in December 1989, shortly before the elections. Giving the independence of the central bank a constitutional footing would, among other things, 'prevent a socialist economy from being introduced in Chile'.[95] The opposition immediately recognized this as an attempt 'to freeze monetary policy at the constitutional level', to perpetuate the neoliberal 'scheme',[96] and to prevent a new government implementing other economic priorities: 'it is evident that this is being legislated at the last minute to guarantee a technical-financial enclave that ensures ... influential groups of power within the present regime a situation of omnipresent veto and control against any alternative economic policy in the future'.[97]

Indeed, through this political and legal act, an institution was created that at the time was considered one of the most independent central banks among the developing and newly industrialized countries. In some respects, it took its lead from the Bundesbank. As in the German system, the finance minister has no vote on the bank's board of governors; and, as in the German system, the members of the executive are appointed for ten years, in other words for longer than a legislative term, and can only be dismissed on formal grounds (for example because of a conflict of interests). The central bank has autonomous control over monetary and credit policy and pursues the primary goal of securing price stability. The 1989 law invests the central bank with further political-economic powers – such as the regulation of foreign debt, control over the exchange rate, foreign trade policy – that intrude on the remits of governmental departments. Above all, the central bank is not permitted, 'under any circumstances', either 'directly' or 'indirectly', to finance governmental bodies, state-owned corporations, or any kind of public spending, except during wartime. The financial services of the central bank are reserved exclusively for private banks and financial institutions.[98] Any kind of deficit spending was thus made impossible or extremely expensive for future governments.

Chile's independent central bank was thus not so much an effect of democratization as a perpetuation of the authoritarian regime by other means and under new circumstances. Taking place alongside measures guaranteeing the political influence of the military beyond the change of regime, the transfer of reserves of sovereignty to a new institution created an isolated enclave that exercised executive power outside the remit of elected governments. The circumstances of this central bank reform suggest that its motivation was not solely economic and technical. Confronted with the prospect of losing power, the regime transferred that power to the central bank, thereby preserving it. What was described as an 'autonomous entity of a technical nature' with an 'indefinite life-span' actualized itself as a political and strategic act.[99] The central bank was a product of the regime change; it installed a constitutionally anchored instrument of control over the economic mechanisms in place since 1973; and, as a remnant of the military junta, it guaranteed the permanence of neoliberal economic policy. It was immediately identified as a 'fourth power of the state' that ensured the continuity of the economic achievements of the past two decades and the political system associated with them.[100]

First, this meant the irrevocability of the hastily ratified reform. The new government under Patricio Aylwin took office with the promise of retracting the legislation on the autonomy of the central bank. It was not only the large parliamentary majority required for the necessary constitutional amendment (four-sevenths in both houses of the congress) that prevented him from doing so. Because of the international integration of the Chilean financial markets and the strong rise in foreign investments from the mid-1980s, any modification of the statute of the central bank seemed out of the question. Events in Venezuela in 1994 illustrated this. When it was announced that the Venezuelan government was planning to reduce the independence of the country's central bank, the market index nosedived within hours, triggering massive capital flight.[101] Chile's independent central bank directly exposed the policy of its government to the risk evaluation of international finance capital.

Second, the central bank reform was devised in connection with a broader set of measures that ensured that a democratically elected government would be 'permanently and tightly constrained' (*todo atado y bien atado*) from the start.[102] Initially this concerned fiscal policy. A tax reform had succeeded in making only minor corrections to VAT and income tax for companies, and although this enabled a slight raise in social spending on the less well-off, existing privatizations remained unaffected. With a few minor alterations, the new government relied on the programmes and structures of the military regime, continuing with a market-based social policy. The same was the case for employment policy. A small increase in the minimum wage meant that by the mid-1990s it had returned to its 1970 level, while initiatives in employment law failed to improve the situation of wage-earners in labour disputes and sectoral pay negotiations significantly. Although it was possible to halve the share of the population living below the absolute poverty line, the relative distribution of income between the poorest 40 per cent and the wealthiest 20 per cent remained more or less stable. While not all these effects can be attributed directly to the autonomy of the central bank, the fiscal restrictions it dictated, together with its commitment to limiting inflation, made the correction of authoritarian redistribution policy more or less impossible. Austerity programmes and repeated warnings from the central bank forced the government to stick to predetermined financial political goals.[103]

It was not solely the absence of coordinating mechanisms between fiscal and monetary policy that became an issue in conflicts between the government and the central bank. The incompatibility between the commitment to price stability and the broader mission of an 'equitable development' suggests that the primacy of monetary policy belonged – third – to a policy of wealth defence.[104] If, in general, a clear correlation can be observed between a strong financial sector, central bank autonomy and anti-inflationary regulations, then this can reasonably be interpreted as resistance to the redistributive side effects of inflation. Although private savers, pensioners and importers can all claim an interest in inflation control, it was the banking and financial sector that succeeded in rallying the expertise, means and legitimacy of independent central banks in support of its interests. The structural and personal overlaps between central banks and the finance industry leads to a homogenization of monetary policy that amounts to more than instances in which the central bank owns private banks (as in the US) or communicates closely with representatives of the finance industry (as in Germany). Monetary policy is dominant not just because the central banks are independent, but also because the interests of central banks fuse with those of the financial sector.[105] While banks, financial institutes, creditors, rentiers and owners of large-scale assets all profit from the control of inflation and its variance, the strict maintenance of price stability increases the cost of national deficits and disadvantages debtors, labour-intensive industries, the primary sector and wage-earners.[106] Central bank autonomy operates as a useful instrument in conflicts over distribution. Not only did the insulation of Chile's central bank against democratic cycles ensure the continuation of neoliberal economic policy, but its monetary priorities also played a major role in securing the distribution of wealth established under the military regime. The central bank reform was connected to guarantees of primitive accumulation and distribution.

One model for this was the German Bundesbank, whose rigid stability policy suppressed wages and inflation more than was the case in other capitalist countries. However, the textbook example was the policy of the US Federal Reserve following Jimmy Carter's appointment of Paul Volcker as its chairman in 1979. Under Volcker, the Fed succeeded in bringing down the inflation of the 1970s by raising the discount rate and rates of interest. Not only did this stabilize the dollar, it also caused a significant redistribution of wealth and income. While profits for banks and financial institutions, securities, bonds, shares and major assets all increased, debt became more expensive and wages dropped. Revenues from manufacturing, small businesses and agriculture also dropped. The growth of the financial sector and increasing profits from financial capital correlated with a shrinking economy and rising unemployment. The share of the national income of the 55 per cent of households with zero or negative financial value was redistributed among the upper 45 per cent. To sink below what was now referred to as the 'natural rate of unemployment' would, so the argument went, raise inflation (and wages) and thus necessitate 'stability' measures'.[107] As in Chile, the much-applauded 'coup' of the Federal Reserve inaugurated a new financial order dominated by central bank autonomy and inflation control.

From the nineteenth century onwards, the embodiment of seignio- Class rial power in the form of central banks and banks of issue Struggle occupied a permanent and key position in the repertoire of modern government. In the process, it became detached from its origins – the symbiosis of sovereign debt and finance, public borrowing and private investment – and became a security apparatus for the banking sector, the financial markets and the currency system. Central banks played a central role in the stabilization of capitalist financing, and hence in the financial-economic regime. Notwithstanding their diversity, a result of the different political and economic conditions under which they emerged, central banks reveal numerous points of convergence concerning the coordination of state structures and economic dynamics. These, in turn, influence central banks' role in the formation of the financial-economic 'world-system'.

Originating in states of fiscal emergency, central banks initially asserted a position of exemption, expressed in the various debates on their legal status and peculiar institutional format. In the course of the twentieth century, their programmatic and increasingly doctrinaire 'independence' entailed an important shift of sovereign powers and rights. This was the consequence of a systematic economization of power and the permanent 'interpenetration' of political and economic functions, of public tasks and private resources. Central banks obtained an incommensurable status within government, accumulating a policy-making power insulated from elected governments and institutions. This allowed them to operate as an unconstrained executive enclave strategically geared to the demands of the financial markets and their agents. In pursuit of the ideal of 'government without government' (as with the ECB and the ESCB), the financial sector was, through central banks, endowed with a quasi-governmental privilege. This allowed it to inoculate itself against electoral cycles, parliamentary majorities and labile governmental policy in the interests of an investing public.

This shapes the role of central banks in 'democratic capitalism' and debunks the equation of capitalism and democracy as an ideological short circuit or conciliatory commonplace. Central banks – as is proven by the Federal Reserve, the German Bundesbank and the ECB – function as constitutive entities of representative systems only at the price of their systematic extraction from democratic processes. The separation of powers aside, steps were taken at the legal, constitutional and administrative levels to create a fourth power made up of what can be called 'para-democratic organs'. From the final decades of the last century – in connection with the liberalization of the financial markets – these have operated as transformers of governmental power, converting their own independence *from* government into the dependence *of* government on the financial markets.

This autonomous, eccentric, exceptional and in a literal sense 'para-sitic' positioning by no means secured a neutral authority beyond all bias and particular interests. With its technocratic concentration on monetary policy, price stability and inflation control, the central banking system preserved the central dogmas of post-war liberalism. As the Bundesbank, the ECB and the Central Bank of Chile demonstrated, monetary agendas obtained constitutional gravitas; competition and free markets now had political priority. Central banks thus intervene directly in the social, prioritizing particular interests and becoming agencies of a 'politics of wealth defence'.[108] The connection between the autonomy of central banks and rigid inflation control led to a monetary policy that reduces fiscal and political latitude, increases the cost of public debt and makes short-term state investments more costly. Moreover, the fixation on currency and price stability – at the expense of other economic and political concerns such as employment – entrenches a programme of distribution that privileges, structurally and permanently, the profit interests of banks, financial institutes, investment groups, portfolio finance, creditor cartels and large-scale capital assets. Easily recognizable in this unrestrained financial authority is the latest permutation of economic government, an alliance of governmental and financial power, and not least a stake in the 'class struggle'[109] waged by the financial public against the rest of the population.

6

Reserves of Sovereignty

From the Bank of England to the European Central Bank, central banks have established themselves as separate powers with their own political functions within governments. Designed as independent enclaves of government, in democratic and representative systems they have become constitutional anomalies. Their roles are historically determined, ranging from financing fiscal policy, money creation through lending to banks, and the monopoly over the issue of banknotes to the stabilization of the monetary and financial system. The varying degree of emphasis placed on these roles has influenced the inherent tensions and interferences in the remit of central banks.

In this context, the fundamental question repeatedly arises as to how, concretely, the correlations between central banks and market dynamics are organized. Are these correlations structured episodically, as events, or constantly and regularly? Do central banks function within or outside the economic system, and how? Are they a necessary condition for the reproduction of the finance sector? The opacity of financial markets also raises the pressing question of the efficacy of their control mechanisms. Predictably, the practical and theoretical uncertainty evoked by modern finance has infected precisely those institutions supposed to regulate it. A general uncertainty surrounds central banks, as attempts to frame them theoretically and systematically attest.

This is the case for the remit and aims of central banks, as well as the means and procedural structuring of their actions and decisions. Despite the urgency of demands that central banks secure the financial system by regulating capital reserves and money supply, it remains unclear what precisely can be regulated and how. Controversy over this issue already existed in the nineteenth century, originally in connection with the monetary policy of the Bank of England, and it persisted in various forms into the twentieth century, by which time the issue was the medium of circulation. For David Ricardo and other economists, money was defined as banknotes and coins in circulation, while price level was to be controlled by money supply and the convertibility of notes into metal. This meant that central banks were responsible for convertibility and restricting the issue of notes, while market mechanisms 'automatically' controlled the rate of interest and hence the value of money. This prompted the objection that the definition of money also needed to include securities and loans; in other words, that price and monetary value were dependent on money surrogates and interest rates. This meant that indirect intervention was required to stimulate or restrict the availability of credit.

What entered the history of economic thought as the debate between currency theory and banking theory cannot only be seen as a post facto attempt to clarify precisely what central banking operations involved.[1] It was also evidence of a perplexity caused by central bank entities concerning the nature of money itself. Mandated with securing the monetary and financial system, it is precisely the central banks whom, in attempting to grasp the object of money, money's essence escapes. What money does and what it means have become unpredictable and erratic; a developed central banking system can probably only be said to exist when its functions have become controversial and mysterious.

After the financial and economic crises of the 1920s, questions of this kind became existential, pointing to a heightening of financial-economic insecurity. It is incontestable that modern systems of finance and credit are made up of a 'chaos' of private business practices, central bank operations, fiscal measures, government bodies and market mechanisms, and put into circulation not only cash and bank money but all kinds of pseudo-money (such as bonds, savings, securities, debentures, money market instruments, etc.). However, there is very little unanimity over the basis of central banks' desire for order. On the one hand, it is conceded that it is impossible for central banks to distinguish between what is and what is not money. Any definition of money is 'artificial' and raises the question of how far the various substitute and surrogate forms of money are to be included alongside notes and coins. According to one canonical study,

> the money-quality of assets is something imposed by the business habits of people; it is attached in varying degree to various assets; and the attachment can be and is varied over time in a completely unpredictable manner. To label something as 'money', the supply of which is to behave according to rules laid down by legal authority, is to build on shifting sand.[2]

For central banks, all forms of money and credit are essentially interchangeable and ultimately based on private credit. The generation of private credit is independent of the limits of available money. It is therefore impossible to base the interventions and decisions of central banks on reliable quantities and rules. They operate on a case-by-case basis, speculatively, using the widest possible margins of discretion. After all, central banks exist precisely because there are no universal definitions and rules governing the circulation of money, credit and capital.[3]

On the other hand, indeterminacies of this kind are also seen as the 'unnatural' and 'perverse' result of developments incompatible with liberal notions of autonomous market mechanisms, developments that challenge the old 'liberal faith' and demand strict reform.[4] Here, the question is how 'genuine' or 'neutral' moneys can be distinguished from impure quasi-moneys or 'near moneys', so that controllable money supplies can be created and a predictable circulation of money guaranteed. In an article on the creation of a 'new religion of money', published in 1936 and still discussed today, the Chicago economist Henry C. Simons proposed returning the monopoly over money to government, reducing monetary interventions, fixing the money supply permanently, guaranteeing bank deposits with a hundred per cent coverage, minimizing short-term bonds and money surrogates, and restricting monetary policy as such to price control.[5] The proposal to introduce rules prohibiting short-term interventions and discretionary decisions, so as to allow free enterprise to operate on free markets with predictable market mechanisms, raises the prospect of limiting or eliminating the 'authorities' incorporated in central banks.

This gave rise to the monetarist doctrines that dominated central banking policy in the late twentieth century. These posited a causal relationship between money supply and price level or inflation rate, confined central bank operations to regulating money supply (however defined), and delegated responsibility for the control of the system to the compensatory mechanisms of the financial markets.[6] These considerations culminated in the radical theory, proposed by Friedrich Hayek, that money could only be understood theoretically by dispensing with central banks and state monopolies, leaving the creation of 'honest money' to the markets, and allowing the private 'free banking' sector, together with the power of competition, to stabilize price levels. If money was merely an innocent commodity among other commodities, then the 'mystery' of the old sovereign monopoly could comfortably be depoliticized and devolved to 'control of value by competition'.[7]

The emergence of modern central banking is connected to a proliferation of various kinds of money, various definitions of money, and various ways of distinguishing between moneys, which wrestle with the difference between honest and impure, neutral and political, genuine, false and 'near' money. Associated with these attempts are, moreover, various ideas of intervention that populate the spectrum of financial dogma and doctrine. On the one hand, there is resistance to understanding central banks as an 'unnecessary, interventionist, artificial, inflationary intrusion into an otherwise idyllic, efficient, self-equilibrating, natural system of "free banking"'; on the other hand, there is the desire to see in them only a 'diabolical' deformation of otherwise perfect market movements.[8] As the latest controversies over the policies of the ECB show, concepts of 'currency' and 'banking', 'discretion', 'rules' and 'free banking' are not obsolete, but continue to inspire, in various ways, classical, Keynesian, post-Keynesian, monetarist, neoclassical, liberal and liquidity-theoretical doctrines of money, proving with their various concepts of intervention that central banking operations remain both potent and controversial.[9]

It was thus logical that central banks were analysed only on the condition that their existence be declared irregular, alien to the system or simply redundant. In the ideal system of efficient markets with perfect competition, banks and serious questions of money were neither necessary nor justified.[10] Conversely, the

Ideas of Intervention

functioning of really existing central banks tended to be treated less as an exact science than as an 'art', an 'esoteric art', or at best an impure mix of 'art and science', and hence as an activity that had to prove itself in a domain without rules.[11] These central institutions of the modern monetary system were supposedly defined by minimal institutional, theoretical and epistemological consistency. Scholarly opinion is divided over the importance of monetary political initiatives, whether monetary policy should be based on fixed rules or discretionary decisions, and whether central banks indeed offer stability or are merely obstacles to the functioning of the financial system. In other words, expertise fails to agree on a solution to the problem of central banking and, if anything, demonstrates that central banks still operate by 'balancing conflicting aims'.[12]

If the ontology of central banks has always been linked to unclear remits and zones of uncertainty in financial knowledge, then the situation became even more difficult from the 1980s, with the deregulation of the financial markets and the proliferation of private credit and money market instruments. The trade in electronic money, securities and derivatives, 'forwards', 'futures', 'options' and 'swaps' caused an exponential growth in the volume of financial transactions. In 1990, the sum of financial market transactions was five times the worldwide nominal GDP; in 2007, it was more than seventy-three times higher. These new instruments have the creative ability to liquidize all kinds of assets and transform them into money surrogates, secondary media of circulation, and 'potential money'.[13] As part of the money supply, they guarantee extreme liquidity, thereby perfecting the logic of the modern capital and credit economy.

Strange Market Behaviour It is not only the exclusive and exceptional status of central banks within government that is at stake; as the latest financial dynamics have shown, the range of their power to exert influence and make decisions itself now encounters boundaries and resistance. At stake is central banks' 'power to influence events', their ability to assert their primacy over the 'regulation of credit' and the stabilization of the financial and monetary systems.[14] From the 'prudential' perspective of central banks, this above all means assessing market risks. From the 1990s onwards, price formation on the financial and securities markets became highly volatile; long-term price movements could no longer be directly explained with reference to core data such as productivity, cost structures, credit ratings and so on. What has been referred to as 'very strange collective market behaviour' manifested itself in erratic price variations, marking the limits of predictable tendencies.[15]

These financial innovations led to the oft-criticized 'opacity' of the financial markets. They are a part of new business practices and belong to 'risk offsetting investments', in other words the compensatory distribution of risks, in which financing requirements are met through securitization. Creditors, i.e. commercial banks or mortgage banks, transform credit (e.g. mortgages) into obligations, cover these with retroactive interest payments, split these up into various tranches and sell them on the secondary markets as asset-backed securities. Investment banks combine these with other bonds, repackage them as assets with varying degrees of risk or prospective yield, and distribute them as collateral debt obligations. It is thus possible, via an unlimited number of cascades, to increase the financing offer to meet growing capital demand, while at the same time removing passive risks from the balance sheets of the original creditors. Risks are disseminated, diversified and to a certain extent covered by derivatives that match the perspectives of low-risk sellers with those of high-risk buyers. A win–win situation.

According to the IMF's 'Global Financial Stability Report' of 2006, 'These new participants, with differing risk management and investment objectives (including other banks seeking portfolio diversification), help to mitigate and absorb shocks to the financial system, which in the past affected primarily a few systemically important financial intermediaries.'[16] This means that the documentation of individual risks is replaced by an aggregative look at the statistical distribution of potential risks, using a method of calculation referred to as 'value at risk'. This bundles together individual risks so that they are supposedly cushioned by the weight of normal distribution. Finally, there is the notorious species of derivative known as 'credit default swaps', a kind of credit default insurance that allows risky entities to be removed from the balance sheets of the creditor by selling them to profit-oriented, high-risk investors. The demand for credit is thus met through the sale of purchased risks; insolvency is made affordable. This fusion of derivatives and borrowed money can be understood as the reflexivization of money creation and hence the potentiated circulation of bankruptcy.[17]

In the 'mark-to-market' method used to balance these values, active and passive risks are calculated according to the price that the respective securities and bonds list or could plausibly list on stock markets and the like. After all, value is no different from price, meaning that a financial instrument can be legitimately valued on the basis of its market price. Current market prices thus directly determine the value of capital stocks. High prices increase the book value of private capital and assets, and hence the willingness to lend and invest; this efficient script completes the financial-economic process. The prospect of a perfect market process emerges. Balance sheets react immediately to price alterations – in other words, rising market prices (e.g. for real estate) are expressed directly in rising capital values, which are expressed in higher returns on investments and lower potential risks.[18] Higher prices for assets cause calculable risks to decrease, capital is released for more plough-backs, and a self-supporting process of financing is set in motion.

Unknowns   This produces a situation where it is impossible to predict or precisely evaluate the risk either to the banking system as a whole, or to individual financial institutions: 'Gone are the happy days when central bankers, by looking at the BIS [Bank of International Settlement] statistics, could assess, for instance, the country risk exposure of individual banking systems.'[19] This uncertainty extends to the balance sheets of individual corporations. The former CEO of Lehman Brothers, Richard Fuld, still insists that in accounting terms Lehman was solvent in 2008; and the CEO of JPMorgan Chase, Jamie Dimon, when asked about the general stability of banking institutions, replied simply: 'I don't know.'[20] Because the new financial instruments make it possible to spread risk through the sale of risk, they reduce the extent to which systemic risks can be known and assessed, and therefore become a concern for central banks' apparatus of security.

However, it is not only distinctions between different kinds and qualities of financial product that are being undermined. The same goes for the boundaries between various areas of the finance sector. Altered parameters – caused by, among other things, financial deregulation, culminating in the repeal of the Glass–Steagall Act in 1999 – perforated dividing lines between commercial   and   investment   banks   (including   insurance companies). Together with the migration of financial transactions to so-called shadow banks (such as hedge funds or private equity funds), the rise of private trading platforms and 'over-the-counter' trade, this created a situation where the distinction and traditional interplay between central banks and commercial banks lost significance. Until the second half of the twentieth century, banks formed the core of the financial system; they guaranteed the issue of credit, the supply of liquidity and the management of cash flows, and were assisted in this by central banks and their reserves. The liquidity of the banking system was tied to governments and central banks, which set targets for growth and money supply. The expansion of the financial markets and the proliferation of private credit instruments (including electronic money and credit cards) weakened this strategic alliance between central banks and the credit system as a whole.

For example, in the 1950s more than three-fifths of credit demand in the US was met by commercial banks. In 2000 it was only one-fifth. Towards the end of the 1990s, debt securities totalled 163 per cent of the American GDP, while bank reserves totalled only 0.5 per cent; in Germany, the ratio was 85.4 per cent to 2.5 per cent.[21] The crucial functions of money creation, liquidity control and credit supply shifted from the banking sector to the deregulated financial markets. Indeed, this transition from a government-controlled financial system to a market-controlled system was forced by central banks themselves,[22] as well as by increased capital mobility. Short-term capital inflows now produced booms in countries that increased interest rates in the hope of breaking the economy. This made monetary policy unpredictable. However, this shift caused the 'intermediate targets' of central banks' regulatory mandate – discount rates and interest rates, bank reserves – to lose their immediate efficacy. Target setting ceased to be addressed directly via commercial banks and was instead addressed indirectly via the very financial markets whose transactions and volumes to a great extent influence credit behaviour, interest rates and exchange rates. The value of currencies depends in the short run on interest rates and exchange rate expectations, which are in turn influenced by the markets, as capital flows stimulate or dampen the economy. A 'dual decoupling' was visible between the instruments of central banks and market movements.[23] The expansion of credit, as well as exchange rates and the price of assets in opaque markets that are heavily influenced by debt-financed speculation, have escaped central banks' intervention.

The integration of worldwide capital markets has restricted the power of central banks to determine and to implement their own monetary policy. Even if their ability to control pricing was always regarded as 'something of a mystery',[24] the growth of the financial sphere and the migration of the monopoly on money supply to the markets have reduced still further the leverage and servomechanism through which central banks can influence the private credit sector and hence the dynamic of the economy as a whole. Relying instead on signal effects, they concentrate their activity on announcing present and future interest rates and trading on the money markets. As their direct purchase of securities in the wake of the recent financial crisis showed (including the notorious Outright Monetary Transactions of the ECB), central banks have ceased being lenders of last resort and are now *investors of last resort*.[25]

Again, it is possible to observe a collapse of traditional definitions of money, and with them the fine distinctions upon which interventions in the name of monetary policy were based. Economists and central bankers still differentiate minutely between various types of money supply – depending on which system is used, monetary base (minimum reserves and cash), M1 (circulating cash including demand deposits with credit institutes), M2 (M1 plus fixed-term deposits of up to two years), M3 (M2 plus shares in money market funds, bonds, re-purchase agreements). However, the financial innovations of the last three decades have eradicated the boundaries between money and financial assets, causing broader money supplies to become indefinable. This is connected to the alarming possibility that a specific and clearly defined quantity of money, one that indicates a sufficiently stable relation to price formation, and which can serve as a target for monetary policy, may be a matter of mere interpretation, and may not be identifiable at all.

This situation has caused debates over the methods and aims of central banks to become more heated than ever (debates whose lack of resolution has prompted the national and European courts to become involved). However, agnosticism has also increased, attesting to an erosion of financial economic knowledge – to the point where thought is overwhelmed by the principle of insufficient reason. Since the 1980s, sober expertise has considered statistics on money supply to be 'somewhat impressionistic', a kind of 'statistical fog' that provides a poor basis for monetary policy. The market behaviour of the new financial instruments continues to be 'terra incognita' for the central banks; and despite hopes being raised of exerting an 'influence' over market phenomena, it is conceded that it is no longer possible to 'exert control in any of the markets'.[26] According to E. Gerald Corrigan, the former president of the Federal Reserve Bank of New York and managing director of Goldman Sachs, it is probably impossible – in the context of globally networked, high-tech, highly competitive financial processes that no longer involve commercial banks – genuinely to comprehend the 'long-term consequences' of the new cash flows for the financial markets.[27] The persistence of incomplete knowledge is a constant torment. Given the massive increase in liquidity, financial innovation, unknowable risk and private money creation, the notion of a determinate and determinable volume of circulating money appears like a 'historical curiosity, like belief in a flat Earth'.[28]

While central banks largely retained legal sovereignty over monetary affairs, their political instruments have lost a good deal of their impact. The increase in central banks' political and governmental power created the conditions for the erosion of their regulatory potential. Since the latest financial crisis, monetarist doctrines, equilibrium theories, ideals of fiscal-political asceticism and other former certainties have become untenable. Alan Greenspan, long-time director of the Federal Reserve and advocate of unregulated currency markets, admitted that the 'view of the world', the 'ideology' of central bankers, the 'whole intellectual edifice' of the financial industry, collapsed astonishingly quickly.[29] The hastily improvised emergency measures of the central banks demonstrated that even vast amounts of cheap money, pressure on discount and interest rates, a policy of zero or negative interest and the resolute purchase of securities were unable to induce significant movement in inflation rates and credit behaviour. The situation resembles a kind of monetary-political double bind. According to dominant opinion, low rates of interest are linked to prospects of elementary growth; yet this is precisely what provides the stimulus for actors on the financial markets to expand 'hazardous activities', increase 'risky

[margin note:] Financialization

investments' and compensate for the minimization of growth risks by raising speculative risk potentials.[30] The effects of central banking operations (including the desperate measure of quantitative easing) have become contradictory and deeply uncertain, and indicate the limits of monetary-political intervention.

The situation is therefore unstable. Over the last decade, central banks have weakened their own monopoly over liquidity, or caused it to migrate, by restricting fiscal leeway, strengthening the financial sector, forcing private money creation, and delegating monetary decisions to market dynamics. These two processes – the political empowerment of central banks and the transition to a market-based regulation of monetary policy – belong together. They occur in unison with liberal hopes that financial resources are better supplied by markets than by public money-creation;[31] and they are part of a global mass experiment that for three decades and more has sought to 'financialize' national economies and economic and social infrastructures as a whole, thus increasing the opportunity for the finance sector to wield political decision-making power.

What has been broadly described as the latest phase in capitalist modernization and as a restructuring of the economy around the financial sector has been realized through a conglomeration of heterogeneous policies, projects and inventions that have enabled finance capital to cast off its welfare-statist yoke. Some of these are notorious: the liberalization of credit and capital markets; technical financial innovations and the promotion of high-yield assets; the privatization of social security, public functions, services and infrastructures; the emergence of new kinds of financial institution (such as investment funds and rating agencies). Counted among them are also such diverse phenomena as the extensive reforms of corporation tax, property tax and income tax (e.g. in Germany: the abolition of property tax; the lowering of the top rate of tax from 53 per cent to 43 per cent; the halving of corporation tax from 57.5 per cent in 1997 to 29.4 per cent in 2009); the increase in the power of international agencies and treaties (such as the IMF, the World Bank and the World Trade Organization, WTO); proposals for the expansion of major corporations into financial service providers (today, the biggest share of the profits made by corporations such as General Electric or Ford Motor Company is made up by revenues from financial services, not industrial products). Connected to this has been a broader process in which the share of industrial profits in overall corporate profits has steadily decreased. In the 1970s, the share of industrial profits in the US dropped from 24 per cent to 14–15 per cent; in the 1990s, it was overtaken by profits from the financial, insurance and real-estate sectors.[32] Financialization has become structural.

Various explanations can be offered for the persistent stimulation of the newest regime of accumulation: the collapse of the post-war international currency system; declining profits from industrial manufacturing since the mid-1960s and the diversion of investment to the financial sector; governments' search for solutions to the social conflicts and economic crises of the 1970s.[33] Yet whatever its causes, the systematic consolidation of financial markets and financial institutions proved to be a programme of wealth and income redistribution; this is now well documented. Although the US government treats the incomes of the highest earners in the country as a state secret, the figures and dynamics are widely known and similar in most contemporary industrial nations.[34] The expansion and perfection of capital markets liberated 'centrifugal forces': since 2000, the volume of private wealth in Europe has been between four and six times larger than the combined annual national income. Capital gains now clearly exceed long-term economic growth. These tendencies are expressed in the discrepancy between high and low incomes, between wages and asset yields.[35] Between 1999 and 2009, the income of the lowest 10 per cent of German households declined by 9.6 per cent, while that of the highest 10 per cent rose by 16.6 per cent; the real wages of employees dropped by around 3 per cent. In 2007, 10 per cent of the wealthiest households owned two-thirds of total private net wealth, while 1 per cent owned more than one-third and the topmost 0.1 per cent owned 22.5 per cent. The entire bottom half, meanwhile, owned 1.4 per cent. Inequality was even starker in the US, where 43 per cent of the total net wealth of private households was owned by the richest 1 per cent, and 83 per cent by the richest 10 per cent. Moreover, nations with particularly dominant financial industries such as the UK and the US count among those western societies with the least upward mobility.[36]

The hyper-concentration of income and property not only Governance indicates the economic transformations in recent decades; it also points to a change in the organization of governmental power.

While the isolation of monetary political powers by autonomous central banks was already a significant factor in the redistribution of governmental functions, this process was augmented by a series of institutional creations that aimed to install mutual conformity between political structures and (financial-)economic dynamics.

This applies to those ideas and policies that have been gathered under the vague concept of 'governance'. In fifteenth-century France, the expression meant 'good attitude' or 'good behaviour' (*gouvernance*); in the eighteenth century, it was occasionally used as a synonym for 'government' (*gouvernement*); and in the first half of the twentieth century, it reappeared in organizational theory and management jargon. The term was picked up by new institutional economics, where it was used to refer to the coordination of economic activities, the efficiency of regulative processes, the optimization of commercial transactions, and the administration of companies and personnel. 'Governance' was to private companies what politics is to society as a whole.

The use of the concept in the political realm since the 1980s brought a proliferation of applications. These included various micro, meso and macro levels of government, ranging from primary schools to international aid, from everyday office life to the operations of the global economy. However, the concept also described a mode of government that operated alongside and apart from governments and state structures. This was defined not so much through established forms and institutions as through informal processes and practices, through bodies and networks with a weak institutional basis, and through a loose coupling of norms and regulatory systems. Broadly speaking, the concept of governance has come to imply a general reform of – or transformation in – governmental organization. Its programmatic vagueness notwithstanding, it operates within a basic set of coordinates.

First, governance refers to the integration of private actors and agencies into the public realm, the proliferation of private–public synapses, and the intensification of reciprocities and interdependencies. The purpose of this interpenetration is, second, to integrate sectoral organizational knowledge. Looser demarcations between the public and private spheres are linked to hopes for a decentralization and diffusion of governmental power and to greater potential for inclusion. This means, third, that hierarchical structures and formal laws are supplemented or replaced by indirect mechanisms of control, including self-organization and auto-regulative processes. The aim is to create support for governments and governmental goals by minimizing friction and potential for conflict. Fourth, governance is geared to bridging the gap between government praxis and institutional, corporate, regional and interest-based particularities, thereby generating a single field of immanence. As a concept of 'good governmental leadership' and a collective term for the political 'management of interdependency', governance is a diagrammatic arrangement marked by the expansion, delimitation, diffusion, intensification and mediation of governmental forces.[37]

Interest in governance goes back to the public sector reforms of the 1980s, which were primarily implemented in the Anglo-Saxon countries and later prescribed by the OECD and the World Bank as the basis for the 'structural adjustment pro-grammes' in developing and newly industrialized countries. With its universalization of the corporate form, post-war liberalism already saw social and political units in terms of company structures; what emerged in the UK and the USA as the new public management advertised itself as the latest version of the economization of government. On the one hand, this was characterized by the use of corporate management techniques and the introduction of market-based regulatory elements into the public sector. The emphasis on stimulus, competition and the 'free-market liberalization of public services' was connected to the promise of cost reduction and increased administrative efficiency.[38]

On the other hand, a systematic process of marketization was carried out that involved outsourcing public services, increasing public–private partnerships, and privatizing a swathe of traditional public services and infrastructures: from the postal and telecom-munications services to public transport and the energy and water boards, from education and social security to policing and other public responsibilities. This created a broad zone of interference characterized by intense public–private relations. Its spectrum encompasses what in recent jargon is referred to as an 'activating state' (concerned with strengthening subsidiarity and extending areas of private self-regulation), a 'negotiating administration' and a 'deal-making state'. Informal agreements and arrangements were intended to reconcile private and public

Entrepreneurial Administration

interests, in which regulatory abstinence was to be compensated for by lower implementation costs. More importantly, this culture of informal arrangement between government and private sector led to the prioritization of what were already powerful interests, and to the formation of new structures of privilege or 'para-constitutional decision-makers'.[39]

The various types of 'entrepreneurial administration' are characterized by a continuum between sovereign rights, government interventions and private regulations.[40] Expanding zones of intermediacy between public and private, government and the market not only challenged older forms of rational authority and bureaucracy. The new model of government, in which 'modern business practices could make government more efficient, economical, and responsive', ultimately caused the apparatus of government to swell.[41] Concomitant with the dietary constraints of lean states was the emergence of 'shadow governments', which, through privatizations, outsourcing, leasing arrangements and subsidiaries, generated proliferating cascades of government and replaced *big government* with *big governance*. In the US, for example, around 50,000 public sector jobs were cut between 1999 and 2002, while the number of subcontractors and concessionaires working for the government increased by almost one million.[42]

Regulatory Capitalism
The youngest and most ambitious form of economic government is, however, what since the 1990s has increasingly been referred to as 'global governance'. The term refers not only to the many initiatives to internationalize various areas of politics, but also to the institutions, treaties and measures that organize relations between states, and between state bodies and private sector actors. Global governance guarantees that governments and government interventions are integrated into the dynamics of global financial markets.[43] Again, it is about coordinating political structures and economic dynamics; again, economic liberalization is the basis for the construction of the objects and aims of governance; again, the market provides the yardstick for governmental activity.

These transformations have primarily taken place in the sphere of finance. In 1974, under the aegis of the Bank for International Settlements, an alliance was formed between the governors of the central banks of the G10 states, the so-called Basel Committee on Banking Supervision, whose guidelines and recommendations set the parameters for the financial markets. This alliance gave rise to a series of treaties and bodies for the regulation of international transactions – for example, the Basel Accords between 1975 and 1992, the International Organization of Securities Commissions (IOSCO) in 1983, the International Association of Insurance Supervisors (IAIS) in 1994, and the Financial Stability Board, founded by the G7 countries in 1999. These committees are not institutions in the strict sense. They have no specific legal status, are not necessarily based on a treaty, and at best represent a transfer of public functions to ad hoc bodies, often without an official address.[44] They also include independent European consultancy groups and supervisory boards such as the Committee of European Banking Supervisors (CEBS), founded in 2014; the Committee of European Securities Regulators (CESR), founded in 2001; and the European Insurance and Occupational Pensions Supervisors (CEIOPS), founded in 2003.

The global financial architecture is structured by further official entities, including international organizations such as the World Bank, the OECD, the IMF and the WTO; multilateral treaties such as the General Agreement on Tariffs and Trade (GATT), the North American Free Trade Agreement (NAFTA), the Transatlantic Trade and Investment Partnership (TTIP); and interest groups and private clubs with their own regulatory mandate. To this latter category belong the International Swaps and Derivatives Association (ISDA), founded in 1986; the lobby group of the major financial institutes, the Institute of International Finance, founded in 1983; the association of creditor nations in the Creditors Club (or Paris Club); the alliance of commercial banks specializing in public debt (London Club); the private accountancy firms commissioned to carry out public tasks (e.g. Ernst & Young or PricewaterhouseCoopers); and the ratings agencies involved in financial-economic decision-making.

This patchwork of public entities, international organizations, treaties and private actors is connected to general transformations in the agencies, processes and aims of government. The liberalization of markets since the 1970s, particularly the financial markets, cannot be understood simply as the withdrawal of regulatory authorities. On the contrary, calls for regulation, and for regulatory practices, regulatory instruments and regulatory bodies, increased in proportion to the privatization of public services and companies.[45] The implementation, consolidation, securitization and legitimation of market mechanisms have engendered a panoply of public, semi-public and private facilities, testifying to a propagation and dissemination of government functions.

These facilities operate pluralistically and at various levels. As elements and forms of financial-economic 'global governance', they are the hallmark of a regime that, originating in North America and Europe, was put in place by the leading economic powers. An intergovernmental or trans-governmental executive was installed that is hard to define in legal and institutional terms; it augments and replaces the formal authority of governments and undermines the distinction between public and private. The interpenetration of national bodies, international organizations and networks, private agencies and market mechanisms has produced a multi-layered fabric of regulatory systems with varying degrees of density and range. Market forces are bolstered by a proliferation of regulatory bodies; conversely, market dynamics and actors appeal to a close system of regulations. Government functions and market-based operations become mutually inclusive, defining an economic and financial system that can be termed 'regulatory capitalism'.[46] The neoliberal fiction of 'free', 'efficient' and 'unregulated' markets, which supposedly evolve happily and autonomously outside government, now becomes redundant. The liberalization of markets and financial markets has called forth a global programme of regulation and re-regulation.

Private Law   The interconnection of markets and regulatory systems of various kinds is connected to debates around 'private law-making'. Here, the question is broadly how individuals and institutions, public and private actors conduct and regulate their business activities. It is argued from a classical liberal legal standpoint that economic relations, operations and contracts provide a model for the ad hoc and autonomous development of legal systems.[47] In view of the proliferation of international treaties and transactions, the key issue is the status of a private law 'beyond the state', its relation to national legal systems and constitutional law, its legitimacy, validity, procedure and autonomy, and thus its legal character as such. General questions aside as to whether private law exceeds national responsibility or whether it adapts itself to existing global markets, the appeal to private law regulations invokes a normative rationality and set of values that become attractive precisely where the reliability and efficacy of political structures are lacking.[48]

Discussions about 'global governance' in international economic transactions prompted a revival of interest in the pre-modern *Lex Mercatoria*, the commercial codex based on the customs and arrangements of medieval merchants that operated independently of royal authorities. This served as a founding myth for the legislative agency of free associations and inspired proposals for rules and treaties created by the market and developed by market forces.[49] Appeals for a 'privatized private law' able to function without state intervention invoked on the one hand the efficacy of the notorious system of arbitration courts, which have grown rapidly into an independent, profit-oriented sector in which private forums rule on conflicts in international business. In connection with the anticipation that they would set the agenda of legal reforms in the twenty-first century,[50] arbitration courts multiplied from a dozen to over one hundred between the 1970s and 1990s, with the cases handled more than doubling. One of the most prominent, the International Court of Arbitration (ICA), based in Paris, produced a statistic showing an average increase of 55 cases a year between 1923 and 1977, rising to 333 in 1991, 450 in 1997 and 580 in 2003. Around 90 per cent of international contracts include an arbitration court clause. The optimistic agenda of this arbitration procedure is based on a circular logic, according to which commercial routine generates laws that, via the arbitration courts, quickly, flexibly, efficiently and autopoietically rebound upon the conditions of commercial praxis.[51]

This is connected, on the other hand, to the hypothesis that obstructive, disadvantageous and regulatory laws can no longer be enforced by states. Financial markets generate competition between states and legal systems, allowing conflicting parties to pick and choose which jurisdiction they apply. For example, derivatives and over-the-counter trading needs to guarantee mutual obligations, regardless of the geographical location of the markets and contracting parties. The most discreet variant of this type of transaction, namely swaps (i.e. agreements over the kind of future payment), requires that each transaction be accompanied by documentation of the guarantees connected to it. In order to avoid impractical and tedious hearings in national courts when these obligations are breached, in 1985 the biggest derivatives traders formed the alliance known as ISDA. This led to the so-called ISDA Master Agreement, which standardized the legal parameters for each unique swap contract. In difficult cases, however, it was still unclear as to how this private statute guaranteeing outstanding obligations (collateralization) stood in relation to national legislation. To bypass this problem, a clause was added to the standard swap contract requiring that all parties agree on a mutually acceptable jurisdiction.[52] Swap transactions were henceforth mostly carried out under British common law or New York law, both of which offer optimal conditions for the resale of securities – and for the creation of secondary markets.

Some saw these privatized legal procedures as a revival of natural law à la Grotius, in which a mutual bond was formed between (financial-)economic actors beyond the interference of the public authorities, and which protected cultural attainments such as the inviolability of property, the principle of good faith and the regulation of injuries. Over-the-counter trading in derivatives was, so it was argued, an ideal example of a form of transaction regulated by private law.[53] Despite doubts whether private regulations, which have become increasingly detached from nation-states, can 'protect politically defined common interests',[54] private law-making and national legislation and judicature continue to interact in multiple ways.

For example, in cases where the conditions contained in standardized derivatives contracts conflicted with national regulations, the ISDA successfully pushed for changes in legal praxis. In the US, this led to amendments to trade and insolvency law. In the EU, a Directive on Financial Collateral Arrangements was passed that catered entirely to ISDA interests. The directive sought to contribute to 'the integration and cost-efficiency of the financial markets' and to encourage 'cross-border transactions backed by collateral', calling on member-states to 'create legal certainty regarding the use of such securities held in a cross-border context'.[55] The issue is not whether the operations of 'global governance' take place privately or publicly, but how the financial market generates projects that enable private actors and national or international legislatures and regulators to collaborate. From concrete business practices and contractual clauses to legislative and judicial processes, reference chains are generated that are characterized by the interaction between financial economic routine and state guarantees.

In international arbitration courts, major corporations and governments meet on an equal footing, namely as private entities. Cases are heard on minimum wages, taxation, environmental protection, labelling obligations on food, health and safety standards, and the shortfalls associated with them. These courts are set up through intense private–public collaboration. They are inaugurated by international treaties, particularly the 3,000 and more investment treaties, which in turn are flanked by projects involving informal collaboration between politicians and international capital. The most influential of these projects is the Transatlantic Business Dialogue, founded in 1995 with the backing of the US Trade Department and the EU Commission. Here, representatives of the US and European governments meet CEOs to discuss measures for the removal of 'disturbances in trade policy' and the liberalization of markets and financial services. Private companies become party to political decision-making, these processes of 'regulatory convergence' collapsing traditional dichotomies of public and private.[56] Broadly speaking, the intersections between private players and public institutions explain the hectic attempts to create an international private legal system; the two sides together produce a 'mixed jurisdiction' of nationally and privately generated rules. The new *Lex Mercatoria* is an intricate web of informal normative structures, national and non-national legal forms.

With the reciprocal adaptation of public and private spheres of activity, a specific *conditioning* of political-economic policy-making emerges. Its logic and processes are most visible in the organizations introduced into the post-war economic order via the Bretton Woods agreement of 1944 in order to expand and stabilize international trade and economic relations: the World Bank, the IMF, and GATT (later the WTO). The IMF, founded in 1945, was mandated with coordinating international monetary policy and moderating potential conflicts via compensatory payments. By the 1950s, a distinction was already being made between the bridging loans and short-term credit issued to the private sector and the loans issued to governments. The latter were seen as the more problematic, since the 'balance of payments problems that brought countries to seek the assistance of the IMF were typically due to bursts of excessive domestic expansion and could usually be cured by the introduction of financial restraint'.[57]

Conditioning

If a strict set of provisos in IMF lending policy thus already existed, then this 'conditionality' was formally adopted in 1969 with a supplementary clause in the IMF's Articles of Agreement. Connected to IMF credit was now a broad range of fiscal, monetary and economic conditions, concerning national budgets, public spending and general volumes of credit, tax rates, subsidies, public companies, public sector employees, consumer benefits and trade policy.[58] After becoming temporarily obsolete following the collapse of the global currency system and the repeal of the Bretton Woods agreement in 1973, the IMF reinvented itself as an institution for monitoring stability criteria in view of fluctuating exchange rates. Alongside the World Bank, which was responsible for long-term economic and development policy, the IMF was also to function as a lender of last resort to central banks and governments on the international financial markets.[59]

This inaugurated the great era of 'structural adjustment programmes' (SAPs), the response of the World Bank and IMF – with the assistance of the OECD – to the debt crises in Asia and Latin America. Loans to developing and newly industrialized countries were made conditional on reforms, thereby generalizing perspectives for social-economic development and, ultimately, preparing the way for an international economic and financial policy. The key points of the SAPs were summarized in the so-called Washington Consensus of 1989. Alongside requirements for budgetary discipline, the reduction of public spending, tax reforms and the privatization of state-owned companies, they included market-based interest and exchange rates, investor rights, the deregulation of markets and prices, the liberalization of capital flows, and relief for foreign investors. For international financial institutions, the principles of financial-economic 'global governance' were intended not only to transform state structures and the conditions of economic policy, but also to support specific interest groups and agencies.[60] Despite repeatedly being declared a failure,[61] the SAPs were the blueprint for the recent governmental experiments in the Eurozone, where austerity programmes already tested on developing nations – stability and fiscal pacts, debt limits, budgetary discipline, privatizations – were again carried out.

The financial-economic conditioning of national economies subjects state institutions to greater competition, strengthens property rights, decentralizes government power, disciplines behaviour that does not conform to the market, opens up markets – in alliance with corporations – to goods, services and financial products, transforms states into attractive locations for long-term and profitable investments, and creates stable conditions for business. This transformation, which has been seen as a rejection of post-war Keynesianism, was by no means a return to the old liberal night-watchman state. 'Global governance' is neither a straightforward liberation of market freedoms nor a suppression of state institutions, nor is it a rigid dichotomization of market and state. Since the 1990s, a mutual embedding has taken place; permeability has been created, allowing credit conditions to dictate the rules of political restructuring. In this process, state institutions function as bodies for the anchoring of market mechanisms.

Numerous 'World Development Reports' of the World Bank from the turn of the century – *The State in a Changing World* (1997), *Entering the 21st Century* (1999), *Building Institutions for Markets* (2002) – refer to the complementarity of governments and markets, emphasizing the importance of a 'strong and capable state' for the implementation of market rules. One needs to 'step beyond the debates over the roles of governments and markets, recognizing that they need to complement each other'. It is about creating 'an effective state, one that plays a catalytic, facilitating role, encouraging and complementing the activities of private businesses and individuals'.[62] This has nothing to do with the decline of the state; on the contrary, the state is seen as a pillar of a regulatory regime that creates incentives for investment, competition and market-compatible activity. Market conditions are directly connected to 'institution building'. 'Global governance' entails a governmental rationale heralding a double convergence; an agenda that subscribes not just to the fusion of political and economic structures, but also to the adaptation of local factors to the dynamics of the global (financial) markets.

Ultimately, all these projects – trans-governmental executives, mixed jurisdictions, conditionality – address a problem of government concerning the functioning of regulatory capitalism at a fundamental level. The question is how to govern a global space that, regardless of national citizenship, is populated by economic subjects; how to coordinate sovereign powers, with their focus on legal subjects, with binds and mechanisms that determine relations between economic subjects.

The Market On the one hand, the financialization processes of the last three
as Prison centuries have led to a form of financial-economic 'global governance' that, by fusing commercial routines and regulatory systems,
public and private bodies, deepens the interdependency between
political institutions and economic dynamics. On the other hand,
they have produced a form of government that, through the
migration of money creation, of the monopoly on liquidity, and
of political-economic regulation, privileges the powers and agents
of the financial markets. This double movement characterizes
the current financial-economic regime, in which the ability of
financial interests to dominate the social and political field is
greater than ever. The international cycles of reproduction of
capital determine how politics and society understand themselves
and their situation. They dictate the agenda of 'competitiveness'
between institutions and states, realizing the old hope of using
the financial markets as a pseudo-judiciary or 'judge of governments', in other words a judge of governments' budgetary and
investment decisions.[63]

What has been referred to as an 'epochal change', an 'erosion
of statehood', and the 'global sclerosis' of politics is expressed
not in a weakening of government, but in a restructuring of its
goals, maxims and procedures.[64] The closeness of the connection
between public and private in regulatory capitalism causes the
accent of regulatory praxis to shift; direct interventions and
executive hierarchies are supplemented by an indirect system of
incentive and inducement. The American economist and political
scientist Charles Lindblom recognized the governmental dimension
of markets back in the 1980s, in connection with the disciplinary
automatisms that restrict political and legal latitude through
bleak scenarios of capital flight, low interest rates, underinvest-
ment, economic stagnation and rising unemployment. Policy-
making is pre-empted by market preference. The liberalization
and opening up of markets – from the financialization of the
global economy to the structuring of the Eurozone – have generated a new milieu of enclosure, in which the market 'imprisons'
political systems and governmental activities. More than ever,
Lindblom's observation holds true: 'no market society can achieve
a fully developed democracy because the market imprisons the
policy-making process'.[65] Modern markets and market societies
did not suddenly become 'post-democratic'; on the contrary,

their architecture has always been defined by the constraint of popular sovereignty and democratic freedoms.

While the financial order claims elementary rights and, thus, a minimum of democracy, the forms of government associated with it are para-democratic. The reality of 'market-compatible' or 'liberal' democracy is that its institutions and subjects are confiscated by the market. Adam Smith's notion of the market as privileged arena of social order and as essential figure of sovereignty in civil society exists in a new form and under altered circumstances. Fanciful ideas about balancing interests and the invisible hand of mundane providence belong to the distant past. As the markets of markets, financial markets have become an arena in which the liberation of financial-economic forces combines with the systematic expansion of interdependencies.

In a complex interactive process, governments, international organizations and private institutions are integrated into overarching agreements and regulatory systems, guaranteeing a 'regime of compliance'. The capacity of nations to determine national economic policy is made conditional upon their status within these structures of obligation, which define the form and content of international transactions. Moreover, the architecture of global finance – including its regulatory systems, its informal bodies, its conditions and its disciplinary automatisms – demands that nations uphold standards with regard to fiscal and monetary policy, the functioning of the financial sector and free-market mechanisms. The 'entrepreneurial state' accepts dependencies in return for creditworthiness, favourable credit conditions, foreign investment, tolerable ratings and solvent treasuries.[66] Market discipline becomes a fundamental criterion of politics that has raised the capacity of financial-economic actors and operations to intervene in government.

The essential lever for structuring these dependencies is the capitalist economy of debt and credit. The rise of permanent public debt and the concomitant expansion of the financial markets caused the nexus of state and finance to establish itself in pockets of seigniorial power, as an exceptional figure of modern government. The operations of the political-economic zone of indeterminacy – in which the formation of capital is directly connected to the organization of government power – range

Debt Imperialism

from the sporadic inclusion of private creditors in political practice and the institutionalization of private sector lending to the securing of the financial sector through central banks. In the more recent processes of financialization, however, seigniorial power has undergone a further and significant transformation. On the one hand, former state monopolies such as money creation and currency sovereignty have migrated to the financial markets and their agencies. On the other hand, a web of international treaties, agreements and organizations has anchored and reinforced creditor protection at the global level. Money and liquidity supply have been privatized, elementary sovereign powers have been denationalized. Financial markets have become 'lenders of last resort', taking over the role of an ultimate and 'eternal' creditor.[67] The financialization of the global economy has caused economic interests to focus on strengthening the power of private creditors. The impact and political weight of traditional reserves of sovereignty, such as money creation and liquidity, have increased in proportion to their dissociation from state authorities and governmental bodies.

After the debt crises in the developing and newly industrialized countries in the 1970s and 1980s, there emerged a rapidly expanding international market for national debts, which brought with it a new politics of 'debt imperialism' (as Michael Hudson has put it). The financing of national debt by the financial markets, and particularly institutional investors such as pension funds, insurance companies and investment funds, led to debt competition and the rise of credit rating agencies such as Moody's Investors Service or Standard & Poor's. It also led to a proliferation of criteria for evaluating nations. These are based on corporate models and include per capita income, public deficit, balance of trade, growth and inflation rates, prospects of economic development, credit history and the quality of government and political institutions. A mechanism of coercion has been established that allows private agencies and investors to regulate access to financial resources and, directly and indirectly, to intervene in nations' economic, monetary, fiscal, tax and social policy. The political and legal distinction between private property and the state collapses or is reduced to absurdity; financial logic and its rules are inserted into the public realm, while budgetary crises serve as opportunities for investors to gain control over national budgets.[68]

The systematic consolidation of the power of private credit became evident in the management of the financial crisis. What began in 2007 as a problem of liquidity on the mortgage and financial markets, and then mutated into a crisis of national debt, created a dilemma: debts had to be nationalized and banking institutions recapitalized; however, national budgets could only be supported if certain stipulations were met. This was particularly apparent in the Eurozone. For most euro nations, the crisis began not with budgetary deficits but with the implosion of the financial markets. However, in the subsequent escalation, what was prioritized was the vital interest of creditors in the profitable circulation of national debt. The shortfalls of private banks were covered by borrowing from other private banks, while the prohibition on the direct financing of national governments by central banks and the ECB's supply of cheap money to private institutions created the incentive for this money to be used to finance national budgets at a higher rate of interest. The effect was to install an automatism of enrichment through which 'seigniorage' – in other words, the net profit earned through the supply and protection of currency – could itself be successfully privatized.

When – as with Greece – state bankruptcy threatened and re-financing by the markets became impossible because of declining ratings and rising interest rates, the IMF and the EU (in the form of the European Financial Stability Facility, EFSF) jumped in to meet the requirements of the debt market. Two-thirds of the total paid to Greece between May 2010 and May 2012 returned to European creditors and holders of Greek national bonds.[69] This might be regarded as a particularly dark episode in the transition of taxation states to debtor states, obliged to spend an increasing portion of their income on financing their debts.[70] The crucial point, however, is that by nationalizing private losses, investors could be re-financed into the position of creditors of last resort. The short-lived movement towards the socialization of finance capital was hindered at enormous public cost. Debt limits, stability mechanisms, fiscal pacts and excessive deficit procedures could claim to have secured the trust and status of private creditors, and to have generated reliable public debtors who, in cases of emergency and with their fiscal sovereignty constrained, prioritized the portfolios and demands of their creditors. For that reason, democratic exercises such as the Greek elections in January 2015 were dismissed as illegitimate revolts against the predominance of the financial sovereign.

It is not only during crises that dependencies of this kind have led to the implementation of notorious austerity programmes, bringing cuts in social spending and interventions in labour and wage policy. In today's financial regime, new forms of social control are combined with a renunciation of the welfare-state consensus that moderated post-war capitalism. Since the middle of the last century, it has been discussed how the laws of the market and the capitalist economy can be made to harmonize with those of social reproduction. Market laws, it is argued, need not apply to market phenomena alone; the aim should also be to 'organize the economy of the social body according to the rules of the market economy'. The principles of optimized social productivity are premised on a greater need for integration into the fabric of economic relations; generally, it is about establishing a form of government in which economic dynamics determine social process. This not only means restructuring institutions and designing an axiomatics whose formal – in other words legal and institutional – structures guarantee that the social order constitutes itself according to the mechanisms of the market economy, creating a space of possibility for the survival of capitalism.[71] It also means interpreting market relations in the broad sense, so that they extend to transactions and interactions as such, in other words to the entirety of 'human actions', to a universal praxeology.

The financial-economic regime becomes a *fait social total* through a universalization of the corporate model. By mobilizing its subjects, economic governance enables competition to penetrate the thicket of social relations. Relations between market competitors are no longer sporadic and local, but permanent, beholden to the expectation that the proliferation of new markets, together with their structures of incentive, will enable the coordination of complex individual behaviour. This means that economic subjects behave not merely as agents of trade, as producers or consumers, but also as corporations with corresponding motivations, activities and structures. Households are defined as 'production units or small factories', individuals as micro-enterprises. When Michel Foucault refers to the formative, formalizing and informative power of corporate culture on society, he means not the gearing of the totality of behavioural forms towards the requirements of the market, but the activation of the traces of market conformity in the entirety of individual practices and motives, projects, objectives and decisions. It is about economizing the everyday, diffusing corporate structures throughout the social body or tissue.[72] The corporate form functions both as an institution for the transformation of life into value, and as the model for the regulation and alignment of social relations.

The 'human' or 'social capital' thus activated is integrated into the profit-generation process of financial markets. The privatization of social security systems not only flexibilized waged labour and introduced a repressive administration of poverty and unemployment, it also de-solidarized welfare burdens, individualized risk and made people's lives dependent on financial cycles. Income and pensions are redistributed; financially defined health and retirement insurance turns wage-earners into players on the financial markets. A governmental power emerges that connects welfare and pensions, savings and healthcare, education and professional biographies to the risks of the financial system. If economic government is understood as a set of measures and procedures that transforms individuals and populations into resources for the production of wealth, then financialization leads to a redistribution of life in the realm of use and value. The conduct of one's life, one's relations to oneself and to the world, become investments through which one attaches oneself to market fluctuations. Since the turn of the millennium, this financial-economic integration has been presented as a new social utopia:

> We need to democratize finance and bring the advantages enjoyed by the clients of Wall Street to the customers of Wal-Mart. We need to extend finance beyond our major financial capitals to the rest of the world. We need to extend the domain of finance beyond that of physical capital to human capital, and to cover the risks that really matter in our lives. Fortunately, the principles of financial management can now be expanded to include society as a whole. And if we are to thrive as a society, finance must be for all of us – in deep and fundamental ways.[73]

The 'democratization' of the financial world, in other words the enclosure of populations in the production of financial capital, has also been guaranteed by the refinement of debt economies. Opportunities for private households to contract debt have

– particularly in the Anglo-Saxon countries – proliferated thanks to consumer credit, credit card systems, education costs and mortgages. With sinking or stagnating real wages, prosperity expectations are realized through a panoply of credit offers, demand for which increased with the property boom. Between 1990 and 2006, the average debt servicing of private households in the US went up from around 11 per cent of available income to 14 per cent; mortgage debts, which amount to more than 79 per cent of GDP, were one of the main areas of expanding consumption. This was enabled through so-called 'remortgaging', which allows mortgages to be renegotiated, in order to contract more debts on the basis of rising property prices (which were resold via debt derivatives and asset-backed securities).[74] The growth of the financial sector was financed primarily by the expansion of the debt market.

The correlate of finance capital and the creditor of last resort is the debt subject who experiences herself as a 'securitized' existence; who, with her bare life, takes on liability for the accidents and upheavals on the financial markets. Systematic risk is transferred downwards. In 2009, 10,000 foreclosures (and occasionally arrest warrants) against insolvent home-owners were applied for in the US daily, forming a further chapter in the history of 'primitive accumulations'. The economic reality of debt subjects represents an elementary financial resource; there can be no better example of what Walter Benjamin referred to as capitalism's 'cult of blame/debt' (*verschuldender Kultus*). Contemporary politics appropriates this cultish dimension and, citing financial emergency, demands a 'sacrifice' from its subjects.[75]

The inclusion of populations in the cycles of financial risk via this mechanism of social diffusion is the social concomitant of the restructuring of the financial system since the 1970s. The 'financialization' of the social field is a process that entails the diversification of market relations, the universalization of corporate culture, the creation of human capital and the economization of the entirety of human relationships. The efficacy of the regime of accumulation, in which all aspects of individual and social existence are fed into the process of financial-economic value creation, manifests itself in dependencies, obligations and bonds that influence behaviour, unite social and economic reproduction, and coordinate the life of the social body through the movements of speculative capital.[76] This marks the dynamic of an apparatus of capture, with which the financial regime suffuses the life-world via the management of risk and debt.[77]

If the magico-theological aspects of sovereign power were once associated with the treasury, and the treasury was in turn associated with the financial aspects of credit, then recognition of sovereign rule also implied the acceptance of primordial debt. The disparity of an ineradicable debt is made manifest, in keeping with the etymology of 'credit', whose Indo-European root *kred*- spans the religio-economic semantics of trust and request, credence and status as creditor.[78] Given the fragility and tension of the actual integration of fiscal affairs and of the monopoly over money and currency into the arcane realm of sovereignty, the sovereign could declare himself as such only by virtue of his status as universal creditor. In his autonomy, he is creditor to his subjects; he is sovereign because he is indebted to nobody and nothing.

> Universal Creditor

Even if justified doubts exist as to whether the canonical doctrines of sovereignty from Bodin to Hobbes were ever embodied in the political regimes of the sixteenth century onwards, it was matters of finance that served to exemplify the erosion of theoretically consistent concepts of sovereignty. The cycle of public borrowing and private credit was already being seen as a ruinous exception to the exceptionality of sovereign power in the early-modern period.[79] It was the persistence of the notion that 'sovereign is he who decides on the exception' that, under the influence of modern economics, caused classical figures of sovereignty to appear antiquated; that caused political form, statehood and clear demarcations to seem non-existent; and that justified the announcement of a new 'age of neutralizations and depoliticizations'.[80] It is therefore no surprise that the contemporary financial regime is once again associated with a fracturing of the conceptual axis, complicating analysis of the political situation. From this perspective, the epoch of sovereign territorial states and nations was a transient episode in world history; the contemporary status quo is now to be apprehended in terms of a 'disaggregated', 'decentred', 'vagabond', 'spread', 'hybrid', 'entrepreneurial', 'imperial' or simply 'new' form of sovereignty.[81]

However, considerations of this kind imply that former sovereign powers have not simply been weakened or eliminated, but altered in form, consistency and location. Such approaches appeal to a new concept of the political that undermines the dichotomies between politics and economics, sovereignty and government. The logic of a permanent state of exception accompanying the genesis of modern finance takes a further twist. For example, the privatization of money creation and of the monopoly on liquidity and currency increases the powers of the financial markets and international institutions. These include not only transnational executive networks and a tapestry of international treaties and organizations, but also the global corporations that form a financial-economic system of representation structured such that it functions as a parallel government or bypass vis-à-vis popular sovereignty and conventional systems of political representation. They define the current era of economic governance.

According to recent system-theoretical and quantitative analyses, around 1,300 corporations dominate 80 per cent of the global economy. In 2007, 147 of these (of which 133 belong to the financial and real-estate sector) controlled 40 per cent of the worldwide profits of transnational corporations, while 35 of them (including Barclays, AXA, JPMorgan Chase & Co., UBS AG, Deutsche Bank AG or Credit Suisse Group) controlled 35 per cent. Here we see not only a concentration of financial capital that limits competition and accumulates systematic risk (Lehman Brothers once belonged to the innermost circle of these corporations). Typifying these corporations is also the fact that they 'cumulatively hold the majority share of each other', thus generating 'a complicated web of ownership relations' consisting of chains of subsidiaries, shares and investments in investments. A close-knit and largely self-regulating bloc of corporations forms an economic 'super-entity' containing a concentration of network control and financial-economic policy-making power.[82]

This accumulation of policy-making power, whose political dimension is so far unpredictable, is indicative of an escalation of what the American economist and sociologist Thorstein Veblen referred to as the 'sovereign rights of absentee ownership'. By this he meant the transition from a stakeholder economy to a shareholder economy, the mobilization of property and the disobligation of owners, the separation of ownership from the hardships of production, the rise of the rentier and the 'sabotage' of industrial manufacture by shareholder interests. From the start, the modern finance sector was marked by a dynamic in which financial capital – in transition from phases of expansion to 'over-accumulation' – detached itself from the material resistances of trade and production, leading to the migration of centres of accumulation (e.g. from northern Italy to the Netherlands, or from England to the US).[83] The contemporary financial industry has set this movement forth via expanding forms of investment capital, funds, investment banks, insurance companies and private equity, through which natural and legal persons, private individuals and consortia are united by anticipations of profit from random shares and investments in random corporations in random places. A global system of financial-economic representation emerges that concentrates the electoral force of the absentee owner and the international finance public in a small number of influential corporations. For example, the financial services company BlackRock, the world's largest asset manager, collects capital from private and institutional investors, controlling assets totalling $3.3 trillion, fifty times the total assets held in the US National Currency Reserve. Simulating 200 million risk scenarios weekly, its primary occupation is the constant redistribution of assets and investments.[84] Corporations like BlackRock have become exemplary incarnations of contemporary capitalist absentee ownership.

If international corporations have developed in parallel with the modern state, obtaining rights of sovereignty in the process, then the financial sector represents the latest phase of this co-evolution. From the privileges and freedoms granted by the state to early-modern trading corporations, to the exemptions through which international regulatory structures privilege investors and creditors, a historical and ontological connection can be traced between capital and sovereign authority.[85] A new geo-economic order has superimposed itself on the old geopolitical order that was dominated by strong territorial states and nations; independence from territories and states, the ability to create money, legal and tax mobility, and the increased mobility of finance capital as such cause a detachment of the new 'cosmopolitan citizen', of the 'super citizen' and its representations.[86] On the one hand, finance's demands for independence are met by the transformation of property owners into rentiers in the sphere of circulation; on the other hand, the authorities and agencies of regulatory capitalism – together with the symbiosis of financial markets, international organizations, national economies and state institutions – guarantee that the decision-making power of the financial public translates into the life-world of state-bound, telluric, territorially distributed majorities. Only when this double and contrary movement of liberation and domination is taken into account can one speak of the becoming-sovereign of the financial markets, of their 'role as a regulator of sovereignty' and their emergence as the latest variant of exceptional seigniorial power.[87] Investment and finance capital, the representation of the worldwide community of investors, can now be understood as the body politic of a collective capitalist. It is generated by processes of financialization, by the liberation of financial-economic dynamics and their regulatory attachment to political and social systems. Forming within it is the universal creditor in a new shape, now as a *persona ficta* of investors, constituting itself as their *makros anthropos*. The sovereign figure of the Leviathan has changed its state and become liquid.

The Sovereignty Effect   The partial privatization of sovereign competencies in the regime of finance has caused a redistribution of reserves of sovereignty. If Hegel's 'civil society' acted as mediator between individual economic interests and sovereign statehood, so the categorical or dialectic antithesis between economy and state, sovereignty and society, sovereign transcendence and social immanence now becomes obsolete. Financialization transforms the static and ideal nature of sovereign authority into a dynamic axiomatic that enables existing relations of power – whether institutions or distributions of wealth – to make the rules themselves.[88]

This means, on the one hand, that the ruptures between rule and government, sovereignty and 'governance', exceptional form and legality, are converted into a single field of immanence. Sovereign competencies perpetuate themselves in governmental practice and mechanisms of social control, realizing the bipolar machine of the political economy. This impacts on the ontology of the act of government in the regime of finance. The political dimension of capital is sovereign insofar as in it, the production of values is transposed directly onto the exercise of power, asymmetrically wedding the agenda of the financial public to societies and national populations.

On the other hand, the old definition of sovereignty – as legally codified decision-making power mandated to act within a particular territory – is broadened. It now refers to the temporal resources accessed through the purchase of liquidity and the liberation of credit cycles, chains of financing and cascades of risk. Financial economic power is geared towards transforming future wealth into present-day profit, and towards capitalizing unpredictable futures; it thereby preserves its dynastic persistence. The financial regime of the last century has not only led to a massive accumulation of capital in a few private hands, and created a powerful oligarchy that operates a policy of radical wealth defence through formally democratic means. With the ongoing collateralization and confiscation of the future, the market itself becomes a creditor-deity, which in the last resort decides the fate of currencies, national economies, social systems, public infrastructures and private savings.

If it is characteristic of the financial market that those who feel the impact of its risks have no say in its decision-making, and if risks differ from dangers insofar as dangers cannot be attributed to one's own actions or failure to act, then for the majority of people who in their complete dependence have nothing to decide, financial systems have turned risks into clear and present dangers. If, in financial capital, the particular character of capital becomes universal, as a uniform power determining the vital processes of society, then with it return, under the most modern conditions, the exceptionality and danger of older figures of sovereignty. This marks the sovereignty effects of the financial regime. It positions itself as para-democratic, exceptional power. It binds through debt and indebtedness. It adapts social and political structures to financial-economic risk. And it returns the forces and uncertainties of a 'perfidious future' (in Keynes' phrase) to the centre of our societies.

Sovereign is he who can transform his own risks into others' dangers, positioning himself as a creditor of last resort.

Notes

Chapter 1 Functional Dedifferentiation

1 For a chronicle and assessment of the unsuccessful bailout of Lehman Brothers, see James B. Stewart, 'Eight Days: The Battle to Save the American Financial System', *New Yorker*, 21 September 2009, 58–81; Alan S. Blinder, *After the Music Stopped: The Financial Crisis, the Response, and the Work Ahead*, New York 2013, 100–73; Gary B. Gorton, *Misunderstanding Financial Crisis: Why We Don't See Them Coming*, Oxford 2012, 147–50; Neil Irwin, *The Alchemists: Three Central Bankers and a World on Fire*, New York 2013, 126–65; Marc Roche, *La banque: Comment Goldman Sachs dirige le monde*, Paris 2010, 160–5; Nouriel Roubini and Stephen Mihm, *Das Ende der Weltwirtschaft und ihre Zukunft*, Munich 2011 (2nd edn), 154–9.

2 See Blinder, *After the Music Stopped*, 409–28; Carmen M. Reinhart and Kenneth S. Rogoff, *This Time is Different: Eight Centuries of Financial Folly*, Princeton 2009, 223–47; Roubini and Mihm, *Das Ende der Weltwirtschaft*, 160–72; Hans-Werner Sinn, *Kasino-Kapitalismus: Wie es zur Finanzkrise kam und was jetzt zu tun ist*, Berlin 2009 (2nd edn), 61–81; Joseph Stiglitz, *Freefall: America, Free Markets and the Sinking of the World Economy*, New York 2010.

3 The expertise was based on the World Economic Outlook of the IMF: see Reinhart and Rogoff, *This Time is Different*, 214–15; Josef Ackermann, 'Kein "Kollaps" bei Lehman', *Capital*, 10 September 2008. Quotes from: Blinder, *After the Music*

Stopped, 119; Stewart, 'Eight Days', 68; Andreas Langenohl, 'Finanzmarktöffentlichkeiten: Die funktionale Beziehung zwischen Finanzmarkt und öffentlichem Diskurs', in Rainer Diaz-Bone and Gertraude Krell (eds), *Diskurs und Ökonomie: Diskursanalytische Perspektiven auf Märkte und Organisationen*, Wiesbaden 2009, 258–9.

4 Claudia Honegger, Sighard Nickel and Chantal Magnin, 'Schlussbetrachtung: Strukturierte Verantwortungslosigkeit', in Honegger, Nickel and Magnin, *Strukturierte Verantwortungslosigkeit: Berichte aus der Bankenwelt*, Berlin 2010, 302–3; referring to Niklas Luhmann, *Soziologie des Risikos*, Berlin 1991, 199.

5 Ben S. Bernanke, *The Federal Reserve and the Financial Crisis: Lectures*, Princeton 2013, 95. The inevitability thesis is relativized by the plausible speculation expressed by several different people that the events of autumn 2008 clearly favoured Goldman Sachs. In 2008, the bank profited directly from the government guarantee programme as well as from the rescue of AIG. Responsibility for these decisions was largely carried by the secretary of the treasury, Henry Paulson, former CEO of Goldman Sachs. See Roche, *La banque*, 159–71; also Janine Wedel, *Shadow Elite: How the World's New Power Brokers Undermine Democracy, Government, and the Free Market*, New York 2009, 208–9.

6 Richard Fuld, the CEO of Lehman Brothers, in Stewart, 'Eight Days', 68. On the law of 'unintended consequences', see Joyce Appleby, *The Relentless Revolution*, New York 2010, 405–6; Irwin, *The Alchemists*, 144.

7 Federal Reserve Act 13(3), online at www.federalreserve.gov/aboutthefed/section13.htm; see also: Irwin, *The Alchemists*, 133–4; Jasmin Fischer, 'Kalter Finanzkrieg: Brown attackiert fast bankrottes Island', *Westdeutsche Zeitung*, 10 October 2008; José Manuel Durão Barroso, 'A Roadmap to Stability and Growth', European Parliament debate ahead of the European Council, Brussels, 12 October 2011, online at europa.eu/rapid/press-release_SPEECH-11-657_en.htm.

8 In the order cited: Evangelos Venizelos, Greek minister of finance, cited in Michael Martens, 'Und täglich droht der Staatsbankrott', *Frankfurter Allgemeine Zeitung*, 6 February 2012, 6; Roubini and Mihm, *Das Ende der Weltwirtschaft*, 156; Christine Lagarde, managing director of the IMF, cited in Susanne Höll, 'Warnung

aus Washington', *Süddeutsche Zeitung*, 12 June 2013, 5; Henry Paulson, cited in Stewart, 'Eight Days', 74.

9 Ernst-Wolfgang Böckenförde, 'Kennt die europäische Not kein Gebot?', *Neue Zürcher Zeitung*, 21 June 2010.

10 Government declaration by Angela Merkel on the stability measures for the euro, 19 May 2010, online at www.bundesregierung.de/Content/DE/Regierungserklaerung/2010/2010-05-19-merkel-erklaerung-eu-stabilisierungsmassnahmen.html.

11 Carl Schmitt, *Der Begriff des Politischen*, Berlin 1991 (3rd edn), 12 (in the introduction to the German edition of 1963).

12 Gabriel Naudé, *Political considerations upon refin'd politicks, and the master-strokes of state, As practis'd by the Ancients and Moderns*, trans. Dr. King, London 1711, 59. Original: *Considérations politiques sur les coups d'État*, Paris 1988, 101.

13 Naudé, *Political considerations*, 69–70. See also: Friedrich Meinecke, *Die Idee der Staatsräson in der frühen Neuzeit*, Munich 1963 (3rd edn), 250; Michel Foucault, *Security, Territory, Population*, trans. Graham Burchell, London 2007, 255–67; Richard Tuck, *Philosophy and Government 1572–1652*, Cambridge 1993, 93; Herfried Münkler, *Im Namen des Staates: Die Begründung der Staatsräson in der frühen Neuzeit*, Frankfurt 1987, 187–93; Ethel Matala de Mazza, 'Notwendige Grenzüberschreitungen: Staatsräson und Arkanismus', in Albrecht Koschorke, Susanne Lüdemann, Thomas Frank and Ethel Matala de Mazza, *Der fiktive Staat: Konstruktionen des politischen Körpers in der Geschichte Europas*, Frankfurt 2007, 177–83. On the baroque character of Naudé's concept, see Louis Marin, 'Pour une théorie baroque de l'action politique: Lecture des *Considérations politiques sur les coups d'État* de Gabriel Naudé', in Naudé, *Considérations politiques*, 6–65.

14 Foucault, *Security, Territory, Population*, 262.

15 Marin, 'Pour une théorie baroque de l'action politique', 19.

16 Knut Wicksell, *Finanztheoretische Untersuchungen nebst Darstellung und Kritik des Steuerwesens Schwedens*, Jena 1896, 111.

17 See Milton Friedman, *Capitalism and Freedom*, Chicago 1962, IX. A more recent variant of the emergency calculus was formulated by, among others, the German FDP politician Guido Westerwelle in 2009, then foreign minister: 'We must use the pressure caused by the crisis to seize the opportunities of the crisis and complete long-overdue re-structuring'; cited in

Hans Jürgen Bieling, 'Neuer Staatsinterventionismus? Brüche und Kontinuitäten im marktliberalen Diskurs', *Widerspruch. Beiträge zu sozialistischer Politik* 57, 2009, 45.

18 Florian Rödl, 'EU im Notstandsmodus', *Blätter für deutsche und internationale Politik*, 5, 2012, 5–8; see also: Andreas Fisahn, 'Stellungnahme zur Anhörung des Haushaltsausschusses des Deutschen Bundestages am 7.5.2012 zum Fiskalvertrag u.a.', online at eurodemostuttgart.files.wordpress.com/2012/05/prof-dr-andreas-fisahn.pdf; Heribert Prantl, 'Das Finale nach dem Ende', *Süddeutsche Zeitung*, 29 June 2012, 2; Steffen Vogel, *Europas Revolution von oben: Sparpolitik und Demokratieabbau in der Eurokrise*, Hamburg 2013, 95–102. It should be mentioned that the crisis politics of recent years made free use of the rhetoric of the 'state of exception'; however, in its actual operation it ought not to be confused with the legal construct proper. What is categorized here under the 'politics of emergency' and illustrated with reference to Naudé's coup d'état refers to an individual case whose emergency measures do not suspend the existing legal order as such. It is not a question of a 'status' or a legal situation *sui generis*, but of a single realm in which existing norms are not applied – as in the way that the exceptional powers claimed by the EU organs were not regulated for in the Treaties on the Functioning of the European Union; see Böckenförde, 'Kennt die europäische Not kein Gebot?'. On the relation between emergency and state of exception, see Carl Schmitt, *Political Theology: Four Chapters on the Concept of Sovereignty*, trans. George Schwab, Chicago 2005, 6–7; Giorgio Agamben, *State of Exception*, trans. Kevin Attell, Chicago 2005, 22–31.

19 Alain Deneault, *Gouvernance: Le management totalitaire*, Montréal 2013; Wolfgang Streeck, 'Markets and People, Democratic Capitalism and European Integration', *New Left Review* 73, January/February 2012, 63–71; Roche, *La banque*, 159–71.

20 *'El Ladrillo': Bases de la Política Econímica del Gobierno Militar Chileno*, Centro Estudios Públicos, Santiago de Chile 1992; see Naomi Klein, *The Shock Doctrine*, London 2008, 75–97, 133–41; Abram Chayes, *The New Sovereignty: Compliance with International Regulatory Agreements*, Cambridge 1995, 254ff; Juan Gabriel Valdès, *Pinochet's Economists: The Chicago School of Economics in Chile*, Cambridge 1995.

21 Stephan Haggard, cited in Klein, *The Shock Doctrine*, 134; on
    Slavoj Žižek's concept of 'authoritarian capitalism' see Vogel,
    Europas Revolution, 109.
22 Carl Schmitt, *The Concept of the Political*, trans. George Schwab,
    Chicago 2007, 80–96 (from the essay, 'The Age of Neutralizations
    and Depoliticizations', 1929); Friedrich Hayek, *The Road to
    Serfdom*, London 1946, 125–39, esp. 125, 136–7.

Chapter 2   Economy and Government

1 Foucault, *Security, Territory, Population*, 109.
2 Jean Bodin, *Six Books of the Commonwealth*, ed. M.J. Tooley,
   Oxford 1955, book 1, 2.
3 Johann Heinrich Gottlob von Justi, *Natur und Wesen der Staaten
   als Quelle aller Regierungswissenschaften und Gesetze*, ed.
   Heinrich G. Scheidemantel, Mitau 1771, 7.
4 See Samuel Pufendorf, *Einleitung in die Historie der vornehmsten
   Reiche und Staaten, so itziger Zeit in Europa sich befinden*,
   Frankfurt 1683.
5 Cited in Wilhelm Roscher, *Geschichte der Nationalökonomie
   in Deutschland*, Munich 1874, 335. On the 'economization' of
   the concept of government in early modernity, see Michel Senellart, *Les arts de gouverner: Du regimen médiéval au concept
   de gouvernement*, Paris 1995, 32–40.
6 Anastasio Sincero (Christoph Heinrich Amthor), *Project der
   Oeconomic in Form einer Wissenschaft: Nebst einem Unmaßgeb-
   lichen Bedencken Wie diese Wissenschaft beydes in Theoria
   und Praxi mit mehrerem Fleiß und Nutz getrieben werden könne*,
   Frankfurt 1716, 1, 4–5, 8–9, 11–13, 17, 22.
7 Thomas Hobbes, *Leviathan, Or the Matter, Forme and Power
   of A Common-wealth Ecclesiasticall and Civil* (1651), ed. J.C.A.
   Gaskin, Oxford 1998, 247.
8 See Reinhard Brandt, 'Das Titelblatt des Leviathan', *Leviathan*
   15, 1987, 165–86, esp. 166.
9 Hobbes, *Leviathan*, 443.
10 Amthor, *Project der Oeconomic*, n.p., 1; Antoyne de Montch-
    rétien, *Traicté de l'œconomie politique* (1615), ed. Théophile
    Funck-Brentano, Paris 1930, 20–1.
11 The image of the ship might also be understood as an allusion
    to the frontispiece of Francis Bacon's *Novum Organon* of 1620,

which replaced the old European dictate 'nec plus ultra' with the motto 'Multi pertransibunt & augebitur scientia'.

12 Amthor, *Project der Oeconomic*, n.p.
13 Montchrétien, *Traicté de l'œconomie politique*, 31, 34. As far as can be proven, the term was first used in Louis Turquet de Mayerne's *La monarchie aristodémocratique, ou Le gouvernement composé et meslé de trois formes de légitimes Républiques* (Paris 1611); here it was synonymous with 'state' or 'community/commonwealth'. See Alfred Bürgin, *Zur Soziogenese der politischen Ökonomie. Wirtschaftliche und dogmengeschichtliche Betrachtungen*, Marburg 1993, 272ff.
14 See Theo Stemmler (ed.), *Ökonomie: Sprachliche und literarische Aspekte eines 2000 Jahre alten Begriffs*, Tübingen 1987; Joseph Vogl, 'Homogenese: Zur Naturgeschichte des Menschen bei Buffon', in Hans-Jürgen Schings (ed.), *Der ganze Mensch: Anthropologie und Literatur im 18. Jahrhundert*, Stuttgart 1994, 88–90; Giorgio Agamben, *The Kingdom and the Glory: For a Theological Genealogy of Economy and Government*, trans. Lorenzo Chiesa (with Matteo Mandarini), Stanford 2011, 17–20; Jean-Claude Perrot, *Une histoire intellectuelle de l'économie politique (XVIIe–XVIIIe siècle)*, Paris 1992, 68–9.
15 According to the *Dictionnaire de l'Académie* of 1762, 1798/9; cited in Agamben, *The Kingdom and the Glory*, 281.
16 Novalis, *Philosophical Writings*, ed. Margaret Mahony Stoljar, Albany 1997, 107.
17 See Gerhard Richter, *Oikonomia: Der Gebrauch des Wortes Oikonomia im Neuen Testament, bei den Kirchenvätern und in der theologischen Literatur bis ins 20. Jahrhundert*, Berlin 2005.
18 Agamben, *The Kingdom and the Glory*, 53–143. See also Birger P. Priddat, 'Benign order and heaven on earth: Kapitalismus als Religion? Über theologische Ressourcen in der Entwicklung der modernen Ökonomie', in Peter Seele and Georg Pfleiderer (eds.), *Kapitalismus: Eine Religion in der Krise. I: Grundprobleme von Risiko, Vertrauen, Schuld*, Zurich 2013, 25–135.
19 I.J. Bibery (Carolus Linnaeus, 'Die Ökonomie der Natur', in Linnaeus, *Auserlesene Abhandlungen aus der Naturgeschichte, Physik und Arzneywissenschaft*, vol. 2, Leipzig 1777, 1–2; Carolus Linnaeus, *Oratio de Telluris*, §96, cited in Camille Limoges, 'Introduction', in Linnaeus, *L'équilibre de la nature*, ed. Camille Limoges, Paris 1972, 11; Henric C.D. Wilcke, 'La

police de la nature' (1760), in Linnaeus, *L'équilibre de la nature*, 103.

20 Gottfried Wilhelm Leibniz, 'On the Ultimate Origination of Things', in Leibniz, *The Shorter Leibniz Texts*, ed. and trans. Lloyd Strickland, London 2006, 31–8, 35; Gottfried Wilhelm Leibniz, *Theodicy: Essays on the Goodness of God, the Freedom of Man, and the Origin of Evil*, ed. Austin Marsden Farrer, trans. E.M. Huggard, London 1951, 253. Joseph Vogl, *Kalkül und Leidenschaft: Poetik des Ökonomischen Menschen*, Zurich and Berlin 2004 (2nd edn), 142–59.

21 Leibniz, 'On the Ultimate Origination of Things', 36.

22 Gottfried Wilhelm Leibniz, 'Von dem Verhängnisse', in Leibniz, *Hauptschriften zur Grundlegung der Philosophie*, ed. Ernst Cassirer, Hamburg 1966, vol. 2, 131.

23 Leibniz, 277; see also Christiane Frémont, 'Komplikation und Singularität', in Friedrich Balke and Joseph Vogl (eds.), *Gilles Deleuze: Fluchtlinien der Philosophie*, Munich 1996, 64.

24 Gottfried Wilhelm Leibniz, 'Discourse on Metaphysics', in Leibniz, *Discourse on Metaphysics*, ed. and trans. R.N.D. Martin and Stuart Brown, Manchester 1988, 74; Leibniz, *Theodicy*, 257.

25 Leibniz, 'On the Ultimate Origination of Things', 33.

26 Gottfried Wilhelm Leibniz, 'On First Truths', in Leibniz, *The Shorter Leibniz Texts*, 29–30. On the problem of the maximization and optimization of existence, see Donald Rutherford, *Leibniz and the Rational Order of Nature*, Cambridge 1995, 22–45.

27 Gottfried Wilhelm Leibniz, 'Dialogue entre Théophile et Polidore', in Leibniz, *Textes inédits*, ed. Gaston Grua, Paris 1948, vol. 1, 285f.

28 Gottfried Wilhelm Leibniz, cited in Michel Guéroult, *Dynamique et métaphysique leibniziennes*, Paris 1934, 189.

29 Leibniz, 'Discourse on Metaphysics', 43, 82–3; see also Jon Elster, *Leibniz et la formation de l'esprit capitaliste*, Paris 1975.

30 Gottfried Wilhelm Leibniz, *Confessio philosophi: Papers concerning the Problem of Evil*, trans. and ed. Robert C. Sleigh, New Haven 2005, 87ff; Leibniz, 'Zur prästabilierten Harmonie', in Leibniz, *Hauptschriften zur Grundlegung der Philosophie*, vol. 2, 271–2; Leibniz, *Theodicy*, 277; Leibniz, 'On the Ultimate Origination of Things', 31–8; Leibniz, 'Discourse on Metaphysics', 74. On the law of the preservation of energy in Leibniz'

concept of force, see the editorial note in Gottfried Wilhelm Leibniz, *Schöpferische Vernunft: Schriften aus den Jahren 1668–1686*, ed. Wilfried von Engelhardt, Marburg 1955, 509ff.

31 See Pierre Legendre, *Le désir politique de Dieu: Étude sur les montages de l'État du Droit (Leçons VII)*, Paris 1988, 101–3.

32 Joseph Vogl, *The Specter of Capital*, Stanford 2015, 14–16, 17–33.

33 Jean-Jacques Rousseau, 'Discourse on Political Economy', in Rousseau, *The Social Contract and Other Later Political Writings*, ed. Victor Gourevitch, Cambridge 1997, 3–38, 3. See also Joseph Vogl, 'Politische Ökonomie (économie politique)', in Iwan-Michelangelo D'Aprile and Stefanie Stockhorst (eds.), *Rousseau und die Moderne: Eine kleine Enzyklopédie*, Göttingen 2013, 250–8.

34 Rousseau, 'Discourse on Political Economy', 5; see also Foucault, *Security, Territory, Population*, 104–6.

35 Johann Heinrich Gottlob von Justi, *Gesammelte politische und Finanzschriften über wichtige Gegenstände der Staatskunst, der Kriegswissenschaften und des Cameral- und Finanzwesens*, Copenhagen and Leipzig 1761, 77; John Locke, *The Second Treatise of Government* (1690), ed. C.B. McPherson, Indianapolis and Cambridge 1980, 20, 55–6.

36 Rousseau, 'Discourse on Political Economy', 6.

37 Rousseau, *The Social Contract*, in Rousseau, *The Social Contract*, 82.

38 Rousseau, 'Discourse on Political Economy', 6.

39 Foucault, *Security, Territory, Population*, 106; for contemporary references to Rousseau's text see Pierre Prevost, *De l'économie des anciens gouvernemens comparée á celle des gouvernemens modernes (Mémoire lû dans l'Assemblée publique de l'Académie Royale des Sciences et Belles-Lettres de Prusse, du 5 Juin 1783)*, Berlin 1783.

40 Rousseau, *The Social Contract*, 83.

41 Rousseau, 'Discourse on Political Economy', 8–9, 12, 13, 20–1, 27.

42 Rousseau, *The Social Contract*, 58.

43 Agamben, *The Kingdom and the Glory*, 265–6, 272–3. On the relation between divine general will and the corresponding concepts in Montesquieu, Rousseau and Diderot, see Michael Sonenscher, *Before the Deluge: Public Debt, Inequality and the Intellectual Origin of French Revolution*, Princeton 2007, 222.

44 Rousseau, 'Discourse on Political Economy', 8–9, 10.
45 Agamben, *The Kingdom and the Glory*, 265–6, 272–3. The uniform figure of divine and political economy circulates up until the end of the eighteenth century; see Johann David Caspar Herrenschwand, *De l'économie politique et morale de l'espèce humaine*, London 1796 (esp. the introduction).
46 Guillaume François Le Trosne, *De l'ordre social: Ouvrage suivi d'un traité élémentaire sur la valeur, l'argent, la circulation, l'industrie & le commerce intérieur & extérieur*, Paris 1777, 302–3; cited in Agamben, *The Kingdom and the Glory*, 282; cf. Vogl, *Kalkül und Leidenschaft*, 233.
47 Thorstein Veblen, 'The Precondition of Economic Science', in Veblen, *The Place of Science in Modern Civilization*, New York 1941 (4th edn), 82–179; Alexander Rüstow, *Die Religion der Marktwirtschaft*, Münster 2002, 21, 107.
48 See Matthias Bohlender, *Metamorphosen des liberalen Regierungs-denkens: Politische Ökonomie, Polizei und Pauperismus*, Weilerswist 2007, 7–143 (esp. 10–24); Pierre Rosanvallon, *Le libéralisme économique: Histoire de l'idée du marché*, Paris 1989.
49 Adam Smith, *The Theory of Moral Sentiments*, ed. Knud Haakonssen, Cambridge 2004, 95.
50 Thomas Paine, *Rights of Man, Common Sense and Other Political Writings*, ed. Mark Philp, Oxford 1995, 214.
51 See Panajotis Kondylis, *Die Aufklärung im Rahmen des neuzeitli-chen Rationalismus*, Stuttgart 1981, 244–7; Paul Oslington, 'God and the Market: Adam Smith's Invisible Hand', *Journal of Business Ethics* 108, 2012, 429–38.
52 Smith, *The Theory of Moral Sentiments*, 44, 90, 91, 216.
53 Paul Oslington (ed.), *Adam Smith as Theologian*, London 2011; Jacob Viner, *The Role of Providence in the Social Order*, Philadelphia 1971, 55–85; Lisa Hill, 'The Hidden Theology of Adam Smith', in Paul Oslington (ed.), *Economics and Religion*, vol. 1, Cheltenham 2003, 292–320.
54 Adam Smith, *An Inquiry into the Nature and Causes of the Wealth of Nations*, vol. 2, ed., James E. Thorold Rogers, Oxford 1869, 272; see also Bohlender, *Metamorphosen des liberalen Regierungsdenkens*, 116–19.
55 Smith, *Wealth of Nations*, 28.
56 On the reduction of the role of the state to securing peace, defence and securing public infrastructures, see Smith, *Wealth of Nations*, 28.

57 Smith, *Wealth of Nations*, 526.
58 Smith, *Wealth of Nations*, 1.
59 See Michel Foucault, 'Omnes et singulatim: Towards a Criticism of "Political Reason" ', in *The Tanner Lectures on Human Values*, ed. Sterling McMurrin, vol. 2, Salt Lake City 1981, 223–54.
60 The insistence on the problem of sovereignty in liberalism is perhaps best seen in the last part of Smith's project, the incomplete or destroyed 'Natural Jurisprudence'; see Bastian Ronge, *Das Adam-Smith-Projekt: Zur Genealogie der liberalen Gouvernementalität*, Wiesbaden 2015, 381–409. The problem of stability in contemporary liberalism also implies a discussion of sovereignty; see Geoffrey Vaughan, 'The Decline of Sovereignty in the Liberal Tradition: The Case of John Rawls', in Martin Peters and Peter Schröder (eds.), *Souveränitätskonzeptionen: Beiträge zur Analyse politischer Ordnungsvorstellungen im 17. bis zum 20. Jahrhundert*, Berlin 2000, 158–85.
61 Michel Foucault, *History of Sexuality*. Vol. 1: *An Introduction*, trans. Robert Hurley, New York 1978, 136; Michel Foucault, *Discipline and Punish*, trans. Alan Sheridan, London 1991, 208. See Thomas Lemke, *Eine Kritik der politischen Vernunft: Foucaults Analyse der modernen Gouvernementalität*, Berlin and Hamburg 1997.
62 See Montchrétien, *Traicté de l'oeconomie politique*, 24. On Jean Baptiste Colbert's population policy, see Karl Erich Born, 'Jean Baptiste Colbert (1619–1683)', in Joachim Starbatty (ed.), *Klassiker des Ökonomischen Denkens*, Munich 1989, vol. 1, 105–6; Perrot, *Une histoire intellectuelle de l'économie politique*, 143ff; Michel Senellart, *Machiavélisme et raison d'état XIIe–XVIIIe siècle*, Paris 1983, 88ff.
63 Johann Friedrich von Pfeiffer, *Lehrbegriff sämtlicher oeconomischer und Cameralwissenschaften*, Mannheim 1777–8, vol. II/2, 1; see Ferdinando Galiani, *De la Monnaie* (1751), ed. Georges-Henri Bousquet and J. Crisafulli, Paris 1955, 98.
64 See Foucault, 'Omnes et singulatim', 248.
65 Gary S. Becker, *The Essence of Becker*, eds. Ramon Ferrero and Pedro S. Schwartz, Stanford 1995, XXI–XXII; Gary S. Becker, *A Treatise on the Family*, Cambridge 1991; Gary S. Becker, *The Economic Approach to Human Behavior*, Chicago 1976; Ludwig von Mises, *Human Action: A Treatise on Economics*, New Haven 1949. See Michel Foucault, *The Birth of Biopolitics*, trans. Graham Burchell, Basingstoke 2010, 129–84, 215–38.

66 Exemplary of these visionary activities in the 1990s is Pierre Levy, *L'intelligence collective*, Paris 1997.

Chapter 3   Seigniorial Power

1 André Félibien, *Entretiens sur les vies et sur les ouvrages des plus excellens peintres anciens et modernes* (1685), vol. 4, London 1705, 28–31; Jean-Paul La Roque, *Journal des Sçavans pour l'Année M.DC.LXXXV* (1685), vol. 13, Amsterdam 1686, 12.

2 See Richard Ehrenberg, *Das Zeitalter der Fugger: Geldkapital und Kreditverkehr im 16. Jahrhundert*, vol. 1: *Die Geldmächte des 16. Jahrhunderts*, Jena 1896 (repr. Hildesheim 1990), 168–71.

3 Jacques Derrida, *Given Time: Counterfeit Money*, trans. Peggy Kamuf, Chicago 1992, 1–32.

4 Helmut Quaritsch, *Souveränität: Entstehung und Entwicklung des Begriffs in Frankreich und Deutschland vom 13. Jahrhundert bis 1806*, Berlin 1986, 54–8; Georges Bataille, 'Die Souveränität', in Bataille, *Die psychologische Struktur des Faschismus: Die Souveränität*, Munich 1978, 48; French original published in *Monde nouveau*, 101–3, June–September 1956.

5 See Cardin Le Bret, *De la souveraineté du roy*, Paris 1632, 428.

6 Bodin, *Six Books of the Commonwealth*, book 1, 25. See Julian H. Franklin, *Jean Bodin and the Rise of Absolutist Theory*, Cambridge 1973, 41–2; Dieter Grimm, *Souveränität: Herkunft und Zukunft eines Schlüsselbegriffs*, Berlin 2009, 16–18; Werner Mäder, *Vom Wesen der Souveränität: Ein deutsches und europäisches Problem*, Berlin 2007, 19; Claudia Opitz-Belakhal, 'Ambivalenzen und Widersprüche: Jean Bodins Souveränitätskonzept im historischen Kontext', in Samuel Salzborn and Rüdiger Voigt (eds.), *Souveränität: Theoretische und ideengeschichtliche Reflexionen*, Stuttgart 2010, 44.

7 Le Bret, *De la souveraineté du roy*, 168 (cf. also 244–5, 396–8); Charles Loyseau, *Traicté des seigneuries*, Paris 1609, 50–9; Bodin, *Les six livres de la république*, livre 1, 331–4.

8 Bodin, *Les six livres de la république*, livre 6, 44, 88–92.

9 Bodin, *Les six livres de la république*, livre 1, 334–8; livre 6, 47, 67–8; Bodin, *Six Books of the Commonwealth*, book 6, 188–90; Loyseau, *Traicté des seigneuries*, 61. On the 'tax paradox' in Bodin, see Franklin, *Jean Bodin and the Rise of Absolutist Theory*, 86–90; Quaritsch, *Souveränität*, 60–2.

10 Bodin, *Les six livres de la république*, livre 6, 44, 88–92.

11 Hobbes, *Leviathan*, 120.

12 Otto von Gierke, *Das deutsche Genossenschaftsrecht*, vol. 3: *Die Staats- und Korporationslehre des Alterthums und des Mittelalters und ihre Aufnahme in Deutschland*, Berlin 1881, 59–61. On the continuation of this question in the Middle Ages, see Ernst Kantorowicz, *The King's Two Bodies*, Princeton 1957, 177–9; Joseph Canning, *The Political Thought of Baldus de Ubaldis*, Cambridge 1987, 86–9, 120–1, 221–7.

13 Otto von Gierke, *Das deutsche Genossenschaftsrecht*, vol. 4: *Staats- und Korporationslehre der Neuzeit*, Berlin 1913, 249–50. For similar considerations in Baldus in connection with the Donation of Constantine, see Canning, *The Political Thought of Baldus de Ubaldis*, 86–7.

14 Gierke, *Das deutsche Genossenschaftsrecht*, vol. 4, 251–2.

15 Bodin, *Les six livres de la république*, livre 1, 337–8; livre 6, 39.

16 Le Bret, *De la souveraineté du roy*, 425, 621–6. 'C'est une maxime que l'on a tenuë de tout temps, qu'il n'y a que le Prince Souuerain qui aye le droict d'auoir un Fisque, c'est a dire, une bourse & une espargne publique.'

17 Alain Guéry, 'Fondements historiques des finances de l'État', in Bruno Théret (ed.), *L'état, la finance et le social: Souveraineté national et construction européenne*, Paris 1995, 394; Marie-Thérèse Boyer-Xambeu, Ghislain Deleplace and Lucien Gillard, *Monnaie privée et pouvoir des princes*, Paris 1986, 78; Ehrenberg, *Das Zeitalter der Fugger*, vol. 1, 379–90; Friedrich Kluge, *Etymologisches Wörterbuch der deutschen Sprache*, Berlin 1995 (23rd edn), 266.

18 On the comparison between the fisc and Christ, see Kantorowicz, *The King's Two Bodies*, 164–92. The phrase 'soul of the state' derives from Baldus. Commentators on Roman law up to modernity associated the holiness of the treasury with the treasures kept in temples and churches, e.g. in phrases such as *sacratissimus fiscus* and *fiscus sanctissimus*. Belonging to this sacralization were notions of fiscal ubiquity, an important precondition for the fusion of treasury and state in modernity. According to Baldus, 'The treasury is omnipresent and in this sense similar to God'; see Kantorowicz, *The King's Two Bodies*, 196–7; Bodin, *Les six livres de la république*, livre 6, 42.

19 Loyseau, *Traicté des seigneuries*, 59. See Boyer-Xambeu et al., *Monnaie privée et pouvoir des princes*, 16, 82–3, 113; Friedrich von Schrötter (ed.), *Wörterbuch der Münzkunde*, Berlin 1930, 419–21, 430–5, 603–4; Michael North (ed.), *Von Aktie bis Zoll: Ein historisches Lexikon des Geldes*, Munich 1995, 263, 267–8, 357.

20 See Raymond de Roover, *L'évolution de la lettre de change: XIVe–XVIIIe siècles*, Paris 1953.

21 See the analyses of Boyer-Xambeu et al., *Monnaie privée et pouvoir des princes*, 179–89, 240–69, which focus on France and serve as the basis for the description here.

22 Boyer-Xambeu et al., *Monnaie privée et pouvoir des princes*, 268, 354.

23 Boyer-Xambeu et al., *Monnaie privée et pouvoir des princes*, 245, 260–1.

24 See David Graeber, *Debt: The First 5000 Years*, New York 2011.

25 See Boyer-Xambeu et al., *Monnaie privée et pouvoir des princes*, 353.

26 Nikolaus Oresme, *Traktat über Geldabwertungen*, ed. E. Schorer, Jena 1937, 43–5; see also: Hendrik Mäkeler, 'Nicolas Oresme und Gabriel Biel: Zur Geldtheorie im späten Mittelalter', *Scripta Mercaturae: Zeitschrift für Wirtschafts- und Sozialgeschichte* 37/1, 2003, 56–94.

27 Jean Bodin, *Discours de Jean Bodin, sur le rehaussement et diminution des monnoyes tant d'or que d'argent, et le moyen d'y remedier, aux Paradoxes de Monsieur de Malestroict*, Paris 1578, 98; Bodin, *Les six livres de la république*, livre 1, 194; livre 6, 117.

28 Bodin, *Les six livres de la république*, livre 1, 332; livre 6, 123; Bodin, *Six Books of the Commonwealth*, book 1, 47–8; Le Bret, *De la souveraineté du roy*, 245.

29 See Bodin, *Les six livres de la république*, livre 1, 331–2; livre 6, 123; Montchrétien, *Traicté de l'oeconomie politique*, 175–6; Le Bret, *De la souveraineté du roy*, 249–54.

30 See Franklin, *Jean Bodin and the Rise of Absolutist Theory*, 71–3; Grimm, *Souveränität*, 25; Quaritsch, *Souveränität*, 52–3.

31 See Grimm, *Souveränität*, 26.

32 Ehrenberg, *Das Zeitalter der Fugger*, vol. 1, 18–31; Jonathan Nitzan and Shimshon Bichler, *Capital as Power: A Study of Order and Creorder*, London 2009, 291–4; Hans Pohl (ed.),

Europäische Bankengeschichte, Frankfurt am Main 1993, 114–20; Guéry, 'Fondements historiques des finances de l'État', 395–6. On the discussion of the serviceability of royal debt in the seventeenth century and the special role of cities, see Le Bret, *De la souveraineté du roy*, 621–7.

33 Gerhard Oestreich, 'Ständetum und Staatsbildung in Deutschland', in Oestreich, *Geist und Gestalt des frühmodernen Staates: Ausgewählte Aufsätze*, Berlin 1969, 277–89.

34 The phrase used by Kantorowicz in connection with the jurisprudential discussion in the high and late Middle Ages on the relation between *necessitas in actu* and *necessitas in habitus* in permanent taxation; see Kantorowicz, *The King's Two Bodies*, 286–8. On the development described here, see Bodin, *Les six livres de la république*, livre 6, 88–93; Ehrenberg, *Das Zeitalter der Fugger*, vol. 1, 28, vol. 2: *Die Weltbörsen und Finanzkrisen des 16. Jahrhunderts*, 82–4; Guéry, 'Fondements historiques des finances de l'État', 398–402; Joseph A. Schumpeter, 'The Crisis of the Tax State' (1918), *International Economic Papers* IV, 1954, 17; Norbert Elias, *The Civilizing Process*, vol. 2: *State Formation and Civilization*, Oxford 1982, 421–39, esp. 437; Earl J. Hamilton, 'Origin and Growth of the National Debt in Western Europe', *American Economic Review* 37/2, 1947, 118–30; David Stasavage, *Public Debt and the Birth of the Democratic State: France and Great Britain, 1688–1798*, Cambridge 2003, 65–6. On the relation between taxation and sovereignty, see Ralph G. Hawtrey, *Economic Aspects of Sovereignty*, London 1952, 4ff.

35 For an exemplary analysis of the development in the German principalities, see Karlheinz Blaschke, 'Finanzwesen und Staatsräson in Kursachsen zu Beginn der Neuzeit', *Der Staat: Zeitschrift für Staatslehre, öffentliches Recht und Verfassungsgeschichte* 25/3, 1986, 373–83 (esp. 379). On the trinity of military, taxation and monetary policy, see Pierre Bourdieu, 'L'État et la concentration du capital symbolique', in Théret, *L'état, la finance et le social*, 73–115.

36 Ehrenberg, *Das Zeitalter der Fugger*, vol. 1, 29.

37 Werner Sombart, *Der moderne Kapitalismus*, vol. 1: *Die vorkapitalistische Wirtschaft* (1902), Berlin 1969 (16th edn), 661.

38 Fernand Braudel, *Civilization and Capitalism, 15th–18th Century*, vol. 3: *The Perspective of the World*, trans. Siân Reynolds,

London 1984, 157 (French original: *Civilisation matérielle, économie et capitalisme, XVe–XVIIIe siècle*, vol. 3: *Le temps du monde*, Paris 1979, 130); Ehrenberg, *Das Zeitalter der Fugger*, vol. 1, 353. For an overview see Andreas M. Andréadès, *History of the Bank of England 1640–1903*, London 1966 (4th edn), 78–9; Giovanni Arrighi, *The Long Twentieth Century: Money, Power and the Origins of Our Times*, London 2010 (2nd edn), 111–29; Boyer-Xambeau et al., *Monnaie privée et pouvoir des princes*, 25–6; Braudel, *Civilization and Capitalism, 15th–18th Century*, vol. 3, 130–74; Ehrenberg, *Das Zeitalter der Fugger*, vol. 1, 324–55; Otto von Gierke, *Das deutsche Genossenschaftsrecht*, vol. 1: *Rechtsgeschichte der deutschen Genossenschaft*, Berlin 1868, 991–2; Jacques Heers, *Gênes au XVe siécle: Activité économique et problèmes sociaux*, Paris 1961, 97–190; Niall Ferguson, *The Cash Nexus: Money and Power in the Modern World, 1700–2000*, London 2001, 199.

39 See Arrighi, *The Long Twentieth Century*, 151–3.

40 G. D. Peri, *Il negociante*, Genoa 1647; cited in Ehrenberg, *Das Zeitalter der Fugger*, vol. 2, 229.

41 Bernardo Davanzati, cited in Ehrenberg, *Das Zeitalter der Fugger*, vol. 2, 229. On the Genoese fairs and the business practices associated with them, see Boyer-Xambeau et al., *Monnaie privée et pouvoir des princes*, 283–309; Fernand Braudel, *Civilization and Capitalism, 15th–18th Century*, vol. 2: *The Wheels of Commerce*, trans. Siân Reynolds, London 1982, 90–2, 344–8; Fernand Braudel, *The Mediterranean and the Mediterranean World in the Age of Philip II*, vol. 1, trans. Siân Reynolds, London 1973, 138–8; Ehrenberg, *Das Zeitalter der Fugger*, vol. 2, 222–42.

42 Karl Marx, *Capital*, vol. 1, trans. Ben Fowkes, London 1990, 919.

43 On the diagram as depiction of power relations, see Gilles Deleuze, *Foucault*, trans. Seán Hand, Minnesota 1988, 34–8; Friedrich Balke, 'Fluchtlinien des Staates: Kafkas Begriff des Politischen', in Balke and Vogl, *Gilles Deleuze*, 169–78. Foucault and Deleuze use the concept of the diagram to describe the informal powers that evade a clear location and (legal) representation. The diagram is on the one hand 'highly unstable or fluid, continually churning up matter and functions in a way likely to create change'. On the other hand, the concept of the diagram implies that the exercise of power is less a question of form

than one of function; the diagram forces certain materials to perform certain functions, in other words it has the ability '*to impose a particular human conduct on a particular human multiplicity*' (italics in original); see Deleuze, *Foucault*, 34–5.

44 Braudel, *Civilization and Capitalism, 15th–18th Century*, vol. 2, 553–5.

45 On Marxist concepts of the state, see Gerold Amborius, *Zur Geschichte des Begriffs und der Theorie des Staatskapitalismus und des staatsmonopolistischen Kapitalismus*, Tübingen 1981, 10ff; Bob Jessop, *State Theory: Putting the Capitalist State in Its Place*, Cambridge 1990, 26ff; Bob Jessop, *The Capitalist State: Marxist Theories and Methods*, Oxford 1982, 1–31; Ralph Miliband, *The State in Capitalist Society*, London 1969; James O'Connor, *The Fiscal Crisis and the State*, New Brunswick 2002 (2nd edn), 2–12.

46 On the 'immediate' relation between individuals in the taxation state, see Blaschke, 'Finanzwesen und Staatsräson in Kursachsen zu Beginn der Neuzeit', 380–1; on the reciprocal conversion of power and capital, see Nitzan and Bichler, *Capital as Power*, 294–300.

47 Marx, *Capital*, vol. 1, 919–21; see also Manuel Gottlieb, 'Political Economy of the Public Debt', *Public Finance* 11/3, 1956, 265–79; on the concept of 'primitive accumulation' in Marx, see André Gunder Frank, *The World Accumulation 1492–1789*, New York 1978, 238ff.

48 Braudel, *Civilization and Capitalism, 15th–18th Century*, vol. 2, 234–5; Sonenscher, *Before the Deluge*, 2.

Chapter 4   Apotheosis of Finance

1 Marx, *Capital*, vol. 1, 916.

2 Louis Turquet de Mayerne, *La monarchie aristodémocratique, ou Le gouvernement composé et meslé des trois formes de légitimes républiques: Aux Estats-Généraux des Provinces Confédérées des Pays-Bas*, Paris 1611, dedication (n.p.), 558.

3 Johan de Witt, *Political Maxims of the State of Holland: Comprehending a General View of the Civil Government of that REPUBLIC, and the Principles on which it is Founded...* (1671), London 1743; Pieter de la Court, *Interesse*

von Holland / Oder Fondamenten von Hollands Wohlfahrt, n.p. 1665. On the singularity of political thought in seventeenth-century Holland, see Tuck, *Philosophy and Government*, 154ff.

4 Simon Stevin, *Livre de compte de prince à la manière d'Italie*, Leyden 1607.

5 See Immanuel Wallerstein, *The Modern World-System*, vol. 2: *Mercantilism and the Consolidation of the World-Economy*, New York 1980, 60–1.

6 See de Witt, *Political Maxims of the State of Holland*, 3; Isaac de Pinto, *Traité de la circulation et du crédit*, Amsterdam 1775, 313ff; Braudel, *Civilization and Capitalism, 15th–18th Century*, vol. 3, 235–45. On the relation between public debt and taxation in the Netherlands, see Stasavage, *Public Debt and the Birth of the Democratic State*, 55–9; Marjolein t'Hart, *The Making of a Bourgeois State: War, Politics and Finance during the Dutch Revolt*, Manchester 1993, 167; Augustus J. Veemendaal Jr, 'Fiscal Crisis and Constitutional Freedom in the Netherlands, 1450–1795', in Philip T. Hoffman and Kathryn Norberg (eds.), *Fiscal Crises, Liberty, and the Representative Government, 1450–1798*, Stanford 1994, 96–124; James D. Tracy, *A Financial Revolution in the Habsburg Netherlands: Renten and Renteniers in the County of Holland, 1515–1565*, Berkeley 1985, 71–107; Ehrenberg, *Das Zeitalter der Fugger*, vol. 2, 279–81.

7 On the 'apparatus of capture', see Gilles Deleuze and Félix Guattari, *A Thousand Plateaus: Capitalism and Schizophrenia*, trans. Brian Massumi, Minneapolis 1987, 424–75, online at http://projectlamar.com/media/A-Thousand-Plateaus.pdf.

8 See Arrighi, *The Long Twentieth Century*, 45ff; t'Hart, *The Making of a Bourgeois State*, 178–9; Stasavage, *Public Debt and the Birth of the Democratic State*, 57–9.

9 See Daron Acemoglu and James A. Robinson, *Why Nations Fail: The Origins of Power, Prosperity, and Poverty*, New York 2012, 254–9; Charles H. Alexandrowicz, *An Introduction to the History of the Law of Nations in the East Indias (16th, 17th and 18th Centuries)*, Oxford 1967, 59; Arrighi, *The Long Twentieth Century*, 130–48; John S. Furnivall, *Netherlands India: A Study of Plural Economy*, Cambridge 1944, 34–9. The Juvenalian motto ('The earth is not enough') was imprinted on a coin celebrating the foundation of the company in 1602. See Joseph de la Vega, *Die Verwirrung der Verwirrungen: Vier*

Dialoge über die Börse in Amsterdam (*Confusión de confusiónes*, 1668), intro. Otto Pringsheim, Breslau 1919, 227 (in keeping with the motto, the coin showed a horse jumping from the earth into the sea).

10 See René Louis d'Argenson, *Réflexions politiques sur le crédit public*, MS, 1734 or 1735, cited in Sonenscher, *Before the Deluge*, 161–2; Pinto, *Traité de la circulation et du crédit*, 14; John Law, *Money and Trade Considered: With a Proposal for Supplying the Nation with Money*, Edinburgh 1705, online at https://archive.org/details/moneytradeconsid00lawj. On the history of the Amsterdam Wisselbank, see Pohl, *Europäische Bankengeschichte*, 126–33; Michel Beaud, *A History of Capitalism: 1500–2000*, New York 2001, 23–5; t'Hart, *The Making of a Bourgeois State*, 164; Larry Neal, 'How It All Began: The Monetary and Financial Architecture of Europe during the First Global Capital Markets, 1648–1815', *Financial History Review* 7, 2000, 117–40.

11 Vega, *Die Verwirrung der Verwirrungen*, 34; Pinto, *Traité de la circulation et du crédit*, 80ff. See also Braudel, *Civilization and Capitalism, 15th–18th Century*, vol. 2, 100–3; Ehrenberg, *Das Zeitalter der Fugger*, vol. 2, 291–9; Oscar Gelderblom and Joost Jonker, 'Completing a Financial Revolution: The Finance of the Dutch East India Trade and the Rise of the Amsterdam Capital Market, 1595–1612', *Journal of Economic History* 64/3, 2004, 641–72.

12 Jacques Accarias de Sérionne, *Les intérêts des nations de l'Europe, développés relativement au commerce*, Leiden 1766, vol. 2, 201.

13 Amiya Kumar Bagchi, *Perilous Passage: Mankind and the Global Ascendancy of Capital*, Lanham 2005, 91.

14 Daniel Defoe, *A Plan of the English Commerce: Being a Compleat Prospect of the Trade of this Nation, as well the Home Trade as the Foreign*, London 1728, 192 (italics in original); see Appleby, *The Relentless Revolution*, 42–3.

15 Karl Heinzen, *Reise eines teutschen Romantikers nach Batavia*, Mannheim 1845 (2nd edn), 19; see Donald Maclaine Campbell, *Java: Past and Present. A Description of the Most Beautiful Country in the World ...* , London 1915, 1074.

16 Simon Schama, *The Embarrassment of Riches*, New York 1988, 44, 265.

17 See Pinto, *Traité de la circulation et du crédit*, 243.

18 Carl Schmitt, *The Nomos of the Earth*, trans. G.L. Ulmen, New York 2006, 42–9, 67–71; Plato, *Laws 1 and 2*, ed. Susan Sauvé Meyer, Oxford 2015, 625c6–632d7.

19 See Fernand Braudel, *La dynamique du capitalisme*, Paris 1985, 50.

20 See Sombart, *Der moderne Kapitalismus*, vol. 1, 319–27; Max Weber, *The Protestant Ethic and the 'Spirit' of Capitalism and Other Writings*, trans. Peter Baehr and Gordon Wells, London 2002, 8–28; Beaud, *A History of Capitalism*, 5.

21 See Nitzan and Bichler, *Capital as Power*, 227–8.

22 Marx, *Capital*, vol. 1, 915; see Nitzan and Bichler, *Capital as Power*, 295–6.

23 Richard B. Wernham (ed.), *The Counter-Reformation and Price Revolution, 1559–1610*, London 1968, 1, cited in Immanuel Wallerstein, *The Modern World-System*, vol. 1: *Capitalist Agriculture and the Origins of the European World-Economy in the Sixteenth Century*, New York 1974, 197.

24 Braudel, *Civilization and Capitalism, 15th–18th Century*, vol. 3, 375; Pinto, *Traité de la circulation et du crédit*, xiii–xiv, 137.

25 Bank of England Act 1694, online at www.legislation.gov.uk/aep/WillandMar/5-6/20/introduction.

26 Huw V. Bowen, 'The Bank of England During the Long Eighteenth Century, 1694–1820', in Richard Roberts and David Kynaston (eds.), *The Bank of England: Power, Money and Influence 1694–1994*, Oxford 1995, 3–6.

27 Lorenz von Stein, *Lehrbuch der Finanzwissenschaft*, Leipzig 1871 (2nd edn), 641.

28 Adam Smith, *An Inquiry into the Nature and Causes of the Wealth of Nations*, ed. Richard H. Campbell and Andrew S. Skinner, Oxford 1976, vol. 1, 320.

29 Michael Godfrey, 'A Short Account of the Bank of England' (London 1695), in Michael Collins (ed.), *Central Banking in History*. Vol. 1: *Central Bank Functions*, Aldershot 1993, 3; Daniel Defoe, *An Essay upon Projects*, London 1887, Project Gutenberg eBook 2014, 20–30.

30 David Hume, 'Of Public Credit', in Hume, *Political Essays*, ed. Knud Haakonssen, Cambridge 1994, 166–78, 174; Anon., *A Review of the Universal Remedy for All Diseases Incident to Coin With Application to Our Present Circumstances: In a Letter to Mr. Locke*, London 1696, 33–4, 52.

31 William Paterson, 'A Brief Account of the Intended Bank of England' (1694), in Michael Collins (ed.), *Central Banking in History* vol. 3: *Discretion and Autonomy*, Aldershot 1993, 7–8; Andréadès, *History of the Bank of England*, 69.

32 For example, in relation to debates on the extension of banking privileges in 1705; see John Broughton, *Remarks Upon the Bank of England, with Regard More Especially to Our Trade and Government...*, London 1705 (repr. Farnborough 1968), 'To the Reader' (n.p.), 45–6.

33 Jonathan Swift (1711) and Lord Chief Justice John Holdt (1702), cited in J.R. Jones, 'Fiscal Policies, Liberties, and Representative Government during the Reigns of the Last Stuarts', in Hoffman and Norberg, *Fiscal Crises, Liberty, and the Representative Government*, 84.

34 Daniel Defoe, *The Chimera: Or, The French Way of Paying National Debts, Laid Open...*, London 1720, 5–9, 22, 55–7.

35 See Arrighi, *The Long Twentieth Century*, 212.

36 Broughton, *Remarks Upon the Bank of England*, 29, 36; Lord King, *Thoughts on the Effects of the Bank Restrictions*, London 1804, 119–20.

37 See Karl Dierschke and Friedrich Müller, *Die Notenbanken der Welt...*, vol. 1, Berlin 1926, 114–15.

38 See Charles Goodhart, *The Evolution of Central Banks*, Cambridge 1988, 123.

39 Karl Brunner, 'The Art of Central Banking', Center for Research in Government Policy and Business, Graduate School of Management, University of Rochester, Working Paper No. GPB 81–6, June 1981, 5, cited in Martin Mayer, *The Fed: The Inside Story of How the World's Most Powerful Financial Institution Drives the Markets*, New York 2001, 15; see William Greider, *Secrets of the Temple: How the Federal Reserve Runs the Country*, New York 1987, 49–55.

40 Philip Geddes, *Inside the Bank of England*, London 1987, 61–4, 63.

41 Josiah Child, *Brief Observation Concerning Trade and Interest of Money*, London 1668, 5. See Peter G.M. Dickson, *The Financial Revolution in England: A Study in the Development of Public Credit 1688–1756*, London 1967, 4–5; Bruce G. Carruthers, *City of Capital: Politics and Markets in the English Financial Revolution*, Princeton 1996, 90.

42 Douglass C. North and Barry E. Weingast, 'Constitutions and Commitment: The Evolution of Institutions Governing Public Choice in Seventeenth-Century England', *Journal of Economic History* 49, 1989, 803–32. See also Carruthers, *City of Capital*, 115–121.

43 See Philip T. Hoffman and Kathryn Norberg, 'Conclusion', in Hoffman and Norberg, *Financial Crises, Liberty, and the Representative Government*, 299–301; Carruthers, *City of Capital*, 54, 83–4; Dickson, *The Financial Revolution in England*, 253–85; Carl Wennerlind, *Casualties of Credit: The English Financial Revolution, 1620–1720*, Cambridge 2011, 169–70; John Brewer, *The Sinews of Power: War, Money, and the English State, 1688–1783*, London 1989, 64ff.

44 Pinto, *Traité de la circulation et du crédit*, 41–2; Carruthers, *City of Capital*, 10. On the 'fiscal military state' in Great Britain, see Brewer, *The Sinews of Power*, 64ff.

45 John Locke, *Further Considerations Concerning Raising the Value of Money*, London 1695, 100, cited in Wennerlind, *Casualties of Credit*, 123.

46 Carruthers, *City of Capital*, 124–48. On the relation between 'thanatocracy' and the economic regime in England from 1690, see Peter Linebaugh, *The London Hanged: Crime and Civil Society in the Eighteenth Century*, London 2003; on the capital-intensive and coercive mode of the English system, see Charles Tilly, *Coercion, Capital, and European States, AD 990–1990*, Cambridge MA 1990, 30, 156–9.

47 John Craig, 'Isaac Newton and the Counterfeiters', *Notes and Records of the Royal Society in London* 18, 1963, 139. See Carruthers, *City of Capital*, 148–52.

48 Wennerlind, *Casualties of Credit*, 169–72.

49 Charles Davenant, *Discourses on the Publick Revenues, and on the Trade of England*, London 1698, 38.

50 Daniel Defoe, 'An Essay upon Publick Credit...' (1710) 1797, Eighteenth Century Collections Online, 8, 12. See overview in Wennerlind, *Casualties of Credit*, 172–87.

51 Joseph Addison, *The Spectator* (March 1711), ed. Donald F. Bond, Oxford 1965, 14–17; Daniel Defoe, 'Review' (1706), cited in John G.A. Pocock, *The Machiavellian Moment: Florentine Political Thought and the Atlantic Republican Tradition*, Princeton 1975, 452–3. See Marieke de Goede, 'Mastering Lady Credit: Discourses of Financial Crisis in Historical

Perspective', *International Feminist Journal of Politics* 2/2, 2000, 58–81.

52 This had already been formulated by the Portuguese-Dutch stock-market specialist Joseph de la Vega in 1688; see Vega, *Die Verwirrung der Verwirrungen*, 65. Cf. Wennerlind, *Casualties of Credit*, 197–234.

53 Kenneth Morgan, *Slavery, Atlantic Trade and the British Economy, 1660–1800*, Cambridge 2000.

54 Daniel Defoe, 'Review' (October 1711), cited in Wennerlind, *Casualties of Credit*, 222.

55 Daniel Defoe, *A True Account of the Design, and Advantages of the South-Sea Trade…*, London 1711, 6. Cf. Wennerlind, *Casualties of Credit*, 197–211.

56 Wennerlind, *Casualties of Credit*, 171.

57 On the concept of the 'financial-market public', see: Langenohl, 'Finanzmarktöffentlichkeiten', 245–66; Andreas Langenohl and Dietmar J. Wetzel (eds.), *Finanzmarktpublika: Moralität, Krisen und Teilhabe in der Ökonomischen Moderne*, Wiesbaden 2014.

58 On the situation in France, where such structures did not yet exist, see Herbert Lüthy, *La banque protestante en France de la révocation de l'édit de Nantes à la révolution*, vol. 1: *Dispersion et regroupement (1685–1739)*, Paris 1959, 104.

59 Immanuel Kant, 'Eternal Peace', *Advocate of Peace*, 59/5, 1897, 111–16.

60 See Geddes, *Inside the Bank of England*, 61; King, *Thoughts on the Effects of the Bank Restrictions*, 120; Robert Pringle, 'Central Bank Co-Operation 1970–1994', in Roberts and Kynaston, *The Bank of England*, 143; Sonenscher, *Before the Deluge*, 7. On the alchemical wedding between king and treasury, see Kantorowicz, *The King's Two Bodies*, 212, 218.

61 Walter Bagehot, *Lombard Street: A Description of the Money Market* (1873), London 1927 (14th edn), 311.

62 Thomas Hobbes, *On the Citizen*, ed. and trans. Richard Tuck and Michael Silverthorne, Cambridge 1998, 36–7, 62.

63 Davenant, *Discourses on the Publick Revenues*, 40; L.R., *A Proposal for Supplying His Majesty with Twelve Hundred Thousand Pounds…*, London 1695, 15, cited in Wennerlind, *Casualties of Credit*, 138; Defoe, 'Review' (February 1711), cited in Wennerlind, *Casualties of Credit*, 191; Anon., *A Review of the Universal Remedy*, 50; John Locke, *Some Considerations of the Consequences of the Lowering of Interest and Raising*

the Value of Money, London 1692, 4; Anon., *An Essay on Publick Credit*..., London 1748, 5; Thomas Mortimer, *The Elements of Commerce, Politics and Finance*..., London 1772, 365; Pinto, *Traité de la circulation et du crédit*, 39–41. On the 'culture of credit' in seventeenth-century England, see Craig Muldrew, *The Economy of Obligation: The Culture of Credit and Social Relations in Early Modern England*, Houndmills 1998, esp. 123–47.

64 Adam Müller, *Versuche einer neuen Theorie des Geldes mit besonderer Rücksicht auf Großbritannien*, Leipzig 1816, 28, 89–90, 94, 163, 255–6.

65 Robert Peel, 1844, cited in Felix Schuster, *The Bank of England and the State*, Manchester 1923, 9. See also Stein, *Lehrbuch der Finanzwissenschaft*, 664–5.

66 Hume, 'Of Public Credit', 174.

67 James Steuart, *An Inquiry into the Principles of Political Economy* (1767), Edinburgh 1966, vol. 1, 181.

68 Emmanuel Joseph Sieyès, 'Überblick über die Ausführungsmittel, die den Repräsentanten Frankreichs 1789 zur Verfügung stehen', in Sieyès, *Politische Schriften 1788–1790*, eds. Eberhard Schmitt and Rolf Reichardt, Munich 1981 (2nd edn), 86.

69 See Sonenscher, *Before the Deluge*, 5–17. The tension between the interests of society at large and those of private creditors, identified by Wolfgang Streeck as a significant feature of the contemporary financial system, can already be seen at the end of the seventeenth century; See Wolfgang Streeck, *Buying Time*, trans. Patrick Camiller, London 2014, 79–96.

70 Niklas Luhmann, *Die Wirtschaft der Gesellschaft*, Frankfurt 1994, 147; see also Brewer, *The Sinews of Power*, 64ff. Niall Ferguson has referred in this connection to the emergence of a 'square of power' consisting of tax bureaucracy, parliament, public debt and central bank; See Ferguson, *The Cash Nexus*, 15–16, 199.

71 Ralph G. Hawtrey, *The Art of Central Banking*, London 1932, 123. On governmentality and government see Foucault, *Security, Territory, Population*, 109.

Chapter 5   Fourth Power

1 See Karl Dierschke and Friedrich Müller, *Die Notenbanken der Welt*, vol. 2, Berlin 1926, 1–7; Bray Hammond, *Banks*

and Politics in America from the Revolution to the Civil War, Princeton 1957, 114–15; Roger T. Johnson, *Historical Beginnings...The Federal Reserve,* Boston 1999, 7–11.

2 Dierschke and Müller, *Die Notenbanken der Welt,* vol. 2, 6.

3 Louis D. Brandeis, *Other People's Money: And How the Bankers Use It* (1914), New York 1967, 3ff, 30ff.

4 See Gabriel Kolko, *The Triumph of Conservatism: A Reinterpretation of American History, 1900–1916,* New York 1963, 139–58; Greider, *Secrets of the Temple,* 268–303.

5 According to contemporary commentaries, cited in Greider, *Secrets of the Temple,* 279; Johnson, *Historical Beginnings,* 26.

6 According to Carter Glass, cited in Kolko, *The Triumph of Conservatism,* 224.

7 *The Statutes at Large of the United States of America from March, 1913, to March, 1915,* vol. 28/1: *Public Acts and Resolutions* (Sixty-Third Congress, Sess. II, Ch. 6, 1913), Washington 1915, 251–75. See Dierschke and Müller, *Die Notenbanken der Welt,* vol. 2, 26–35; Fabian Amtenbrink, *The Democratic Accountability of Central Banks: A Comparative Study of the European Central Bank,* Oxford 1999, 138–54.

8 According to the director of Chase National Bank at the time, A. Barton Hepburn; cited in Kolko, *The Triumph of Conservatism,* 235.

9 According to the records of the second chair of the Federal Reserve Board (previously the director of the First National Bank of Birmingham and president of the Alabama State Bankers Association). See William P.G. Harding, *The Formative Period of the Federal Reserve System (During the Crisis),* Boston 1925, 32–3.

10 Cited in Harding, *The Formative Period of the Federal Reserve System,* 233. See also John Maynard Keynes, *A Treatise on Money* (1930), London 1953, vol. 2, 235–6.

11 The question considered by the secretary of the treasury at the time, William Gibbs McAdoo; cited in Harding, *The Formative Period of the Federal Reserve System,* 9.

12 See Greider, *Secrets of the Temple,* 49.

13 Online at www.federalreserve.gov/faqs/about_14986.htm.

14 Wright Patman, Democrat congressman, and Philip E. Coldwell, long-serving head of the Federal Reserve Bank of Dallas, cited in Greider, *Secrets of the Temple,* 49–50. See Amtenbrink, *The Democratic Accountability of Central Banks,* 231–2.

15 Walter Lippmann, *Public Opinion* (1922), New York 1946, 274; see Kolko, *The Triumph of Conservatism*, 146, 285; Greider, *Secrets of the Temple*, 284–5.

16 Charles A. Beard, *An Economic Interpretation of the Constitution of the United States*, New York 1914, v.

17 Cited in Stasavage, *Public Debt and the Birth of the Democratic State*, 12.

18 Amtenbrink, *The Democratic Accountability of Central Banks*, 144; Greider, *Secrets of the Temple*, 313; Mayer, *The Fed*, 83–4.

19 See Amtenbrink, *The Democratic Accountability of Central Banks*, 231ff. On the personalization of the executive power of the Fed, see Susan Strange, *Mad Money: When Markets Outgrow Government*, Ann Arbor 1998, 144–5.

20 See Bagehot, *Lombard Street*, 311.

21 See Charles Goodhart, Forrest Capie and Norbert Schnadt, 'The Development of Central Banking', in Forrest Capie, Charles Goodhart, Stanley Fischer and Norbert Schnadt (eds.), *The Future of Central Banking: The Tercentenary Symposium of the Bank of England*, Cambridge 1994, 2, 66–9.

22 Greider, *Secrets of the Temple*, 11, 277.

23 *The Statutes at Large of the United States of America* (Sixty-Third Congress, Sess. II, Ch. 6, Sec. 10), 260.

24 On the well-known personal links between the Federal Reserve and Investment Banks (above all Goldman Sachs) in the present day, see the investigative journalism of Éric Laurent, *La face cachée des banques: Scandales et révélations sur les milieux financiers*, Paris 2009, 119–22; Roche, *La banque*, 160–5.

25 See Kolko, *The Triumph of Conservatism*, 247–51; Greider, *Secrets of the Temple*, 73.

26 Carter Glass in a speech of 1916, cited in Kolko, *The Triumph of Conservatism*, 254; see also Greider, *Secrets of the Temple*, 252–3.

27 See statements made by Alexander Hamilton, cited in Hammond, *Banks and Politics in America from the Revolution to the Civil War*, 46, 117–18.

28 Donald F. Kettl, *Leadership at the Fed*, New Haven 1986, 153, 159. On the politics of secrecy, see Marvin Goodfriend, 'Monetary Mystique: Secrecy and Central Banking', *Journal of Monetary Economics* 17, 1986, 63–92.

29 Alan S. Blinder, *Central Banking in Theory and Practice*, Cambridge 2000, 55. Cf. Mayer, *The Fed*, 15; Greider, *Secrets of the Temple*, 55, 313.

30 Antonio Fazio, 'Role and Independence of Central Banks', in Patrick Downes and Reza Vaez-Zadeh (eds.), *The Evolving Role of Central Banks*, Washington 1991, 121–7.

31 Blinder, *Central Banking in Theory and Practice*, 60; Lucas Zeise, *Geld: Der vertrackte Kern des Kapitalismus. Versuch über die politische Ökonomie des Finanzsektors*, Cologne 2013 (3rd edn), 214.

32 Mayer, *The Fed*, 286; Greider, *Secrets of the Temple*, 240, 534; Ethan B. Kapstein, 'Architects of Stability? International Cooperation among Financial Supervisors', in Claudio Borio, Gianni Toniolo and Piet Clement (eds.), *Past and Future of Central Bank Cooperation*, Cambridge 2008, 151; Stanley Fischer, *Modern Central Banking*, in Capie et al., *The Future of Central Banking*, 303; Hugo J. Hahn, 'Preface', in Amtenbrink, *The Democratic Accountability of Central Banks*, vii.

33 See Blinder, *Central Banking in Theory and Practice*, ix.

34 Goodhart et al., 'The Development of Central Banking', 53; Ferguson, *The Cash Nexus*, 162; Marjorie Deane and Robert Pringle, *The Central Banks*, London 1994, 4.

35 According to Karl Otto Pöhl, a former president of the Bundesbank; cited in David Marsh, *The Bundesbank: The Bank That Rules Europe*, London 1992, 169.

36 'Gesetz über die Deutsche Bundesbank: Vom 26. Juli 1957', *Bundesgesetzblatt*, I/ 33, 30 July 1957, 747.

37 The president and the vice-president of the Executive Board are 'appointed by the Federal President on the advice of the Federal Government'. The central executive body, the Central Bank Council, consists of the Executive Board and the presidents of the central banks of the federal states, who are again appointed by the Federal president on the advice of the second chamber (Bundesrat). The eight-year terms of the members of the Central Bank Council are supposed to inoculate against legislative cycles (§7 and §8 BBankG).

38 According to §13(2) BBankG. On the independence of the Bundesbank, see Amtenbrink, *The Democratic Accountability of Central Banks*, 216–24, 276–8.

39 Wilhelm Könneker, *Die Deutsche Bundesbank*, Frankfurt am Main 1967, 68–9.

40 John B. Goodman, *Monetary Sovereignty: The Politics of Central Banking in Western Europe*, Ithaca 1992, 99.

41 See Amtenbrink, *The Democratic Accountability of Central Banks*, 218; Friedrich Wilhelm Dörge and Ralf Mairose, 'Die Bundesbank: Eine Nebenregierung?', *Gegenwartskunde: Eine Zeitschrift für Gesellschaft, Wirtschaft, Politik und Bildung* 18/1, 1969, 91–122; Zeise, *Geld*, 123.

42 Amtenbrink, *The Democratic Accountability of Central Banks*, 92.

43 'Basic Law for the Federal Republic of Germany', version of 23 May 1949, online at http://www.documentarchiv.de/brd/1949/grundgesetz.html.

44 Amtenbrink, *The Democratic Accountability of Central Banks*, 159–62. On the controversies surrounding the drafting of the Bundesbank Law, see Volker Hentschel, 'Die Entstehung des Bundesbankgesetzes 1949–1957: Politische Kontroversen und Konflikte', *Bankhistorisches Archiv: Zeitschrift für Bankengeschichte* 14, 1988, 3–31 (part I), 79–115 (part II).

45 According to Joseph Dodge (the former president of the Detroit Bank and Trust Company and from 1945 leader of the financial department of the Office of Military Government of the United States, OMGUS); cited in Marsh, *The Bundesbank*, 148.

46 Article I §3, Law No. 60/Regulation No. 129/Regulation No. 203 of the American, British and French Military Governments of 1 March 1948 and 26 March 1949 on the 'Establishment of the Bank of the German States', online at www.verfassungen.de/de/de45–49/bizone-gesetz48–1.htm.

47 See article II and its revision by the law of 10 August 1951; see article I §3, Law No. 60/Regulation No. 129/Regulation No. 203. On the debate on the independence of the Bank of the German States, see Theo Horstmann, 'Die Entstehung der Bank deutscher Länder als geldpolitische Lenkungsinstanz in der Bundesrepublik Deutschland', in Hajo Riese and Heinz-Peter Spahn (eds.), *Geldpolitik und ökonomische Entwicklung: Ein Symposion*, Regensburg 1990, 202–18.

48 Konrad Adenauer in a speech to the Federation of German Industry on 23 May 1956; cited in Marsh, *The Bundesbank*, 57.

49 Report of 1 April 1948, in Bundesministerium für Wirtschaft (ed.), *Der Wissenschaftliche Beirat beim Bundesministerium*

für Wirtschaft: Sammelband der Gutachten von 1948 bis 1972,
Göttingen 1973, 1–4.

50 Rainer Salzmann (ed.), *Die CDU/CSU im Frankfurter
Wirtschaftsrat: Protokolle der Unionsfraktion 1947–1949,*
Düsseldorf 1988, 218, 226, 229–32; see also Bernhard
Löffler, 'Einführung', in *Rede Ludwig Erhards während der
14. Vollversammlung des Wirtschaftsrates des Vereinigten
Wirtschaftsgebietes am 21.4.1948 in Frankfurt am Main,*
online at: www.1000dokumente.de/index.html?c=dokument_
de&dokument=0010_erh&object=context&st=&l=de.

51 'Gesetz über Leitsätze für die Bewirtschaftung und Preispolitik
nach der Geldreform', *Verordnungsblatt für die Britische Zone,*
issued in Hamburg, 13 July 1948, No. 33, 202.

52 Ludwig Erhard, 'Der Weg in die Zukunft: Rede vor der
14. Vollversammlung des Wirtschaftsrates des Vereinigten
Wirtschaftsgebietes am 21. April 1948 in Frankfurt am Main',
in Erhard, *Deutsche Wirtschaftspolitik: Der Weg der Sozialen
Marktwirtschaft,* Düsseldorf 1962, 52. See Foucault, *The Birth
of Biopolitics,* 75–100.

53 Erhard, 'Der Weg in die Zukunft', 52; Ludwig Erhard, *Wohlstand für alle,* Düsseldorf 1957, 12. See also Walter Eucken,
Grundsätze der Wirtschaftspolitik, Bern 1952, 1ff.

54 'Gesetz über Leitsätze für die Bewirtschaftung und Preispolitik
nach der Geldreform', in *Gesetzblatt der Verwaltung des
Vereinigten Wirtschaftsgebietes* (WiGBl.), issued in Frankfurt,
7 July 1948, No. 12, 59.

55 Ludwig Erhard, 'Vorwort', in Erhard, *Deutsche Wirtschaftspolitik,* 5–6; Erhard, 'Der Weg in die Zukunft', 51–2; Erhard,
Wohlstand für alle, 14.

56 Foucault, *The Birth of Biopolitics,* 82.

57 Erhard, 'Der Weg in die Zukunft', 52.

58 Foucault, *The Birth of Biopolitics,* 83–4.

59 'Entwurf eines Gesetzes über die Deutsche Bundesbank', §3,
in *Deutscher Bundestag, 2. Wahlperiode, Drucksache 2781,*
18 October 1956, 4.

60 'Entwurf eines Gesetzes über die Deutsche Bundesbank', §3,
23–5.

61 Alfred Müller-Armack, *Genealogie der Wirtschaftsstile: Die
geistesgeschichtlichen Ursprünge der Staats- und Wirtschaftsfor-
men bis zum Ausgang des 18. Jahrhunderts,* Stuttgart 1941;
see also Foucault, *The Birth of Biopolitics,* 101–28.

62 Erhard, *Wohlstand für alle*, 16 (italics in original).
63 Foucault, *The Birth of Biopolitics*, 86.
64 'Entwurf eines Gesetzes über die Deutsche Bundesbank', 27.
65 Erhard, 'Der Weg in die Zukunft', 42, 45; cf. Hayek, *The Road to Serfdom*, 91–104, esp. 93–4.
66 Hans Tietmeyer, 'The Role of Independent Central Banks in Europe', in Downes and Vaez-Zadeh, *The Evolving Role of Central Banks*, 177–9; see also Alex Cukierman, 'Central Bank Independence and Monetary Policy Making Institutions: Past, Present, and Future', *European Journal of Political Economy* 24/4, 2008, 722–36.
67 See Ulrich Haltern, *Was bedeutet Souveränität?*, Tübingen 2007, 99–104.
68 Streeck, *Buying Time*, 174.
69 According to Marius Holtrop, the chair of the committee and director of the Dutch Central Bank in the inaugural session. See *Procès-verbal de la première séance du comité des gouverneurs des banques centrales*, 6 July 1964, in ECB Archive, Frankfurt am Main, Committee of Governors, 122/1–2.
70 Anne-Marie Slaughter, *A New World Order: Government Networks and the Disaggregated State*, Princeton 2004, 44; see also Ulrich Haltern, *Europarecht und das Politische*, Tübingen 2005, 148–57.
71 On the reconstruction of this process, see Harold James, *Making the European Union: The Role of the Committee of Central Bank Governors and the Origins of the European Central Bank*, Cambridge 2012.
72 James, *Making the European Union*, 268, 278.
73 Council of the European Communities, Commission of the European Communities, 'Treaty on the European Union', 7 February 1992, online at http://europa.eu/eu-law/decision-making/treaties/pdf/treaty_on_european_union/treaty_on_european_union_en.pdf.
74 Council of the European Communities, Commission of the European Communities, 'Treaty on the European Union'.
75 'Beschlußempfehlung und Bericht des Sonderausschusses "Europäische Union (Vertrag von Maastricht)"', *Deutscher Bundestag, 12. Wahlperiode, Drucksache 12/3896*, 1 December 1992, 21–2.
76 See Friedrich Hayek, *Denationalisation of Money: The Argument Refined. Analysis of the Theory and Practice of Concurrent*

Currencies (1976), London 1990 (3rd edn); James, *Making the European Union*, 6–7; Élie Cohen, 'L'Union Économique et Monétaire ou l'Échec d'un Procès Fédératif Subreptice', in Théret, *L'état, la finance et le social*, 463ff; Alexandre Lamfalussy, 'Central Banks, Governments, and the European Money Unification Process', in Borio et al., *Past and Future of Central Bank Cooperation*, 156; Mäder, *Vom Wesen der Souveränität*, 75–6; Haltern, *Was bedeutet Souveränität?*, 100.

77 See Amtenbrink, *The Democratic Accountability of Central Banks*, 180–5.
78 The Maastricht Judgment of the Federal Constitutional Court, 12 October 1993 (BVerfGE 89, 155), C II. 3a), 153, online at www.servat.unibe.ch/dfr/bv089155.html#Rn152.
79 The Maastricht Judgment of the Federal Constitutional Court, 154.
80 See Amtenbrink, *The Democratic Accountability of Central Banks*, 185–6.
81 Alex Cukierman, *Central Bank Strategy, Credibility, and Independence: Theory and Evidence*, Cambridge 1992, 16–22; Sylvia Maxfield, *Gatekeepers of Growth: The International Political Economy of Central Banking in Developing Countries*, Princeton 1997, 11–12.
82 Maxfield, *Gatekeepers of Growth*, 69–70; Adam S. Posen, 'Declarations Are Not Enough: Financial Sources of Central Bank Independence', *NBER Macrooeconomics Annual* 10, 1995, 253–74.
83 According to Tim Koopmans, advocate general at the Supreme Court of the Netherlands; see Tim Koopmans, 'Rechter, D-mark en democratie: het Bundesverfassungsgericht en de Europese Unie', *Nederlandsch Juristenblad* 69/8, 1994, 249, cited in Amtenbrink, *The Democratic Accountability of Central Banks*, 185.
84 Ingolf Pernice, 'Das Ende der währungspolitischen Souveränität Deutschlands und das Maastricht-Urteil des BVerfG', in Ole Due, Marcus Lutter and Jürgen Schwarze (eds.), *Festschrift für Ulrich Everling*, Baden-Baden 1995, vol. 2, 1068. Pernice does, however, concede that the 'legal and institutional precautions for securing the goal of stability' as regards the ECB exceed those of the Bundesbank; 1064.
85 Pernice, 'Das Ende der währungspolitischen Souveränität Deutschlands', 1064.

86 'Protocol on the Statute of the European System of Central Banks and of the European Central Bank', 1992, online at http://www.ecb.europa.eu/ecb/legal/pdf/en_statute_2.pdf.

87 According to the dictum that 'currency markets' are 'judges of governments'; see Herbert Giersch, 'Beschäftigung, Stabilität, Wachstum: Wer trägt die Verantwortung?', in Giersch (ed.), *Wie es zu schaffen ist: Agenda für die deutsche Wirtschaftspolitik*, Stuttgart 1983, 31; Rainer Hank, *Die Pleiterepublik: Wie der Schuldenstaat uns entmündigt und wie wir uns befreien können*, Munich 2012, 18. See also Michael Hudson, 'Die Herrschaft der Finanzoligarchie: Der Krieg der Banken gegen das Volk', *Frankfurter Allgemeine Zeitung*, 3 December 2011, online at www.faz.net/aktuell/feuilleton/die-herrschaft-der-finanzoligarchie-der-krieg-der-bankengegen-das-volk-11549829.html; James, *Making the European Union*, 280–1; Streeck, *Buying Time*, 165–6; Zeise, *Geld*, 119–20.

88 Giersch, 'Beschäftigung, Stabilität, Wachstum', 28.

89 See Cukierman, *Central Bank Strategy, Credibility, and Independence*, 722–36; Alberto Alesina and Lawrence H. Summers, 'Central Bank Independence and Macroeconomic Performance: Some Comparative Evidence', *Journal of Money, Credit and Banking* 25/2, May 1993, 151–62. On the boom in literature on 'credibility', see Delia M. Boylan, *Defusing Democracy: Central Bank Autonomy and the Transition from Authoritarian Rule*, Ann Arbor 2001, 6–7.

90 See Boylan, *Defusing Democracy*, 28–31; Amtenbrink, *The Democratic Accountability of Central Banks*, 15–17; Posen, 'Declarations Are Not Enough', 253–56; Ulrike Herrmann, *Der Sieg des Kapitals: Wie der Reichtum in die Welt kam. Die Geschichte von Wachstum, Geld und Krisen*, Frankfurt 2013, 134–41.

91 Sergio de Castro, minister of the economy and finance in the Pinochet regime and one of the founders of the economic reforms from the Chicago School circle, cited in Boylan, *Defusing Democracy*, 89. On the following, see also Boylan, *Defusing Democracy*, 75–138. On the initial resistance of the Junta to the free-market reforms, see Jeffrey M. Chwieroth, 'Shrinking the State: Neoliberal Economists and Social Spending in Latin America', in Rawi Abdelal, Mark Blyth and Craig Parsons (eds.), *Constructing the International Economy*, Ithaca 2010, 23–46.

92 Statement from Pinochet's political and legal advisors, cited in Boylan, *Defusing Democracy*, 90.
93 Fernando Agüero, chairman of the Industrialists Association (Sociedad de Fomento Fabril, SOFOFA) in an editorial, cited in Boylan, *Defusing Democracy*, 93.
94 In a survey held after the referendum; see Boylan, *Defusing Democracy*, 101.
95 Admiral Merino, head of the Chilean navy, in August 1989, cited in Boylan, *Defusing Democracy*, 112.
96 Roberto Zahler, 'La inserción institucional del Banco Central de Chile', *Cuadernos de Economía* 26/77, April 1989, 101–92, cited in Boylan, *Defusing Democracy*, 112.
97 Ramón Briones Espinosa, legal advisor to the Concertación, in a memo, cited in Boylan, *Defusing Democracy*, 112–13.
98 Law 18,840 (Basic Constitutional Act of the Central Bank of Chile), Section 27, online at www.bcentral.cl/eng/about/basic-constitutional-act/law03.htm). See Boylan, *Defusing Democracy*, 114–16.
99 Law 18,840, Section 1. See Boylan, *Defusing Democracy*, 114–16.
100 Zahler, 'La inserción institucional del Banco Central de Chile', 102, cited in Boylan, *Defusing Democracy*, 122.
101 See Boylan, *Defusing Democracy*, 58–9, 125, 132–7.
102 As Pinochet put it; cited in Brian Loveman, 'Democracy on a Tether', *Hemisphere* 2/2, May 1990, 24–8.
103 See Boylan, *Defusing Democracy*, 127–32; Delia M. Boylan, 'Taxation and Transition: The Politics of the 1990 Chilean Tax Reform', *Latin American Research Review* 31/1, 1996, 7–31.
104 Boylan, *Defusing Democracy*, 131.
105 See Posen, 'Declarations Are Not Enough', 253–74.
106 See Boylan, *Defusing Democracy*, 52–9, 83; Goodhart et al., 'The Development of Central Banking', 60; Maxfield, *Gatekeepers of Growth*, 22–3; Thomas Piketty, *Capital in the Twenty-First Century*, Cambridge MA 2014, 544–8; Adam S. Posen, 'Central Bank Independence and Disinflationary Credibility: A Missing Link?', *Oxford Economic Papers* 50, 1998, 335–59; Streeck, *Buying Time*, 34ff.
107 Milton Friedman, 'The Role of Monetary Policy', *American Economic Review* 58/1, March 1968, 1–17; see Zeise, *Geld*, 124–5; Greider, *Secrets of the Temple*, 46–7, 75–123, 168–9,

404–11, 551–3; Greta R. Krippner, *Capitalizing on Crisis: The Political Origins of the Rise of Finance*, Harvard 2011, 103–4, 116–20.
108 The term used by Jeffrey Winters, *Oligarchy*, Cambridge 2011, 213.
109 See Hudson, 'Die Herrschaft der Finanzoligarchie'.

Chapter 6   Reserves of Sovereignty

1 See e.g. Karl Munk, *Zur Geschichte und Theorie der Banknote mit besonderer Rücksicht auf die Lehren der klassischen Nationalökonomie*, Bern 1896, 17ff; Alfred Kruse, *Geschichte der volkswirtschaftlichen Theorien*, Berlin 1959 (4th edn), 81ff; Karl Erich Born, 'Geld und Währungen im 19. Jahrhundert', in Pohl, *Europäische Bankengeschichte*, 177–95.
2 Richard S. Sayers, *Central Banking After Bagehot*, Oxford 1957 (repr. Westport 1982), 5.
3 Sayers, *Central Banking After Bagehot*, 7. See Suzanne de Brunhoff, *État et capital: Recherches sur la politique économique*, Paris 1982, 34; Rudolf Hilferding, *Das Finanzkapital: Eine Studie über die jüngste Entwicklung des Kapitalismus* (1910), Berlin 1955 (2nd edn), 68.
4 See Henry C. Simons, 'Rules versus Authorities in Monetary Policy', *Journal of Political Economy* 44/1, 1936, 1–30; Milton Friedman and Anna J. Schwartz, 'Has Government Any Role in Money?', *Journal of Monetary Economics* 17, 1986, 37–62.
5 Simons, 'Rules versus Authorities in Monetary Policy', 4–8, 17, 22–5; see also Thorvald Grung Moe, 'Control of Finance as a Prerequisite for Successful Monetary Policy: A Reinterpretation of Henry Simons's "Rules versus Authorities in Monetary Policy"', *Levy Economics Institute Working Paper Collection*, Levy Economics Institute of Bard College, Working Paper No. 713, April 2012, online at www.levyinstitute.org/pubs/wp_713.pdf.
6 See the inaugural works of modern monetarism, e.g.: Milton Friedman and Anna J. Schwartz, *A Monetary History of the United States 1867–1960*, Princeton 1963; Milton Friedman, 'The Quantity Theory of Money: A Restatement', in Friedman, *The Essence of Friedman*, ed. Kurt K. Leube, Stanford 1987, 285–303; Milton Friedman, 'Notes on Quantity Theory of Money', in Friedman, *The Essence of Friedman*, 370–84.

7 Hayek, *Denationalisation of Money*, 23, 28, 48, 100ff. On early discussions of free banking, see the dissertation of the Hayek student Vera C. Smith, *The Rationale of Central Banking and the Free Banking Alternative* (1936), Indianapolis 1990.

8 Goodhart, *The Evolution of Central Banks*, vii; Hayek, *Denationalisation of Money*, 23.

9 On the various positions and debates, see Goodhart et al., 'The Development of Central Banking', 80ff; Fischer, 'Modern Central Banking', 288–94; Goodman, *Monetary Sovereignty*, 14ff; Reinhard Kohler and Peter Stahlecker, 'Monetäre Theorie und Politik', in *Gablers Wirtschaftslexikon*, Wiesbaden 1993 (13th edn), vol. 5, 2305–12.

10 Eugene Fama, 'Banking in the Theory of Finance', *Journal of Monetary Economics* 6, 1980, 39–57; Hayek, *Denationalisation of Money*, 23, 28, 48, 100ff. See Gary B. Gorton and Joseph G. Haubrich, 'Bank Deregulation, Credit Markets, and the Control of Capital', in Karl Brunner and Allan H. Metzler (eds.), *Bubbles and Other Essays: Carnegie-Rochester Conference Series on Public Policy*, vol. 26, Amsterdam 1987, 289–334.

11 See Goodfriend, 'Monetary Mystique', 64; Hawtrey, *The Art of Central Banking*; Blinder, *Central Banking in Theory and Practice*, 23.

12 Blinder, *Central Banking in Theory and Practice*, 3.

13 Elena Esposito, *The Future of Futures: The Time of Money in Financing Society*, Cheltenham 2011, 51, 107–18.

14 Hawtrey, *The Art of Central Banking*, vii; Goodman, *Monetary Sovereignty*, xi.

15 Alexandre Lamfalussy, 'Central Banking in Transition', in Capie et al., *The Future of Central Banking*, 334–5; Stephan Schulmeister, 'Geld als Mittel zum (Selbst)Zweck', in Konrad Paul Liessmann (ed.), *Geld: Was die Welt im Innersten zusammenhält?*, Vienna 2009, 168–206.

16 IMF, *Global Financial Stability Report*, April 2006, 51, online at http://www.imf.org/external/pubs/ft/GFSR/2006/01/pdf/chp2 .pdf. See John Cassidy, *How Markets Fail: The Logic of Economic Calamities*, New York 2009, 251–316; Michel Aglietta and Sandra Rigot, *Crise et rénovation de la finance*, Paris 2009, 17–47.

17 Ralf Heidenreich and Stefan Heidenreich, *Mehr Geld*, Berlin 2008, 133; see Vogl, *The Specter of Capital*, 120–1.

18 Hyun Song Shin, *Risk and Liquidity*, Oxford 2010, 4–13; Esposito, *The Future of Futures*, 107–18; Cassidy, *How Markets Fail*, 307–9; Michel Aglietta, *La crise: Pourquoi est-on arrivé là? Comment en sortir?*, Paris 2008, 17–31. See also Vogl, *The Specter of Capital*, 121.

19 Lamfalussy, 'Central Banking in Transition', 336.

20 Cited in Nils Rüdel and Rolf Benders, 'Ein Sturm im Wasserglas', *Handelsblatt*, 13 June 2012, online at www.handelsblatt .com/unternehmen/banken/jpmorgan-anhoerung-ein-sturm-im-wasserglas/6747700.html; see also Stefan Frank, 'Von Lehman nichts gelernt', *Die Zeit*, 28 September 2011, online at www.zeit.de/wirtschaft/unternehmen/2011–09/banken-krise-euro.

21 Mayer, *The Fed*, x–xi; Benjamin M. Friedman, 'The Future of Monetary Policy: The Central Bank as an Army with only a Signal Corps?', *NBER Paper Series*, National Bureau of Economic Research, Working Paper 7429, November 1999, 28, online at www.nber.org/papers/w7420.pdf.

22 Piet Clement, 'Introduction', in Borio et al., *Past and Future of Central Bank Cooperation*, 6.

23 See Hasan Cömert, *Central Banks and Financial Markets: The Declining Power of US Monetary Policy*, Cheltenham 2013, 4.

24 Friedman, 'The Future of Monetary Policy', 1–2.

25 Ferguson, *The Cash Nexus*, 167–8; Friedman, 'The Future of Monetary Policy', 1–2; Christian Marazzi, *Sozialismus des Kapitals*, Zurich 2012, 137–8; Roubini and Mihm, *Das Ende der Weltwirtschaft und ihre Zukunft*, 208. On the concerns of the ECB with regard to the extent of electronic money and credit card payments, see European Central Bank, *Report on Electronic Money*, Frankfurt 1998, online at www.ecb.europa.eu/ pub/pdf/other/emoneyen.pdf. See Dirk H. Ehnts, *Modern Monetary Theory and European Macroeconomics*, Abingdon 2016, for a balance-sheet view of the monetary and fiscal policy of the Eurozone.

26 In the words of an insider of the Bank of England as well as its former governor, Edward George; cited in Geddes, *Inside the Bank of England*, 83, 86; Lamfalussy, 'Central Banking in Transition', 333.

27 Cited in Mayer, *The Fed*, 21.

28 Mayer, *The Fed*, x–xi, 21–7. See Lamfalussy, 'Central Banking in Transition', 335–7; Ferguson, *The Cash Nexus*, 167–8.

29 Alan Greenspan, cited in Justin Fox, *The Myth of the Rational Market: A History of Risk, Reward, and Delusion on Wall Street*, New York 2009, xi–xii. See Roman Frydman and Michael D. Goldberg, *Beyond Mechanical Markets: Asset Price Swings, Risk, and the Role of the State*, Princeton 2011, 8–9, 225–6; Thomas Lux, *The Financial Crisis and the Systematic Failure of Academic Economics*, in *Kiel Working Papers*, Kiel Institute for the World Economy, Working Paper 1489, February 2009, online at www.ifw-members.ifw-kiel.de/publications/the-financial-crisis-and-thesystemic-failure-of-academic-economics/KWP_1489_ColanderetalFinancial%20Crisis.pdf.

30 Gerhard Illing, *Zentralbanken im Griff der Finanzmärkte: Umfassende Regulierung als Voraussetzung für eine effiziente Geldpolitik*, Bonn 2011, 6–7.

31 Carl-Johan Lindgren, 'The Transition from Direct to Indirect Instruments in Monetary Policy', in Downes and Vaez-Zadeh, *The Evolving Role of Central Banks*, 307–25.

32 Elmar Altvater, 'Die Politik "im Schlepptau" der Finanzmärkte', in Detlef Horster (ed.), *Markt und Staat: Was lehrt uns die Finanzkrise?*, Weilerswist 2011, 69–80; Colin Crouch, *The Strange Non-Death of Neoliberalism*, Cambridge 2011, 19–20; Jacob S. Hacker and Paul Pierson, *Winner-Take-All Politics: How Washington Made the Rich Richer – And Turned Its Back on the Middle Class*, New York 2010, 66–7; Krippner, *Capitalizing on Crisis*, 3–4 and ch. 2; Paul Windolf, 'Was ist Finanzmarkt-Kapitalismus?', in Windolf (ed.), *Finanzmarkt-Kapitalismus: Kölner Zeitschrift für Soziologie und Sozialpsychologie*, special issue 45/2005, 20–57; Christian Marazzi, *Verbranntes Geld*, Zurich 2011, 32–3.

33 Robert Brenner, *The Boom and the Bubble: The US in the World Economy*, London 2002, 50–9; Krippner, *Capitalizing on Crisis*, 2, 16–23.

34 Even in anonymized form, details about the incomes of the highest earners in the US are available from the Internal Revenue Service only for the period between 1992 and 2006 – and this is only because the Obama administration lifted the regulations imposed by the previous Bush government. See Winters, *Oligarchy*, 213.

35 Piketty, *Capital in the Twenty-First Century*, 493–514.

36 Nicola Liebert, 'Fataler Reichtum: Zuviel Geld in falschen Händen', *Le Monde Diplomatique*, 10 August 2012, 1, 10–11.

See also: Hacker and Pierson, *Winner-Take-All Politics*, 15–16; Tony Judt, *Ill Fares the Land*, London 2010, 14.

37 See Deneault, *Gouvernance*, 9–11; Arthur Benz, Susanne Lütz, Uwe Schimank and Georg Simonis (eds.), *Handbuch Governance: Theoretische Grundlagen und empirische Anwendungsfelder*, Wiesbaden 2007, 9–25 (introduction); Arthur Benz and Nicolai Dose, 'Governance: Modebegriff oder nützliches sozialwis-senschaftliches Konzept?', in Arthur Benz and Nicolai Dose (eds.), *Governance: Regieren in komplexen Regelsystemen*, Wiesbaden 2010 (2nd edn), 13–27; Alexander Demirović and Heike Walk (eds.), *Demokratie und Governance: Kritische Perspektiven auf neue Formen politischer Herrschaft*, Münster 2011; Mark Bevir, *A Theory of Governance*, Berkeley 2013, 149–53; Mark Bevir, 'Governance', in Bevir (ed.), *Encyclopedia of Governance*, Thousand Oaks 2007, vol. 1, 364–81; David Levi-Faur, 'From "Big Government" to "Big Governance"', in Levi-Faur (ed.), *Oxford Handbook of Governance*, Oxford 2012, 3–18. For an exemplary document, see 'European Govern-ance: A White Paper', *Official Journal of the European Com-munities*, 12 October 2001, C 287/1–29, online at eur-lex. europa.eu/legal-content/EN/TXT/PDF/?uri=CELEX:52001DC0 428&rid=2.

38 Kuno Schedler, 'Public Management und Public Governance', in Benz et al., *Handbuch Governance*, 253–68. See Eric Hans Klijn, 'New Public Management and Governance: a Comparison', in Levi-Faur, *Oxford Handbook of Governance*, 201–14; Stephen Cohen and William Eimicke, 'Contracting Out', in Mark Bevir (ed.), *The SAGE Handbook of Governance*, Berkeley 2011, 237–51; Carolyn J. Heinrich, 'Public Management', in Bevir, *The SAGE Handbook of Governance*, 252–69; Foucault, *The Birth of Biopolitics*, 240–3.

39 Dieter Grimm, *Die Verfassung und die Politik: Einsprüche in Störfällen*, Munich 2001, 319–24; Everhard Holtmann, 'Die öffentliche Verwaltung', in Oscar W. Gabriel and Everhard Holtmann, *Handbuch politisches System der Bundesrepublik Deutschland*, Munich 2005 (3rd edn), 333–72 (esp. 357–8); Wolfram Lamping, Henning Schridde, Stefan Plaß and Bernhard Blanke, *Der aktivierende Staat: Positionen, Begriffe, Strategien*, Friedrich-Ebert-Stiftung, Bonn 2002; Crouch, *The Strange Non-Death of Neoliberalism*, 71–96.

40 David Osborne and Ted Gaebler, *Reinventing Government: How the Entrepreneurial Spirit is Transforming the Public Sector*, Wiesbaden 1997.

41 Ronald Reagan during the 1976 presidential campaign, cited in Wedel, *Shadow Elite*, 29.

42 Wedel, *Shadow Elite*, 27–33, 77–82; Paul C. Light, *Fact Sheet on the New True Size of Government*, Wagner School of Public Service, New York University 2003, online at https://wagner.nyu.edu/files/faculty/publications/lightFactTrueSize.pdf.

43 Jonathan Joseph, *The Social and the Global: Social Theory, Governmentality and Global Policies*, Cambridge 2012, 132.

44 Slaughter, *A New World Order*, 42–3.

45 See David Levi-Faur, 'The Global Diffusion of Regulatory Capitalism', *Annals of the American Academy of Political and Social Science* 598: *The Rise of Regulatory Capitalism: The Global Diffusion of a New Order*, 2005, 12–23; Fabrizio Gilardi, 'The Institutional Foundations of Regulatory Capitalism: The Diffusion of Independent Regulatory Agencies in Western Europe', *Annals of the American Academy of Political and Social Science* 598, 2005, 84–101.

46 See John Braithwaite, *Regulatory Capitalism: How It Works, Ideas for Making It Work Better*, Cheltenham 2008, 1–31; Slaughter, *A New World Order*, 36–64; Anastasia Nesvetailova and Carlos Belli, 'Global Financial Governance: Taming Financial Innovation', in Sophie Harman and David Williams (eds.), *Governing the World? Cases in Global Governance*, London 2013, 46–61; see also n.45 in this chapter.

47 See Commission on Global Governance, *Our Global Neighborhood*, New York 1995, 95, cited in Joseph, *The Social and the Global*, 89–90; Bruce R. Scott, *Capitalism: Its Origins and Evolution as a System of Governance*, New York 2011, 518–19.

48 Nils Jansen and Ralf Michaels, 'Beyond the State? Rethinking Private Law: Introduction to the Issue', *American Journal of Comparative Law* 56/3, Summer 2008, Special Symposium Issue: *Beyond the State: Rethinking Private Law*, 527–39.

49 Benn Steil and Manuel Hinds, *Money, Markets, and Sovereignty*, New Haven 2009, 23–9. Critical: Ralf Michaels and Nils Jansen, 'Private Law beyond the State? Europeanization, Globalization, Privatization', *American Journal of Comparative Law* 54/4, Fall 2006, 843–90; Jürgen Basedow, 'The State's Private Law

and the Economy: Commercial Law as an Amalgam of Public and Private Rule-Making', *American Journal of Comparative Law* 56/3, Summer 2008, 703–21; Nicholas H.D. Foster, 'Foundation Myth as Legal Formant: The Medieval Law Merchant and the New Lex Mercatoria', *forum historiae juris*, 18 March 2005, online at www.forhistiur.de/2005-03-foster.

50 *The Economist*, 18–24 July 1992, 17, cited in Walter Mattli, 'Private Justice in a Global Economy: From Litigation to Arbitration', *International Organization* 55/4, Autumn 2001, 920. See Corporate Europe Observatory, Transnational Institute, Campact and Power Shift, *Profit durch Un-Recht: Wie Kanzleien, SchiedsrichterInnen und Prozessfinanzierer das Geschäft mit dem Investitionsschutz befeuern*, Brussels 2014.

51 Mattli, 'Private Justice', 919–47; Steil and Hinds, *Money, Markets, and Sovereignty*, 29.

52 Annelise Riles, 'The Anti-Network: Private Global Governance, Legal Knowledge, and the Legitimacy of the State', *American Journal of Comparative Law* 56/3, Summer 2008, 605–30.

53 Steil and Hinds, *Money, Markets, and Sovereignty*, 26, 31–2.

54 Moritz Renner, *Zwingendes transnationales Recht: Zur Struktur der Wirtschaftsverfassung jenseits des Staates*, Baden-Baden 2010, 21.

55 'Directive 2002/47/EC of the European Parliament and of the Council of 6 June 2002 on Financial Collateral Arrangements', online at http://eur-lex.europa.eu/legal-content/EN/TXT/?uri=celex:32002L0047. The argument here follows Riles, 'The Anti-Network', 614–17. On the relation between 'financial sovereignty' and 'transnational law' in the case of ISDA, see Johan Forst, 'Lex Financiaria: Das transnationale Finanzmarktrecht der International Swaps and Derivative Association', *Archiv des Völkerrechts* 53, 2015, 491–500.

56 Riles, 'The Anti-Network', 624; David V. Snyder, 'Contract Regulation, With and Without the State: Ruminations on Rules and their Sources: A Comment on Jurgen Basedow', *American Journal of Comparative Law* 56/3, Summer 2008, 723–42; A. Claire Cutler, *Private Power and Global Authority: Transnational Merchant Law in the Global Political Economy*, Cambridge 2003, 1–15, 180–4. Cf. Lori Wallach, 'The Corporate Invasion', *Le Monde Diplomatique* (English edn), November 2013, online at http://mondediplo.com/2013/12/02tafta; Corporate Europe Observatory et al., *Profit durch Un-Recht*, 7, 14.

57 According to the so-called 'Polak Model'. See Jacques J. Polak, 'The IMF Monetary Model: A Hardy Perennial', *Finance & Development*, December 1997, 17, cited in Mark Blyth, *Austerity: The History of a Dangerous Idea*, Oxford 2013, 164.

58 Stephen D. Krasner, 'Compromising Westphalia', *International Security* 20/3, Winter 1995/6, 131–2.

59 *External Evaluation of IMF Surveillance: Report by a Group of Independent Experts*, International Money Fund, Washington 1999, 20; Strange, *Mad Money*, 163–7.

60 Blyth, *Austerity*, 161–2; Krasner, 'Compromising Westphalia', 132.

61 Joseph, *The Social and the Global*, 95–6; John Micklethwait and Adrian Wooldridge, *A Future Perfect: The Essentials of Globalization*, New York 2000, 178–9.

62 World Bank, *Building Institutions for Markets*, Oxford 2002, 26; World Bank, *Entering the 21st Century*, Oxford 1999, 2; World Bank, *The State in a Changing World*, Oxford 1997, iii; Ajay Chibber, 'The State in a Changing World', *Finance & Development* 34/3, September 1997, 17, online at www.imf.org/external/pubs/ft/fandd/1997/09/pdf/chhibber.pdf. See also World Bank, *Reforming Public Institutions and Strengthening Governance*, Oxford 2000; cf. Joseph, *The Social and the Global*, 216–24, 248.

63 Giersch, 'Beschäftigung, Stabilität, Wachstum', 31.

64 Grimm, *Die Verfassung und die Politik*, 11–12; Marazzi, *Verbranntes Geld*, 85.

65 Charles E. Lindblom, 'The Market as Prison', *Journal of Politics* 44, 1982, 324–36, 332.

66 See Abram Chayes and Antonia Handler Chayes, *The New Sovereignty: Compliance with International Regulatory Agreements*, Cambridge MA 1995; Jacob Vestergaard, 'Disciplining the International Political Economy through Finance', in Stefano Guzzini and Iver B. Neumann (eds.), *The Diffusion of Power in Global Governance: International Political Economy Meets Foucault*, Houndmills 2012, 172–202.

67 Marazzi, *Sozialismus des Kapitals*, 137–9; Michel Aglietta and André Orléan, *La monnaie entre violence et confiance*, Paris 2002, 248.

68 Ingo Malcher, 'Nach dem Neoliberalismus? Linkswende in Lateinamerika und ihre Perspektiven', in Christina Kaindl, Christoph Lieber and Oliver Nachtwey (eds.), *Kapitalismus*

Reloaded: Kontroversen zu Imperialismus, Empire und Hegemonie, Hamburg 2007, 220–42; Jeremy Bulow and Kenneth Rogoff, 'Sovereign Debt: Is to Forgive to Forget?', *American Economic Review* 79/1, March 1989, 43–50; Strange, *Mad Money*, 178–80; Hudson, 'Die Herrschaft der Finanzoligarchie', 3; Marazzi, *Verbranntes Geld*, 121. The fusion of private property and public finances can be observed in numerous developing and newly industrialized countries. One of the best-known and most bizarre examples: in the 1990s, Zambia was unable to service a debt of $15 million that it had contracted in 1979 for the purchase of Romanian tractors. Romania sold this debt for $3 million to a hedge fund, Donegal International, based in the Caribbean. The Zambian government agreed to the deal in return for a donation of $2 million. Donegal then sued Zambia at a London court of arbitration for $55 million, including interest, interest on interest, and a risk fee. Because the donation paid to the Zambian government was ruled to be a bribe, the payment demand was lowered in 2007 to $15.5 million and declared legal. Zambia serviced the debt – and the tidy profit made by the hedge fund – by cuts in health spending. See Andreas Oldag, 'Albtraum der Armen', *Süddeutsche Zeitung*, 21 May 2010, online at www.sueddeutsche.de/geld/geierfonds-albtraum-der-armen-1.793842; 'Geierfonds: Das lukrative Geschäft mit Schulden', *Südwind Magazin: Internationale Politik, Kultur und Entwicklung*, September 2013, online at www.suedwind-magazin.at/start.asp?ID=254591&rubrik=31&ausg=201309.

69 Vogel, *Europas Revolution von oben*, 50–2; Altvater, 'Die Politik "im Schlepptau" der Finanzmärkte', 76–8.

70 Streeck, *Buying Time*, 72–5.

71 Alexander Rüstow, in *Compte-rendu des séances du colloque Walter Lippmann* (26–30 August 1938), Travaux du Centre International d'Études pour la Rénovation du Libéralisme, vol. 1, Paris 1939, 83, cited in Foucault, *The Birth of Biopolitics*, 242, footnote 5; von Mises, *Human Action*, 2; see also Joseph Vogl, *Das Gespenst des Kapitals*, Zurich 2010, 133–40.

72 Foucault, *The Birth of Biopolitics*, 333; cf. 208, 210–11, 246, 312. See also Joshua Barkan, *Corporate Sovereignty: Law and Government under Capitalism*, Minneapolis 2013, 12.

73 Robert J. Shiller, *The New Financial Order: Risk in the 21st Century*, Princeton 2003, 1–2.

74 David Harvey, *The Enigma of Capital and the Crises of Capitalism*, London 2010, 18; Marazzi, *Verbranntes Geld*, 34–43.

75 According to Mario Monti before his appointment as prime minister in 2011; cited in Jean-Pierre Dupuy, *L'avenir de l'économie: Sortir de l'économystification*, Paris 2012, 11.

76 Max Haiven, 'Financial Totalitarianism: The Economic, Political, Social and Cultural Rule of Speculative Capital', *truthout*, 12 June 2013, online at truth-out.org/news/item/16911-financial-totalitarianism-the-economicpolitical-social-and-cultural-rule-of-speculative-capital; Stefano Lucarelli, 'Financialization as Biopower', in Andrea Fumagalli and Sandro Mezzadra (eds.), *Crisis in the Global Economy: Financial Markets, Social Struggles, and New Political Scenarios*, Los Angeles 2007, 119–38. On 'indebted persons' in the financial regime, see Maurizio Lazzarato, *Die Fabrik des verschuldeten Menschen: Essay über das neoliberale Leben*, Berlin 2012; Walter Benjamin, 'Capitalism as Religion', in Benjamin, *Selected Writings*, vol. 1, eds. Marcus Paul Bullock et al., London 1996–2003, 288–91; also the articles of Marcel Hénaff, Elena Esposito, Birger P. Priddat, Christina von Braun, Jochen Hörisch, Roberto Esposito and Martin Treml, in Thomas Macho (ed.), *Bonds: Schuld, Schulden und andere Verbindlichkeiten*, Munich 2014.

77 Deleuze and Guattari, *A Thousand Plateaus*, 424–75.

78 Emile Benveniste, *Le vocabulaire des institutions indo-européennes* (1969), Paris 1993, 135–41; Bruno Théret, 'Finance, souveraineté et dette sociale', in Théret, *L'état, la finance et le social*, 571–5.

79 Bodin, *Les six livres de la république*, livre 6, 44, 88–92.

80 Schmitt, *The Concept of the Political*, 80–96; Schmitt, *Political Theology*, 5.

81 Jessica Matthews, 'Power Shift', *Foreign Affairs* 76/1, January/February 1997, 50–66; Slaughter, *A New World Order*, 266–71; Saskia Sassen, *Losing Control? Sovereignty in the Age of Globalization*, New York 1996, 31; Ernst Forsthoff, *Der Staat der Industriegesellschaft*, Munich 1971, 14; Barkan, *Corporate Sovereignty*; Michael Hardt and Antonio Negri, *Empire*, Cambridge MA 2000, 195–216; Chayes and Chayes, *The New Sovereignty*.

82 Stefania Vitali, James B. Glattfelder and Stefano Battiston, 'The Network of Global Corporate Control', *PLos ONE* 6/10, October 2011, doi:10.1371/journal.pone.0025995; Daniel Baumann and

Jakob Schwandt, '147 Unternehmen kontrollieren die Welt', *Frankfurter Rundschau*, 24 October 2011, online at www.fr-online.de/wirtschaft/maechtige-konzerne-147-unternehmen-kontrollieren-die-welt,1472780,11055250.html.

83 Thorstein Veblen, *Absentee Ownership and Business Enterprise in Recent Times*, New York 1938 (2nd edn), 3; Nitzan and Bichler, *Capital as Power*, 321–5; see also Arrighi, *The Long Twentieth Century*, 225–6, 232–44.

84 David Rothkopf, *Power, Inc.: The Epic Rivalry Between Big Business and Government – and the Reckoning That Lies Ahead*, New York 2012, 311, 323–4.

85 Barkan, *Corporate Sovereignty*, 12.

86 Joseph S. Nye, *The Future of Power*, New York 2011, 51; Rothkopf, *Power, Inc.*, 309–15; Manuel Castells, *The Information Age: Economy, Society and Culture. Vol. 1: The Rise of the Network Society*, Oxford 1996, 470–6.

87 Walter Opello and Stephen Rosow, *The Nation-State and Global Order*, Boulder 2004 (2nd edn), cited in Rothkopf, *Power, Inc.*, 313.

88 Deleuze and Guattari, *A Thousand Plateaus*, 460–73; see also Hardt and Negri, *Empire*, 332–58.

Index